HOUSE HISTORIES

D1421821

61 200 329

HOUSE HISTORIES

THE SECRETS BEHIND YOUR FRONT DOOR

UPDATED EDITION

MELANIE BACKE-HANSEN

To mum and dad — who allowed me to move to
the other side of the world to pursue my dreams

First published 2011
This paperback edition first published 2019

The History Press
97 St George's Place, Cheltenham,
Gloucestershire, GL50 3QB
www.thehistorypress.co.uk

© Melanie Backe-Hansen, 2011, 2019

The right of Melanie Backe-Hansen to be identified as the Author
of this work has been asserted in accordance with the
Copyright, Designs and Patents Act 1988.

All rights reserved. No part of this book may be reprinted
or reproduced or utilised in any form or by any electronic,
mechanical or other means, now known or hereafter invented,
including photocopying and recording, or in any information
storage or retrieval system, without the permission in writing
from the Publishers.

British Library Cataloguing in Publication Data.
A catalogue record for this book is available from the British Library.

ISBN 978 0 7509 9230 5

Typesetting and origination by The History Press
Printed in Turkey by IMAK

Contents

Preface

With close to fourteen years' experience researching the history of houses, I have been fortunate in being able to delve into the history of many houses across the country, uncovering an inordinate number of stories that bring a property to life. This book is an opportunity to share some of those stories and offers a glimpse into the world of our ancestors and the way they lived, as well as the bigger picture of the social and cultural history of their experience.

You can be forgiven for thinking that only the large stately homes have interesting histories, but every house, whether the Victorian terraced house, the small country cottage or the modern apartment block, hides a story behind its front door. By examining a range of old documents, including maps, deeds, and occupational records, I am able to compile the history of the house and the stories of people who have called it home. This collection of house histories illustrates the great variety of stories that can be discovered, whether the house was home to a famous author, a military hero, or pioneering men and women of the past.

This second edition includes some new house histories, as well as providing an update on the sources available to those embarking on researching the history of their own home.

In recent years, researching the history of houses has become far more popular due to the increased interest in family history as well as the interest in property restoration. Whether you're restoring a Tudor farmhouse or renovating a Victorian two-up two-down, understanding the history of your house can not only help you in the restoration process, but allows you to imagine the past lives of your home.

This knowledge can inevitably change the financial and emotional value you place on your home and give you a stronger sense of history, but ultimately it can inspire you to look beyond the bricks and mortar to find the secrets behind your front door.

Acknowledgements

There have been many people who have helped me on the journey of writing this book: family, friends, colleagues and archivists, simply too many to thank individually, but know that you are very much appreciated. However, there are two people who deserve special thanks. Firstly, Neville Page, former Marketing Director at Chestertons, who first saw the value of an estate agent having an in-house historian and gave me the opportunity of a lifetime. Secondly, Katharine Reeve, who discovered me in the Twitter crowd and guided me through the ups and downs of writing my first book.

Introduction

Researching the history of a house can be a fascinating adventure, uncovering the mysteries and secrets of the past. Exploring the lives of former residents can become addictive and tricky questions can see you obsessively following up intriguing clues as you become a house detective. Every house is different and will inevitably take you on a different journey; some will not require all sources, but with some you may need to broaden your research depending on the story of your house.

Throughout the stories in this book I refer to key documents that I've used to uncover the history, but if you're embarking on researching the history of your own home, here is a brief overview of how to get started.

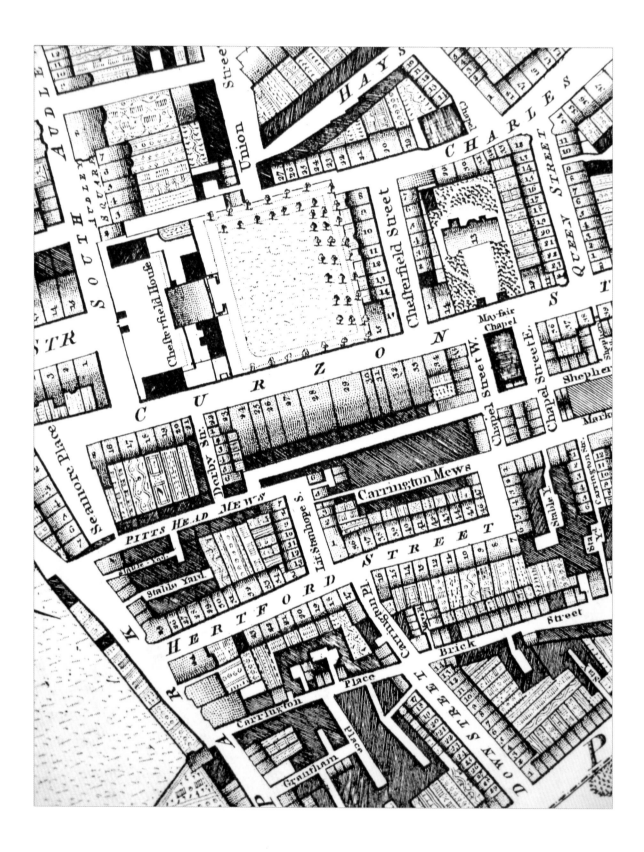

WHERE TO START

When researching the history of a house, many things change over time, including county and ward boundaries, along with street and house names. There may also be gaps in the records, so to avoid pitfalls and dead ends it is easier to work backwards through time. By working backwards from information of which you're sure – i.e. the most recent homeowner – you'll spot the changes where they occur. It can be very tempting to jump back to the early history, but details change and you may discover later that you're researching the wrong house.

Street names and house numbers have changed a lot in the last few hundred years. House numbering only began to be used during the eighteenth century and prior to this it is most likely your home was identified by a name or even by location, for example, 'John Smith's farm on the London road'. After each reorganisation of streets, the names and numbers changed; in fact, some houses have had a few different numbers or names. For houses within London there is a book provided by the former London County Council (LCC) which records the changes made and when. You can also refer to maps at the London Metropolitan Archives which illustrate exactly which numbers were assigned to which house. However, this is unfortunately not available for areas outside of London.

YOUR LOCAL AREA

To get a good understanding of how a house fits into the history of the area and guide you in uncovering key pieces of information, it is good to start by reading about the development of your area. Was the area part of a large landed estate? Did it belong to the Church? Did it expand at a key point in history, perhaps after the discovery of a local resource or the building of the railways? Discovering this information will also guide you as to where to go next, for example, if you discover it was part of a manor you can then extend your research into the manorial records.

Within each borough or county there will be books and studies to refer to, and local archives to visit, but two key sources are: The Survey of London, which has been in production since 1894; as well as The Victoria County History series (produced since 1899 and named after Queen Victoria).

MAPS & PLANS

Maps can be a vital tool in researching the history of a house. There are a number of different maps and plans that are extremely useful, including the Ordnance Survey maps, which were produced in detail across the country at periodic intervals since the 1860s. There are a number of other maps available for London, including those of Richard Horwood (1792–99), and Christopher and John Greenwood (1827–30). Across other parts of the country there will be local parish or county maps.

Tithe maps were produced during the 1830s and '40s when a survey was undertaken across most parts of the country to establish the value of lands in order to determine tithe payments. These maps will give the location of the property with a number, and in a corresponding tithe apportionment you will find the number, which gives you the name of the landowner, the occupant and the extent of the land and the value of the tithe.

Enclosure maps were produced in the late eighteenth and early nineteenth centuries. They were provided as a survey of lands that were being enclosed (a consolidation of smaller plots of land or common land under one owner) and were accompanied by records of the transfer of land, giving details of the owner and sometimes the occupant. These maps

Census enumeration form (handwritten). Page 2] The undermentioned Houses are situate within the Boundaries of the — Civil Parish: Highworth; Parliamentary Borough of Cricklade, Highworth; Town of Bo Blunsdon.

No. of Schedule	ROAD, STREET, &c. and No. or NAME of HOUSE	HOUSES	NAME and Surname of each Person	RELATION to Head of Family	CON-DITION	AGE	Rank, Profession, or OCCUPATION	WHERE BORN	Whether Deaf-and-Dumb / Blind / Imbecile or Idiot / Lunatic
3	Rectory	1	Samuel F. Auchmuty	Head	Mar		Rector of Bo Blunsdon	Ireland	
			Louisa Car.?	Wife		55		Hadsey Beauchamp, Worcestershire	
			Arthur Compton	Son	Unm		Curate of do	Blunsdon St Andrew, Wilts	
			Louisa Mar. do	Dau.		27		do	
			Frances Car.? do	Dau.		24		do	
			Stanus Jas do	Son				Devonport, Devon	
			Samuel F. B. do	Son-grnd				Dartington, Middlesex	
			Arthur Woods do	Grn.son		4		Great Wolford, Warwicks.	
			Sarah Fletcher	Servant			Cook	Oddington, Devon	
			Mary Ann Brown	"			Parlour Maid	Wroughton, Wilts	
			Jane Collier	"		21	Housemaid		
4	Church Green	1	Mary Hamblard	Head	Widow	80	Nil	Bo Blunsdon, Wilts	
			Elizabeth do	Dau.	Unm	40	Washerwoman	do	
			Rose Hannah do	Grd. dau	"	19	Labourer	do	
			Arthur do	Grd. son			Labourer	do	
5	Church Farm	1	John Esmonds	Head	Mar		Farmer - 200 acres (11 men 4 boys 6 women)	Calne - Wilts	
			Fanny Smith do	Wife	mar			Swindon "	
			John do	Son	Unm	12		Bo Blunsdon "	
			Hannah A. do	Dau.	"	6		do	
			Ada Leziah do	"	"			do	
			Louisa Hiscocks	Servant	"	70	General Serv. (Domestic)	Swindon "	
			Frances May Esmonds	Dau.				Bo Blunsdon "	
	Total of Houses.. 3		Total of Males and Females..			8 / 14			

* Draw the pen through such of the words as are inappropriate.

rarely give details about individual houses, but they are useful in tracking land ownership.

Along with these maps you can also find information on estate maps (undertaken by a private landowner on his personal estate); Goad Fire Insurance maps, which show details of houses surveyed for insurance purposes; Charles Booth poverty maps, highlighting the economic and social level of the occupants' property in London; and bomb damage maps, which provide valuable information about damage caused during the Second World War, plus the accompanying reports may tell stories about what happened when the bombs fell.

As well as maps, you can be fortunate enough to discover plans for your house. These may be found in sales particulars, deeds or even drainage plans. They are not always available, but if you do manage to locate any, you can find details of the builder, the owner and even fittings that were planned for the house. Drainage plans can also give information about changes to the property over time, for example if it was converted into apartments.

TAX RECORDS

There are a number of national and parish taxes that are very useful for researching the history of a house. The first is the 1910 Valuation Office Survey, undertaken when Prime Minister David Lloyd George introduced a new land tax. A survey was required to gain a correct valuation of property across the UK; this included the land, house and accompanying buildings. The corresponding field books give details for the property at this time, including the owner, occupant and a description of the house. The Valuation Survey maps and field books are held in The National Archives, although some local studies libraries and county record offices have accompanying valuation books.

Parish rate books can give a wealth of information: like an early version of council tax, they covered taxes for sewerage, lights and the poor rate. Records list the owner and occupant, as well as the valuation attributed to the house, and the tax to be paid. However, the retained records vary from county to county so check with the county records office in your area. Land tax records are another possible source, giving details about the owner, occupant and the extent of the land.

CENSUS RETURNS

The census is a vital source of information for the study into the history of a house, giving details of all the residents in the home, including all children and servants, as well as personal information such as ages, birth place and occupations. The census has been undertaken every ten years since 1801, but it is only since 1841 that the census gives specific personal information. The 1911 census was the most recent census to be made available. The census returns give details of all the occupants recorded in the house at the time the census was taken. For some rural areas, however, the house may not be clearly identified – a whole village may simply be recorded under the name of the village rather than by street or house details. This may mean some real detective work is in order to determine which house you are looking at.

The 1939 Register is a source that has recently been released and provides a fascinating glimpse of the occupants of a house at the outbreak of the Second World War, in September 1939. Like a census, it was compiled for the production of ration books and ID cards. The records, only available online, provide personal information for occupants, including age, occupation, and in some cases war work.

ELECTORAL REGISTERS

The electoral registers are a great source of information, giving details of occupants eligible to vote going back to the nineteenth century. However, it is worth remembering a few key facts. The electoral register does not give details of family relationships. You may find a long list of names and not be sure who were the parents, the children, or the servants. Be aware that non-nationals were not eligible to vote and before 1928 not all women could vote. Despite these hurdles you can find out a vast amount of information about the residents of the house.

STREET DIRECTORIES

Directories can also be a fabulous resource for the house historian as they record the head of the house (like an early version of the phone book). Early directories record occupants because they were operating

a trade from the address (i.e. butcher) or they were a prominent local farmer or member of the local gentry. There are a number of different types of directories, including county directories, local area directories, as well as the Post Office Directory. Nevertheless, it is worth remembering that the further back you go, the harder it may be to find specific address information. It is also worth noting that earlier directories can occasionally have a few errors. Court directories or Court Guides are an excellent source for London houses whose former occupants were members of the nobility or gentry, as they record residents in London for the social season.

DEEDS, ARCHIVES & DOCUMENTS

You may be fortunate to hold the original deeds, but in a lot of cases these no longer exist. You can sometimes access them through your solicitor or mortgage provider, or in some cases they have been retained in local archives. They can provide a full overview of the transfer of the property and details of former owners and occupiers. The county record office may hold leases and mortgage details, along with details of the

land ownership through estate or manorial records. Other documents that may give clues in tracking the history of a house include wills, probate and legal disputes. Land Registry also hold a small amount of detail regarding the historic ownership of a house.

Local libraries and archives may have additional resources, such as old sales catalogues, photographs and illustrations. Newspapers are an excellent source of information and are increasingly available online through the British Newspaper Archive. There are also records at the British Library and local newspapers held in local archives and record offices.

ONLINE

Today we are very fortunate to have access to many more documents online. To be able to search through archives and catalogues without leaving the house is incredibly helpful, but this is only one element of research. The majority of the sources used to research the history of a house are found in the county record office of local studies libraries, as well as The National Archives and other depositories, such as the London Metropolitan Archives. In recent years more and more sources have become available online, which has made initial research easier, but in a great number of cases the resources still need to be viewed in libraries and archives.

17 DUNRAVEN STREET

Dunraven Street in Mayfair, originally named Norfolk Street, was first laid out for building by Edmund Rush during the 1750s, with all houses completed and occupied by 1761. However, since that time, the house numbers have changed, with No 17 originally being No 15. The houses on the east side of Dunraven Street were also all rebuilt between 1897 and 1916, with today's No 17 rebuilt in 1897, along with Nos 16, 18 and 19. The houses were rebuilt using red brick and stone dressings, popular during the late nineteenth century and described as 'Baroque exuberance'. Norfolk Street was renamed Dunraven Street in 1939 after politician and yachtsman Windham Thomas Wyndham-Quin, fourth Earl of Dunraven and Mount Earl, who lived at No 27 in 1895.

MURDER IN NORFOLK STREET

A scandalous murder took place at No 14 Norfolk Street in 1840. Lord William Russell, youngest son of Francis Russell, 5th Duke of Bedford and brother of the 6th Duke of Bedford, was murdered and robbed by his own valet, Benjamin Francis Courvoisier. This was headline news throughout May and June 1840. It has also been claimed that it was only on the evidence of a witness, who saw a naked man by candlelight through the fanlight, that brought about the conviction, but reports in *The Times* and from the Old Bailey archives show that the valet, Courvoisier, was immediately suspected. He confessed to the murder and robberies on 22 June 1840 and was hanged at Newgate prison on 6 July.

RIGHT HO, JEEVES

P.G. Wodehouse, well known for his fictional characters Bertie Wooster and his 'gentleman's personal gentleman' Jeeves, lived at 17 Dunraven Street from 1924 until 1934, during which period his books were receiving much critical acclaim in Britain and America. During this time Wodehouse published *Very Good, Jeeves*, *Meet Mr Mulliner* and *Right Ho, Jeeves*. He created such memorable characters as Gussie Fink-Nottle, Bingo Little and, of course, Aunt Agatha. A blue plaque was unveiled by Her Majesty Queen Elizabeth the Queen Mother in June 1988 to commemorate his residency.

Notable Residents

Lillie Langtry, the famous actress, socialite and mistress of Albert, Prince of Wales (later Edward VII), lived at No 19 from 1877–80. The interior of the house was decorated with the help of renowned artist James McNeill Whistler, and included a painted ceiling in the drawing room. The Admiral of the Fleet, John Fisher, lived at No 18 from 1887–91; Dowager Duchess of Beaufort, widow of the 4th Duke of Beaufort, lived there from 1760–63; and Sir Lucas Pepys, physician to George III, in 1816–21. It is understood that No 17 was also home to Alexander Mountbatten, 1st Marquess of Carisbrooke, shortly before the author P.G. Wodehouse made it his home.

St Benedicts Priory

Authentic Features

Today, this Jacobean house retains a number of beautiful original historic features, most significantly the original seventeenth-century dogleg staircase with turned balusters. Other features include a number of stone fireplaces; the original heavy studded wooden front door; and even a carved stone face on the western chimney stack. Originally owned by great men who were in the favour of successive kings, for most of its history it has been home to gentleman farmers, who played significant roles in the life of the village. At one point the house was at the centre of a farm covering almost 3,000 acres, but today it has been sympathetically restored to become a comfortable family home.

St Benedicts Priory Indenture, 1659.

St Benedicts Priory is a grand seventeenth-century home built on the site of a twelfth-century Benedictine priory that sat at the centre of Deeping village in Lincolnshire until 1539. It was founded by Baldwin Fitz Gilbert in 1139 and dedicated to St James. The priory was a small cell attached to Thorney Abbey and suffered the same fate as the abbey during Henry VIII's Dissolution of the Monasteries in 1539. The land and buildings were given to Thomas, Duke of Norfolk (Anne Boleyn's uncle), in 1540, and it is believed to have been constructed with the stone from the dismantled medieval priory buildings.

The Wymondsold Family

The Manor of Deeping St James was in the hands of the Wymondsold (or Wymonsole) family during the seventeenth century and it is most likely that they were responsible for building on the old priory lands. An indenture dated 1659 between William Wymondsold of Putney and his grandsons clearly identifies the transfer of the manor of Deeping St James, 'late called the cell of Thorney otherwise called the late priory of Deeping St. James', encompassing all the land, church, parsonage and houses, along with the yards, orchards, barns, meadows and cottages.

William Wymondsold was from a prominent family, mainly residing in Putney, south-west London, and was also High Sheriff at the time of the Civil War. Most notably he was present at the time of the Putney Debates

in 1647 and General Fairfax was billeted at Wymondsold's house (believed to have been located where Putney train station sits today). However, the Wymondsold family were noted Royalists and at the Restoration were rewarded for their loyalty to the king. Sir Dawes Wymondsold was favoured by Charles II and William Wymondsold was 'Royall Ayd unto the King' in 1664–65 and again in 1672 and 1679 ('Ayd' given in the form of finance), while Robert Wymondsold was knighted by James II in March 1684.

THE WHICHCOTE FAMILY

By the early 1700s, the manor had transferred into the hands of the Whichcote family, a prominent local family thanks to Sir Jeremy Whichcote, who was created baronet by Charles II in 1660. By the mid eighteenth century the family seat was Aswarby Hall near Sleaford. It is during this period that records directly related to the priory farmhouse emerge, in particular the direct relationship between lord of the manor, Sir Christopher Whichcote, and later his son Sir Thomas Whichcote, with the tenants of the house. In 1775 receipts and rent records show that the occupant of the house was Mr John Pawlett, although it is not certain how long the Pawlett family had been residing at the priory farmhouse prior to this as no previous records survive.

Active in the Community

John Pawlett farmed 400 acres of surrounding land and by the turn of the nineteenth century this was increasing. The poor rate assessments during the early nineteenth century show that John Pawlett was actively involved in the parish of Deeping St James, acting as Vestryman (early council member) and was responsible for the distribution of the poor rate funds to the needy in the parish. At some point during the early 1800s, John's son, also called John, took over the running of the farm and in the 1840s became the Chief Constable of the village.

Restoration & Renovation

By 1959, after a period of change during the twentieth century, the house had become the home of Mrs Hall, who continued in the house for many years, until she sold it to Mr and Mrs Rickard in 1987. By this time the house was almost 400 years old and in dire need of some care and attention. The Rickard family set about restoring the once grand seventeenth-century home to bring it back to its former glory.

THE PAWLETT FAMILY

The 1841 census clarifies that John Pawlett (junior), then aged 55, was a farmer, living there with his wife Elizabeth and their two sons, 30-year-old Samuel, a merchant, and 25-year-old Edmund, a farmer. The family also had a visitor and three live-in servants in 1841. By the time of the 1851 census, John was recorded as 'farmer of 250 acres employing six labourers'. Elizabeth was recorded as 'farmer's wife' and son Edmund as 'farmer 440 acres employing 15 labourers'. John Pawlett died in 1853, and by the 1861 census Edmund was recorded as 'farmer about 700 or 800 acres employing 20 men, 14 boys and 4 women'. At this time, Edmund's mother Elizabeth was still in the house, but she died the following year at the age of 81.

Edmund followed family tradition as a prominent member of the community and was involved with the formation and running of the school board from 1876. By the 1881 census Edmund was occupant of 'The Priory' aged 66 and 'farmer and grazier of 2900 acres employing 40 men & boys'.

RICHARD & ALBERT WARD

Edmund Pawlett passed away in 1885 without marrying, so for the first time in over 100 years the priory farmhouse became the home of a new family, and the 1889 Lincolnshire Directory and the 1891 census reveal it became the home of Richard Ward and his children, Ada and Albert. By the turn of the twentieth century, Albert was head of the household at only 27 years old, with his wife Sarah and their 1-year-old daughter Doris. The family remained at the priory throughout the early 1900s and Albert was still recorded as 'farmer and grazier' in 1919. However, shortly after this time, the priory passed to Albert's son John and his wife Alberta. When John Ward died in 1920, his widow Alberta took over the house and farm.

WHITEHALL COURT

Whitehall Court, situated prominently along Victoria Embankment, was the former home of George Bernard Shaw; former Prime Minister William Gladstone; Lord Kitchener; Grand Duke Michael of Russia; and was even home to MI6 during the First World War. It was built in 1884–87 in a French Chateau Renaissance style by architects Thomas Archer and Arthur Green (also responsible for the Hyde Park Hotel, now the Mandarin Oriental in Knightsbridge). Whitehall Court is Grade II* listed, as is the building next to it: the National Liberal Club designed by Alfred Waterhouse, who is most remembered for creating the Natural History Museum.

In *London of To-Day: an Illustrated Handbook for the Season* (1890), Whitehall Court was described as a 'Palace of Flats'. It features a number of decorative architectural features, including two central projecting bays, iron and glass canopied doorways, decorative iron work, ornamental chimney stacks, and the prominent towers and gables that rise above the trees along the embankment. When completed, it was noteworthy not only for its ornate architecture, but for its use of electricity, lifts and even sound-proofing for the flats.

MI6 & THE EMBASSIES

This was an early location for the Secret Intelligence Service, or MI6, who occupied Flat No 54 from 1916 until after the First World War. During the Second World War a number of government departments were housed in Whitehall Court, including the Russian and American embassies and the Air Training Corps. The section formerly known as No 2 Whitehall Court was converted into the Royal Horseguards Hotel in 1971–72. Today it is home to the Liberal Association, the Farmers Club and United Nations Association.

George Bernard Shaw

George Bernard Shaw lived here from around 1928 until the start of the Second World War. During this period Shaw would often entertain friends, including writers H.G. Wells and Aldous Huxley, actor Maurice Chevalier and T.E. Lawrence – known as 'Lawrence of Arabia'. This imposing building has been home to many eminent residents, including publisher and author Douglas Francis Jerrold; Australian artist Sir Sydney Nolan; poet Margaret Stuart Pollard; author and politician Sir Gilbert George Parker; author and barrister Sarah Caudwell, and politician Sir Richard Stafford Cripps.

57 CHURCH STREET

This ordinary worker's house was built in 1883 as part of Didcot New Town after the introduction of Brunel's Great Western Railway. First owned by a railway inspector and later the home of a blacksmith, then a family of engine drivers, the history of the house is directly linked to the spread of the railways which transformed Britain.

It took some time for new houses and the town itself to be developed, despite the great need of new houses for railway workers from the 1840s. This is believed to have been mainly due to a lack of available land. In 1844, when the branch terminus at Didcot opened, there were still very few new homes for railway workers. This all changed in 1866 when local farmer Stephen Dixon purchased 119 acres of land to the north of East Hagbourne, which became known as North Hagbourne or Northbourne. He divided the land into building plots and sold them off to individual builders and developers, with the first eight plots sold in 1868 along Wallingford Road, today's Lower Broadway. Dixon continued to sell off sections of North Hagbourne throughout the 1870s and 1880s. This approach resulted in a variation of architectural styles rather than any unified plan.

Didcot Railway Station, 1917.

NORTH HAGBOURNE, BERKS. CHURCH ROW.　　TAUNT & CO. 1692

Church Street in the early 1900s.

God's Wonderful Railway

The history of Didcot is synonymous with the development of Victorian engineer Isambard Kingdom Brunel's Great Western Railway (GWR). Prior to the development of the railway, Didcot was a small country village with a predominately agricultural community. The GWR, affectionately called 'God's Wonderful Railway', was founded in 1833, with the first trains running by 1838. The construction of the tracks, tunnels, bridges and station buildings brought new work to the area, as well as rowdy navvies who came to dig the line. In 1839–40 the train line was laid down through Didcot, with the grand opening of this stretch of track, from Reading to Steveton, opened on 1 June 1840. Four years later, on 12 June 1844, Didcot Junction and station opened with an additional line to Oxford.

By 1873 sixty-three new houses had been built in Northbourne. Most streets were not clearly named, and it was only in 1897, when the East Hagbourne Parish Council were asked to name the streets for the planning of new drainage, that these were finally named, somewhat unimaginatively, as West Street (now Mereland Road) and South Street (Wessex Road). Most houses were built specifically to rent to railway workers, creating a new community known as New Town. Didcot remained as two separate communities (old Didcot village and the New Town) until the twentieth century.

THE FIRST OWNER

No 57 Church Street was one of many homes in the heart of the development of Northbourne or Didcot New Town in the 1860s and '70s. It is known from the documents of sale that in 1866 Stephen Dixon mortgaged the land to local solicitor Edward Ormond, along with Joseph Lewis, James Clark and Richard Hart. It was a few years later, in 1874–75, that the plot was leased to contractors John George Brewer and John Peters. In 1882 the site was sold to a railway inspector, Joseph Lintern, who it is believed was responsible for the building of the house, completed in 1883. The original deeds for the house show that Lintern continued as the owner into the 1890s, but he was living in Station Road. The 1881 census records him as railway inspector, 42 years old, in the house with his wife Kezia and their five children. As railway inspector (of trains, tracks and stations), he held a highly responsible position in the railway community. The 1871 census also shows that Lintern had formerly been based at the heart of the Great Western Railway in Paddington, London.

Original deeds of ownership.

23

No 57 & the Railway Workers

The full occupational records for No 57 Church Street during the late nineteenth and early twentieth century are difficult to decipher, as Didcot had numerous names – North Hagbourne, Northbourne and New Town – and also the streets were unnamed and houses not numbered. However, the 1891 census shows New Town occupants were predominately railway employees: signalmen, engine drivers, porters, inspectors, engine cleaners, railway labourers, ticket collectors and locomotive stokers. Unfortunately, given the lack of clear documents, it isn't always clear who was living at 57 Church Street, but it is certain they would have been working on the railway.

Engine Drivers

The deeds for 57 Church Street reveal that the house stayed in the Warr family for many years. Albert Warr rose to become an engine driver for the railway, a much respected and sought-after role. At a time when horse power was the most common form of transport, the speed of a train was thrilling. Into the 1930s and '40s the position of engine driver was still highly valued, and a driver was seen as someone with a strong sense of duty and service to inspire complete respect, not only from travellers but also fellow employees.

BLACKSMITH FREDERICK BELCHER

From the late 1890s into the early years of the twentieth century, No 57 became the home of blacksmith Frederick Belcher. He was recorded as living in North Hagbourne, 48 years old, with his wife Emma and their eight children, the eldest being 16 and the youngest, Ernest, aged 3. The eldest son, Thomas, was listed as assistant to his father. Blacksmiths were important in supporting the rail industry, making many parts for the trains, tracks and even station buildings, as well as the tools for labourers and tradesmen.

RAILWAY CLERK GEORGE WISE

The deeds show that Belcher continued as the house's owner, but at the time of the 1910 valuation survey the occupant was a 'F. Berry [or Perry]'. By the 1911 census the house was the home of George Wise, a 36-year-old GWR railway clerk, and his wife of three years, Lavinia, who was 41 years old, along with George's niece, 21-year-old Ellen Bustin. The house was still not numbered but the Wise family were shown as occupying four rooms.

THE WARR FAMILY

We know from the deeds that in March 1915 the house passed from Belcher to railway signalman Mr Albert Warr. The 1911 census recorded Warr as 49 years old, living with his 49-year-old wife of thirty years, Mary Ann, and their five children. The census offers an interesting picture of the Warr family: the eldest son, also Albert, was 22 years old and an 'engine stoker'; their only daughter, Hilda, was 19 years old and worked as a cashier in the local butchers, most likely Bosley's on Wallingford Road; their middle son, Richard Warr, 17, was an 'engine cleaner'; William, 14, was a 'butchers' errand boy'; and the youngest, Arthur Warr, 12, was still at school.

Albert Warr senior passed away in 1935 and the house passed to his eldest son, now also an engine driver, and his wife Florence. The family continued in the house until 1976 when Albert Warr junior and Florence passed away in March and November respectively, leaving the house to their sons, Reginald, William and Raymond. They sold the house to Robert and Linda Pryor in 1977.

This Indenture made the *twentieth* day of *March*

One thousand nine hundred and fifteen B E T W E E N FREDERICK BELCHER
of Number 36 Wilton Road in the County Borough of Reading Retired Builder
of the one part and ALBERT WARR of Wallingford Road Didcot in the County of
Berks Railway Signalman of the other part W I T N E S S E T H that in -
consideration of the sum of Two hundred and twelve pounds and ten shillings
to the said Frederick Belcher this day paid by the said Albert Warr for the
purchase of the fee simple of the hereditaments expressed to be hereby --
granted (the receipt whereof the said Frederick Belcher doth hereby -- -
acknowledge) he the said Frederick Belcher as Beneficial Owner doth hereby
grant and convey unto the said Albert Warr his heirs and assigns A L L
T H A T messuage or tenement with the Gardens and appurtenances thereto
situate in the Parish of East Hagbourne in that part now called North -
Hagbourne in the County of Berks and having a frontage to a street called
Church Street formerly occupied by Alfred Smith and now by Mrs. J. Darby
which said premises are delineated in the plan in the margin of an Indenture dated the seventeenth day of December One thousand nine hundred and
one being a conveyance to the said Frederick Belcher therein coloured -
Green and Red T O   H O L D the said premises Unto and to the use of the

CHELSEA STUDIOS

Artists & Designers

Chelsea Studios has been home to many creative residents, including royal artist Pietro Annigoni and sculptor Winifred Turner. Annigoni is often remembered for his paintings of royalty, in particular the queen in 1954, but he also painted former presidents of the United States, including John F. Kennedy and Lyndon B. Johnson. Turner's sculptures have been exhibited at the Victoria & Albert Museum and the Royal Academy, and her piece *Thought* (1933) is held in the Tate collection. Another prominent resident was portrait painter Aubrey Davidson-Houston. He is noted for his paintings of Somerset Maugham and Prince Charles, but he also painted the queen, the Duke of Edinburgh and the queen mother. Later residents of Chelsea Studios have included artist Derek Ashley; writer Noel Barber; designer Annie Brown; garden designer and sculptor Joan Edlis; and sculptor Jan Kepinski.

Chelsea Studios in Fulham was established as an artists' enclave known as 'The Italian Village' during the late 1920s. It is made up of two large 1840s Victorian homes: the original Nos 410/412 and 414/416 Fulham Road. In the early years of the twentieth century No 410 Fulham Road was home to prominent Victorian artist John William Godward, and No 416 was a bronze and iron casting foundry. John William Godward was a successful artist for many years working in a style similar to artists Lawrence Alma-Tadema and Frederick Leighton. He produced many paintings including *The Betrothed* (1892), *Dolce Far Niente* (1904) and *Crytilla* (1908). Godward's works have been exhibited at the Royal Academy, as well as galleries in Rome and Paris, and today his work appears in galleries in New York, Los Angeles and the UK..

The two houses, now listed as Buildings of Merit, were bought by artist and sculptor Mario Manenti in 1925–30, who then set about creating the Italian Village, inspired by the artists' colonies near his home in Florence. Situated behind the two larger Victorian homes, Manenti built communal studios varying in design and size, and established a place of beauty where artists could live and work. The first residents moved into the village in 1928. Mario Manenti specialised in bronze and is most remembered today for his First World War memorials.

STUDIO X: FILM & FASHION

During the mid 1950s Studio X became the home of Academy-Award-nominated art director and production designer John Michael Stringer. Stringer worked on over thirty films as a production designer, including *Casino Royale* (1967), *The Awakening* (1980), and the Pink Panther film *A Shot in the Dark* (1964). Stringer was also art director for another twenty films, including *Fiddler on the Roof* (1971). Another prominent resident of Studio X was John Taylor, mannequin designer for Adel Rootstein and Co. and renowned for his role in the revolution of the appearance of the high street mannequin. Along with creator Adel Rootstein, Taylor transformed the lifeless 1950s-style mannequins into the more lifelike ones we have today. He sculpted mannequins based on popular icons of the day, including the quintessential Twiggy.

Tranquillity

Today, Chelsea Studios still manages to maintain a secluded air of tranquillity, despite its busy location in central London, and even features a picturesque garden with an Italian-style water fountain, as well as a porter's lodge that has been likened to something out of a fairy tale.

SYERSTON HALL

This Grade II listed Georgian home in Lincolnshire was built in 1793–95 by William Fillingham, surveyor and land agent to the Duke of Rutland. The house remained in the Fillingham family for almost 200 years, with descendants of William Fillingham still in the house until the late 1970s.

Originally the estate was owned by Robert Sutton, Lord Lexington, later passing to his daughter Bridget, wife of John Manners, 3rd Duke of Rutland, and by the 1770s the estate was in the hands of Lord George Sutton, the youngest son of the Duke and Duchess of Rutland. In 1777 the manor passed to Lewis Disney Fytche, before being sold to William Fillingham in 1792 for £12,375, at which point the estate covered over 500 acres.

THE BUILDING OF SYERSTON HALL

William Fillingham rose from being a humble farmer's son and acquired the manor and estate of Syerston, as well as additional land and property in Newark. His most prominent role was as agent for the Duke of Rutland at Belvoir Castle in Leicestershire, but he also acted for a number of other prominent families across Nottinghamshire and Lincolnshire. With an eye for an opportunity, he invested wisely in a number of new canal schemes that were making their way across the country, including Birmingham, Derby, Leicester and Nottingham. During this time many common fields were being enclosed and each parish appointed three enclosure commissioners to oversee the process. William Fillingham was appointed as enclosure commissioner for over thirty parishes, further adding to his reputation – and his wealth.

When William acquired the Syerston estate he immediately set about building a grand new home. Few documents survive from this time, but it is believed that he had direct involvement in the design and layout of the house and grounds (not a surprise given his experience as a land agent and surveyor). However, in 1795, William died unexpectedly before seeing the house completed, and Syerston passed to William's eldest son, George.

BUILDER & LOCAL LEADER

George Fillingham took over the building of the house, as well as taking over his father's role as agent for the Duke of Rutland and various estates in north Nottinghamshire. He made improvements to Syerston, constructing a number of new buildings which included a chaise house, dovecote and garden house, in 1801, and The Croft for his mother in 1803. George also built new farm buildings and extended the house in 1812. By 1835 the estate had grown from 507 to 670 acres. In 1803, with the feared threat of invasion by Napoleon, George joined the Belvoir Castle Corps of Volunteers as captain, and in the same year was appointed Justice of the Peace. He also held the position of Sheriff of Nottingham in 1829 and 1830.

When George died in 1850 the estate passed briefly to his son, also George, who died only a few years later in 1856. It then went to George junior's 15-year-old son, George Henry Fillingham. George Henry attended Harrow and then St John's College, Oxford, before taking over the estate. By the time of the 1881 census he was recorded in residence with his aunt, Elizabeth, aged 73, and his two sisters, Frances and Caroline. George Henry Fillingham was a keen sportsman, playing cricket for the first XI at Harrow and later the 'Gentlemen of the South', but sadly died from injuries when he fell off his horse while hunting in 1895.

Second World War

The late 1930s saw the grounds around Syerston Hall completely transformed with the creation of an airfield. By 1940 this was being used as a bomber station with Polish airmen flying Vickers Wellington bombers. It was also used by Canadian airmen and by 1942 was home to members of the RAF flying Lancaster Bombers. In 1943 Flight Lieutenant Bill Reid was awarded the Victoria Cross for a mission flown from Syerston. From 1944 it was used as a training ground for aircraft including Spitfires and Hurricanes. After the war, in 1948, the airfield became a training base for Flying Training Command, until it closed in 1970. Since 1975 Syerston has been used by the Air Cadets Central Gliding School and the Volunteer Gliding School.

By the 1970s Syerston Hall was still in the hands of the Fillingham family, the last occupants being the son of George Henry, George Augustus, his wife Mary, and their son Anthony and his wife Janet. George Augustus died in 1974 and by the early 1980s the house had been sold. At this time Syerston Hall, along with the former farm buildings, was completely renovated. Today, it features a renovated interior whilst retaining the ambience of a Georgian stately home set amongst acres of parkland.

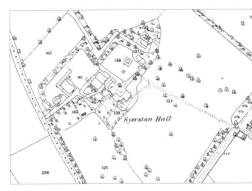

Ordnance Survey map, 1884–85.

2 PALACE GARDENS TERRACE

Famous Residents

The artist and writer Percy Wyndham Lewis lived at No 61, where a plaque commemorates his residence. No 57 was home to actor and stage manager Sir Herbert Beerbohm Tree, and his half-brother, caricaturist Henry Maximilian (Max) Beerbohm; a blue plaque commemorates Sir Max Beerbohm's birth in 1872. No 16 was home to physicist James Clerk Maxwell from 1860 to 1866 and a plaque also commemorates his residence. Architect Henry Ashton lived at No 23 until 1872, artist Henry Brittan Willis lived at No 12 until 1884, and artist Martha Darley Mutrie lived at No 36 until 1885.

This street has been the home of many successful creative artists, and today it is one of the most sought-after residential streets in Kensington. The name originated from its close association with Kensington Palace, whose gardens had originally extended further west. It is situated on the old glebe lands, to the east of Kensington Church Street, formerly owned by the vicars of St Mary Abbots. The lands can be traced back to 1260, and are also believed to be the same lands attributed to the priest of Kensington mentioned in Domesday Book in 1086. It was in 1854 that the church released the land to Thomas Robinson for building development.

ORIGINS

The street plan of this area, including Palace Gardens Terrace, Brunswick Gardens and Inverness Gardens, is likely due to architect David Brandon, who laid the sewer system in 1854. Construction of the street began in 1859 with Robinson's builder, William Lloyd Edwards, favouring unique classical ornament and a renaissance or mannerist style. No 2 was completed in 1860 as part of the eastern terrace numbered 2–40, with all the houses featuring white stucco exteriors with Doric pillar entrances and balustrade balconies along the first floor.

ARISTOCRATIC & FASHIONABLE RESIDENTS

The first resident of No 2 Palace Gardens Terrace was Mrs Cecilia Chambers and her son George Frederick Chambers. George was a barrister and author of many books on a range of subjects, including a *Handbook of Astronomy* and *Hints on Sanitary Law*.

Of all the former residents, the most notable were two musician sisters who had performed in front of Queen Victoria while children. Jeanne and Louise Douste lived here for thirty years and the house was often open to enthusiasts, who would come to hear the two sisters' weekly two-hour musical performances. Their sell-out concerts included the Prince's Hall and Royal Albert Hall Theatre during the late nineteenth century. *The Times* in 1937 said: 'This room, known then as the "sanctuary of music" was unique as a meeting-place for genius.'

Another resident of the house was politician, author and angler John Waller Hills. He married the half-sister of Virginia Woolf and was a good friend of Virginia and Vanessa Bell. He wrote a number of books on economics, but is most noted for his highly successful books on fly fishing, including *A Summer on the Test* (1924). Hills died at No 2 in 1938 and was named a Baronet in the 1939 honours list.

BUTE TOWN

Model Village

Bute Town consists of three terraces: Lower Row, Middle Row and Collins Row; a planned fourth terrace was never completed. Nikolaus Pevsner described Bute Town as constructed in a 'Palladian way', with the parallel terraces made up of a three-storey central section and the two-storeyed ends projecting slightly. The terraces were constructed with coursed stone walls and low-pitched stone-tile roofs with overhanging eaves. Another feature is that the lower terraces had vaulted cellars designed to be separate dwellings, making room for more residents while taking up the same amount of ground space. This double-dwelling design is unique in South Wales and few examples have been retained. The central three-storey sections are commonly understood to have been built as barracks accommodation for single men.

Richard Johnson's designs took into consideration his workers' need for sanitation, light, ventilation, as well as solid construction. He also provided a community chapel, a school and a pub.

Bute Town or Y Drenewydd is a small enclave of miners' cottages situated at the top of the Rhymney valley, just south of the Brecon Beacons, in what is known as the Heads of the Valley.

Ironworks developed in what had been quiet rural landscape during the mid eighteenth century, and by the end of the eighteenth century Rhymney was selected as the site of the new Union Ironworks, with the first furnace completed in 1801. The housing was constructed in 1802–04 and is believed to have been designed by the mine manager, Richard Johnson. It was first known as 'New Town' or Trefnewydd, and was created as a model village for the mining workers of the ironworks. The village is believed to be based on Lowther Village in Cumbria, designed by James Adams in 1765.

IRON MINING

In 1825 the ironworks were extended to include the Bute Ironworks, on land owned by the Marquess of Bute in the Upper Rhymney Valley, and this new association inspired the renaming of the town to Bute Town. The ironworks flourished during the early nineteenth century and by 1830 east Glamorgan and Monmouthshire were producing half the iron exported by Britain. In 1837 the Bute Ironworks merged with the Union Ironworks to become the Rhymney Ironworks.

The later shift to coal power, for use in industry as well as the domestic home, spelt the death of this once great ironworks, and by the late nineteenth century coal mining was the dominant industry in South Wales. This move away from iron in Rhymney was further supported by the expansion of the railways into Wales in the 1840s as Rhymney train station was placed in

Plan and elevation of the terrace in Bute Town.

the heart of Rhymney, with its new coal industry, leaving Bute Town rather isolated. Today, it is still separated from the larger residential area of Rhymney. The Rhymney Ironworks officially closed in 1890, although it continued to produce coal until the 1920s.

Restoration

A 1970s unified restoration programme was implemented to return the houses back to their original design. Bute Town became a conservation area and residents worked with the County Council and other historic associations on the renovation. This involved the removal of exterior additions, such as pebble-dash and cement, and the replacement of doors and windows; even overhead wires were relocated underground. The scheme was so significant it won a Prince of Wales Award for improving the quality of the Welsh Environment. A museum has also been created at Nos 26–27 Lower Row to recreate life in Bute Town during the nineteenth century.

68 Old Church Street

Walter Gropius

Walter Gropius established his successful architectural career in Germany during the early twentieth century while working with another ground-breaking architect, Peter Behrens. He was appointed master of a school of Arts and Crafts in Weimar in 1919, which he transformed into the renowned Bauhaus. Gropius was responsible for establishing a new architectural style which utilised recent developments in technology and industry, combined with a daring new aesthetic. His modernist style focused on the use of steel, glass and concrete as building materials, with the designs heavily influenced by industrial building types. Like many other artists and designers, Gropius fled an increasingly hostile Nazi Germany, moving to England in 1934 where he worked with Edwin Maxwell Fry. This collaboration led to the commission for Old Church Street. Gropius left England for the United States in 1937 to take up the Chair of Architecture at Harvard University.

This unique house in Chelsea is the only residential home in England designed by the founder of the Bauhaus, Professor Walter Gropius, in the twentieth-century 'modernist' style. Gropius' obituary in *The Times* described him as 'one of the most influential architects of modern times'. The house was built for well-known West End playwright Benn Levy – who also worked on Alfred Hitchcock's first 'Talkie', *Blackmail*, in 1929 – and his Hollywood actress wife, Constance Cummings.

The Modern Movement

Benn Levy and his cousin, publisher Dennis Cohen, purchased the vacant land (previously a row of cottages) to build neighbouring family homes. Levy commissioned Gropius and Edwin Maxwell Fry in 1936, while Cohen commissioned a similar 'Modern' home by Eric Mendelsohn and Serge Chermayeff (today's No 64 Old Church Street).

The house along Old Church Street (originally No 66) was completed in 1936 to critical acclaim. *The Times* in October called it '[one] of the most "advanced" buildings in London'. Original drawings from May 1935 are kept by the Royal Institute of British Architects in the Victoria & Albert Museum; they detail the day and night nursery for the Levy children, along with the 'best bedroom', 'sleeping porch', 'Mr Levy's bedroom', 'butler's room' and a 'secretary's room'.

The house was also completely fitted with staff bells, had a washing yard (behind the garage) and included specialised architectural lights. Large sections of the house were rendered with a new (and untried) form of rendering known as 'Brizolite', which Gropius brought from Germany. Other features included glass crete, reeded glass and the specialist 'Nori' bricks, which were used in the construction of the Empire State Building.

From Stage to Screen

Apart from his career as a playwright, Benn Levy was part of the intelligence service during the Second World War. He was appointed MBE in 1945 and from 1945–50 was a Labour MP for Eton and Slough. Levy regularly contributed to the *New Statesman* and *The Tribune*, and continued to write and produce plays, one of his last being *The Tumbler*, staged by Laurence Olivier in New York in 1960. Constance Cummings was a successful American-born Broadway and later Hollywood actress. Her Broadway debut at the age of 18 was the George and Ira Gershwin musical *Treasure Girl*, and she went on to star opposite Mae West in *Night After Night* in 1932.

Benn and Constance married in 1933 and shortly afterwards moved to England. Cummings made her West End debut in 1934 in *Sour Grapes* and continued to act in the burgeoning film industry, most notably in Noel Coward's *Blithe Spirit* opposite Rex Harrison in 1945, and Peter Sellers' *The*

Actress Constance Cummings and her husband Benn Levy live in one of the show modern houses in London, specially designed for them. Outer walls are rust and grey. Echoing the gleaming white paintwork, curtains are lined with white.

CONSTANCE CUMMINGS AND BENN LEVY
AT HOME

The owners' bedroom, bathroom and study form a suite along the garden side of the first floor. Brown, blue-grey and white make the restful colour scheme of the study (above) with its built-in bookshelves. Walls are faced with polished wood. Carpet is vandyke brown; chairs and settee are covered in dark brown corduroy. The modern fireplace is made of silver-grey ribbed glass topped with black.

Leading from the study, the main bedroom (below) has a delightful view of the garden. Polished sycamore gleams on walls, doors and built-in bedside tables. Bed-ends and small desk are covered in natural leather. Curtains are red and white, carpet is sage green and armchair is covered in striped yellow material. The bedspread is of white crochet. Wonderful fitted dress cupboards complete this very unusual bedroom.

36

Alterations

The couple remained in the house from 1936 until Levy's death in 1973, Cummings then moved upstairs to the flat where she stayed until she was in her nineties.

After the Second World War, the house was altered to create a separate apartment on the upper floor, which became 68 Old Church Street and was home to Mrs Rachel M. Lloyd from 1948. The plans by Jane Drew show that many of the original materials were re-used, including timber handrails and light fittings. The house was again renovated during the 1970s, slightly changing the original external appearance, but maintaining Gropius' unique design.

The Times, 31 October 1936.

Battle of the Sexes (1959). Levy even directed Cummings in a 1937 adaptation of *Madame Bovary*.

Cummings went on to act with Sir Anthony Hopkins, Sir Michael Redgrave, Sam Wannamaker and Sir Laurence Olivier, winning the *Evening Standard* drama award for best actress in *Long Day's Journey into Night* in 1971. She also won a Tony award for her performance in *Wings* in 1979 and has a star on the Hollywood Walk of Fame.

A CHELSEA HOUSE.—One of two new houses in Church Street, Chelsea. "In a sense they are the most 'advanced' buildings in London, but . . . they not only tone in with the general character of the neighbourhood, but seem to have a definite relationship to some old houses in the same street." Designed by Professor Walter Gropius.

8 GAY STREET

Bath's City Architect

John Wood the Elder came to Bath in the 1720s with grand dreams of creating a modern city out of the local limestone, using classical or more specifically 'Palladian' design features and innovative construction techniques. His schemes for grand squares and imposing terraces, with wide pavements for window shopping and promenading, transformed what had been a small town into the most fashionable Georgian city in Britain.

The guiding designs and plans were John Wood the Elder's, but the construction was undertaken by builders who purchased building leases. This meant that although the exterior facade followed the design laid down by Wood, the interiors and rear elevations varied depending on the builder undertaking the work.

Gay Street was constructed between 1735 and 1753 and was designed by the man responsible for Bath's stunningly consistent architectural style, John Wood the Elder. This street has long been a fashionable address in Bath and home to many notable residents, including Jane Austen (No 25), John Wood the Younger, and the infamous resident of No 8, Mrs Piozzi (Hester Thrale).

John Wood the Younger lived at No 41 Gay Street, at the south-eastern end. It is most notable for the ornate bow situated on the corner looking out over Queen Square.

Gay Street was first known as Barton Street, but also known as Montpelier for a time. It was renamed when fully completed to honour the former landowner, Robert Gay. John Wood the Elder laid it out as a main thoroughfare between his first speculative development, Queen Square (1728–34), and his grand Circus at the top of the hill. It was built in sections, with the first south-eastern section, as far as George Street, completed in 1735, and the remaining eastern section and the entire western terrace completed by 1753.

THE CARVED HOUSE

No 8 Gay Street, on the western side of the street, was completed in 1753 and has been nicknamed The Carved House for its ornate exterior decoration. The first lease for No 8 was purchased by brothers Prince and William Hoare in 1755. Prince Hoare was a well-respected sculptor who completed a number of works of celebrities from the eighteenth century, including Beau Nash and Alexander Pope. William Hoare was a celebrated artist well known for his portrait painting. During his training in Italy William Hoare met a number of other Grand Tourists who would later become his patrons, including the 3rd and 4th Dukes of Beaufort, George Lyttelton and Charles Hanbury Williams.

The constant influx of wealthy visitors to fashionable Bath, and William Hoare's close connection to the Royal Mineral Water Hospital, meant he was able to establish a very successful business in portrait painting. He painted a number of personalities, including George Frederic Handel, Beau Nash, and Prime Ministers Robert Walpole and William Pitt the Elder. In 1769, at the king's special request, he was also a founding member of The Royal Academy, alongside Joshua Reynolds and Thomas Gainsborough.

However, records reveal that during the 1760s the house was occupied by celebrated physician Dr Rice Charleton, who treated many who came to Bath, including Princess Amelia, the second daughter of King George II, and artist Thomas Gainsborough, for 'Nervous Fever'. Throughout this time, William Hoare continued as the owner of No 8 until his death in 1792, at which time it passed to his youngest son, also named Prince Hoare. Records reveal that

between 1775 and 1784 the house became the home of another prominent physician, Dr Francis Woodward. He is remembered for treating the great naval hero Admiral Lord Nelson, who arrived in Bath in January 1781, at which time it was believed he was suffering from a tropical disease. Nelson took the waters, as well as instructing Dr Woodward as his personal physician.

MRS PIOZZI

Dr Woodward continued at No 8 Gay Street until his death in 1785 and it was several years later, during the early 1800s that the house became the home of Mrs Piozzi, the former Mrs Hester Thrale.

Mrs Piozzi was a prolific writer, diarist and biographer of Samuel Johnson. During her first marriage to wealthy brewer Henry Thrale, she had run a famous literary salon at their country house in Streatham and had been at the heart of fashionable society. She visited Bath a number of times, during the late eighteenth and early nineteenth centuries, where she continued at the centre of a lively literary circle, which included, most famously, Samuel Johnson. However, after Mr Thrale passed away in 1781 Hester shocked society by marrying an Italian Roman Catholic musician, Gabriel Mario Piozzi, in 1784, and for many years was shunned by her former friends, including Samuel Johnson, who it was thought might become her second husband. Records, including her own personal diaries, reveal Mrs Piozzi lived at No 8 Gay Street from 1816 through to 1819, when she moved to Bristol. She died in May 1821, at the age of 80. In 1899, a plaque was unveiled at No 8 to honour her residence at the house.

OTHER RESIDENTS

From 1825 into the 1840s, No 8 became the home of the Severs family, with Benjamin and Elizabeth and their two daughters, Elizabeth and Jane. At the 1841 census, Severs was widowed, in his seventies, and 'independent', while his two daughters were unmarried and in their fifties. The sisters remained in the house after their father's death, in 1847, and the 1851 census records Elizabeth was 62 years old, Jane, 61, and both were recorded as 'fund holder'. After their deaths in 1866 (Jane) and 1870 (Elizabeth), the house became the home of a surgeon, Dr Samuel P. Budd, who was recorded in the 1881 census as from Plymouth, unmarried, 37 years old and living with his mother, Jane St John Budd. Samuel P. Budd came from a family of surgeons, including his uncle, William, who was the first to establish how disease spreads, in particular cholera and typhoid. However, Samuel established a lucrative practice in Bath with 'fashionable clientele' and was also noted as an authority on the Bath waters. Budd remained at Gay Street until 1899, when he passed away at the age of 55.

Budd's practice partner since 1898, Dr Gilbert John King-Martyn, took over the home and continued the practice for the next twenty-five years. The 1901 census records Dr King-Martyn as single, aged 32, with two live-in servants, but by the time of the 1911 census, he had married Annie Louise from New Zealand and the couple were living in the twelve-bedroom house with three servants. In 1913 King-Martyn was appointed as consulting physician for The Mineral Water Hospital (today the Royal National Hospital for Rheumatic Diseases). His obituary in the *British Medical Journal* explains that his health suffered greatly from overwork during the First World War and the Bath Directory records show that he kept No 8 on until 1925. From the end of the Second World War until the early 1950s No 8 continued as a private home when, like much of Gay Street, it was converted into offices.

1881 Census showing surgeon Samuel Budd.

HORSESHOE COTTAGE

Agriculture

Wixford is set in the middle of a vast agricultural landscape and even up until the late twentieth century this was the dominant form of work. By the seventeenth century, records show the cottage and land were owned by yeoman farmer Mr John Allen. It appears most likely that the property continued in the Allen family for generations, with records (at the time of enclosure in 1767) and land tax records (from 1775) detailing another John Allen as owner-occupier until the 1790s.

This 300-year-old cottage in Wixford was originally built as a yeoman's house and appears at first sight to be a typical Warwickshire timber-framed house.

The cottage has been altered over the centuries, leaving behind a number of architectural mysteries which make the study of this house history quite a challenge. Horseshoe Cottage (which was unnamed and unnumbered until the 1960s) has witnessed changes in rural life, domestic history, as well as in architectural style. On a first walkabout inside, Horseshoe Cottage appears to be quite an enigma: it is often unclear where one room ends and another starts. There is a trap door through to the dining room, hidden doorways in the kitchen and cupboards that don't belong, but still somehow fit. So, how to make sense of the history of Horseshoe Cottage?

SHAKESPEARE & WIXFORD VILLAGE

The village was immortalised by William Shakespeare, who lived nearby in Stratford-upon-Avon. In fact, his wife's house, Anne Hathaway's Cottage, shows distinct similarities to Horseshoe Cottage and is only a few miles away. It is commonly believed that after a heavy night drinking Shakespeare wrote this short poem in a pledge never to drink with the men of:

> Piping Pebworth, dancing Marston,
> Haunted Hillborough, hungry Grafton,
> Dodging Exhall, *Papist Wixford*,
> Beggarly Broom and drunken Bidford.

The reference to 'Papist' was aimed at the influential local Catholic Throckmorton family. They were involved in the plot to place Mary Queen of Scots on the throne in 1583 ('The Throckmorton Plot') and were also involved in the 1605 Gunpowder Plot. Records for the village date back to the tenth century. These show that the manor passed to Sir George Throckmorton in 1541 (in whose family it remained until 1919), after the Dissolution of the Monasteries in the sixteenth century removed it from the Abbey of Evesham, its owner since AD 973.

CONVERSIONS & MYSTERIES

Building work on the cottage began around the late seventeenth or early eighteenth century. The timber construction features wall posts and tie-beams, and the exterior shows a square panel style with the occasional diagonal brace; all common techniques in the county at the time. The original interior layout would also have been very different to what we see today, as fireplaces, doors and windows have all been moved over time.

Old postcard of Horseshoe Cottage, 1916.

Sources

The Warwickshire County Record Office has an insurance certificate for the house, taken out by the new owner, Joseph Fisher, on 25 March 1868 with the Phoenix Assurance Company. The cottage to the right was valued at £100 and described as 'brick, timber and tiled in tenure of Bennett, labourer', while the other cottage was valued at £80 and described as 'brick, timber and thatched in tenure of Beasley, labourer'.

It was during the Regency period, around 1830, that the first major change took place at Horseshoe Cottage. It was at this time that the cottage appears to have been divided into two (a left and a right-hand side) and the neighbouring Stone House was added to the right of the cottage. Some of the mysterious anomalies in the house now begin to make sense. Given the connections between the right-hand side of Horseshoe Cottage and Stone House, one theory is that Stone House was originally joined to the cottage. This explains the old doorway that appears to have led through to Stone House, as well as a former space looking directly into Stone House from the upper floor of Horseshoe Cottage, and also the cupboard overhang that still survives today.

CHANGING OCCUPANTS

The 1830 land tax records show Thomas Duffin as owner, with the two sides of the cottage occupied by agricultural labourers William Simpson and George Mucklow. By the late 1830s Duffin had moved into one side of the cottage house and Mucklow was still living in the cottage to the left. By the time of the 1841 census the cottage was clearly two separate homes: one belonging to Mucklow and his family and the other to architectural labourer, Charles Forester, with his wife and two children.

At the time of the 1851 census, a 61-year-old cordwainer (leather shoe-maker), William Bennett, his wife Hannah (aged 57) and their four children were occupying the cottage to the right (next to Stone House). The eldest daughter, 21-year-old Amanda, was working as a governess, while George, aged 19, and Edwin, aged 18, were following in their father's footsteps as cordwainers; the youngest, 13-year-old Frederick, was still at school. The cottage to the left was home to 39-year-old gardener William Beasley and his family.

By 1863 both families remained, but the two sides of the cottage and Stone House were now owned by Elizabeth Charles. By 1868 documents show that she sold the whole property to a gentleman farmer, Mr Joseph Fisher, for the sum of £500. Interestingly, the archives still hold the letters sent to the occupants of the cottages giving eight months' notice for them to quit the premises in September 1868.

Joseph Fisher left the freehold of Stone House and the cottages to his nephews, William Wadams Fisher and John Wadams, in the late 1870s. William remained as freeholder until 1896, when it appears to have passed to his daughters. From the 1870s to the 1880s William Beasley continued in his cottage, but by the 1891 census he had been replaced by a shepherd, Charles Hickson, and his wife Sarah Jane, who now lived in the three-roomed cottage. An independent 63-year-old woman, Elizabeth Osbourne, was listed in the 1881 census as living on her own in the right-hand cottage.

TWENTIETH-CENTURY COTTAGE

In 1901 the cottage to the right was occupied by agricultural labourer John James and his wife Anne, both 76 years old, their 30-year-old unmarried daughter Annie, working as a domestic servant, and 10-year-old Geoffrey James, recorded as a son, who is believed to possibly be the illegitimate son of Annie.

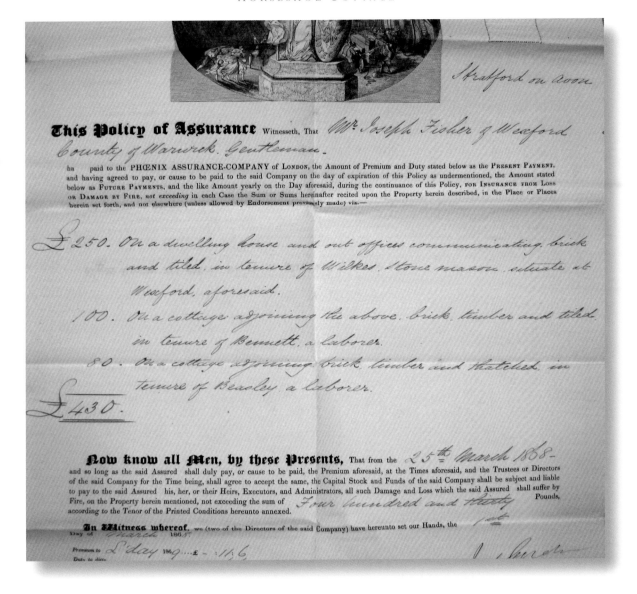

Stratford on Avon

This Policy of Assurance Witnesseth, That *Mr Joseph Fisher of Wexford County of Warwick. Gentleman.*

ha paid to the PHŒNIX ASSURANCE-COMPANY of LONDON, the Amount of Premium and Duty stated below as the PRESENT PAYMENT, and having agreed to pay, or cause to be paid to the said Company on the day of expiration of this Policy as undermentioned, the Amount stated below as FUTURE PAYMENTS, and the like Amount yearly on the Day aforesaid, during the continuance of this Policy, FOR INSURANCE FROM LOSS OR DAMAGE BY FIRE, not exceeding in each Case the Sum or Sums hereinafter recited upon the Property herein described, in the Place or Places herein set forth, and not elsewhere (unless allowed by Endorsement previously made) viz.—

£250. *On a dwelling house and out offices communicating. brick and tiled, in tenure of Wilkes. Stone mason. situate at Wexford. aforesaid.*

100. *On a cottage adjoining the above. brick. timber and tiled. in tenure of Bennett. a laborer.*

80. *On a cottage adjoining brick. timber and thatched. in tenure of Beadley a laborer.*

£430.

Now know all Men, by these Presents, That from the *25th March 1868* and so long as the said Assured shall duly pay, or cause to be paid, the Premium aforesaid, at the Times aforesaid, and the Trustees or Directors of the said Company for the Time being, shall agree to accept the same, the Capital Stock and Funds of the said Company shall be subject and liable to pay to the said Assured his, her, or their Heirs, Executors, and Administrators, all such Damage and Loss which the said Assured shall suffer by Fire, on the Property herein mentioned, not exceeding the sum of *Four hundred and thirty* Pounds, according to the Tenor of the Printed Conditions hereunto annexed.

In Witness whereof, we (two of the Directors of the said Company) have hereunto set our Hands, the Day of *March* 1865

Premium to *L'day 1869....£ - :11; 6*
Duto to ditto.

Insurance certificate for the two cottages and Stone House, 1868.

The Inland Revenue valuation survey and the 1911 census give a good picture of life in the cottages. Firstly, the valuation survey shows that the cottage to the left was occupied by 46-year-old farm labourer Henry Bailey, his wife Sophia and four children, including 24-year-old James, a brick maker. It was described as having two bedrooms on the first floor and a kitchen, scullery and washhouse on the ground floor. The slightly larger five-roomed cottage on the right was occupied by 27-year-old John Robbins, his wife Ellen and their 1-year-old son. It was described as tiled and in good repair, with the same layout as its neighbour. As a blacksmith, John would have been paid more than Henry the labourer. The Baileys remained here until the outbreak of the Second World War in 1939.

It appears that there was a period of transition after the Second World War and one or both cottages may have been vacant for a time. The name of Horseshoe Cottage only appeared during the mid 1960s when the house had been converted back into a single family home.

LAVENDER COTTAGE

L avender Cottage and its surrounding rural area is a unique remnant of the smallholding farm system that was popular during the first half of the twentieth century, after the government introduced the Small Holdings Act in 1908. Local councils were required to buy land to lease out as smallholdings and allotments, to allow people to grow food through small dairy farms, orchards and vegetable plots.

THE LEMONS

The area surrounding today's Lavender Cottage, down as far as Little Woodcote Lane, originally covered over 71 acres and was purchased by the Surrey Agricultural Committee – for £5,500 in December 1912 – for small-holdings. At this time, the area was commonly referred to as 'The Lemons', named after the first detached cottage to be built there (today's No 274 Woodcote Road), where the former owner had cultivated 8 acres of fruit plantations. New semi-detached cottages were built, including Lavender Cottage, completed in 1913. There are no clear records as to the cottage's occupancy at the time, possibly due to the outbreak of war in 1914 halting the whole development.

'Homes for Heroes'

After the First World War, the need for smallholdings, to allow returning servicemen to get back into work, was a high priority for the government. In 1919 Surrey County Council purchased more land to the west of 'The Lemons', the 370-acre 'Little Woodcote Estate'. This formed part of an initiative offering 'Homes for Heroes' under the Land Settlement Act. The Estate was initially divided into ten smallholding farms ranging from 17 to 50 acres in size. Prior to this, a large part of the Little Woodcote Estate was used for growing lavender and peppermint – clearly the inspiration for the name 'Lavender Cottage'.

Records for Surrey smallholdings show that Mr Charles Machell moved into Lavender Cottage shortly after the First World War. His annual rent of £11 18s 6d included the house and 8 acres of arable land. He continued to work his land until his death in 1952. Military records for his son, Leslie George Machell, reveal he fought as a private with the 21st London Regiment during the war. Leslie joined his father in becoming a smallholder, moving to 68 Little Woodcote Lane in 1925.

The Machell family were closely linked with farming in the area throughout the twentieth century, and after Charles passed away, Lavender Cottage and the land passed to his grandson, Godfrey. In 1953 the annual rent was re-evaluated to become £58 15s 10d. The house consisted of 'three bedrooms, bathroom, two living rooms, kitchen, larder, hall and outside W.C.' As the house was improved, so too the rents rose at each evaluation through the 1950s, going up to £87 after a bathroom and hot water system was installed. In 1968 Godfrey took over his father's farm, bringing the two Machell farms together.

7–9 PRINCELET STREET

Huguenot Refugees

The turning point for Spitalfields came late in the seventeenth century from a change in the political situation in France, when King Louis XIV revoked the Edict of Nantes (which had been created by King Henry IV for the protection of Protestants in France). French Protestants, known as Huguenots, fled to England to escape persecution. Many found their way to Spitalfields, creating a new community of highly skilled silk weavers.

Richard Horwood map, 1799.

Built in 1718 as one of Spitalfields' original Georgian homes, this was formerly the residence of a Huguenot silk dealer, two Jewish jewellers and a cigar-making family. Princelet Street was first known as Princes Street and was part of the complete transformation of this area, from rural fields during the seventeenth century to a thriving Huguenot and then Jewish urban community. Today, it is one of the most popular places to live in central London.

DEVELOPMENT OF SPITALFIELDS

The name 'Spitalfields' originated from the hospital of St Mary Spital, a large monastery that gave refuge and lodging to the poor, established in 1197. This land, however, was sold off in 1537 at the time of Henry VIII's Dissolution of the Monasteries. Later in the sixteenth century, part of the land was used by the Honourable Artillery Company for shooting grounds and testing guns (hence street names like Artillery Row and Gun Street nearby). Until the early 1700s, the area south of Hanbury Street, down to

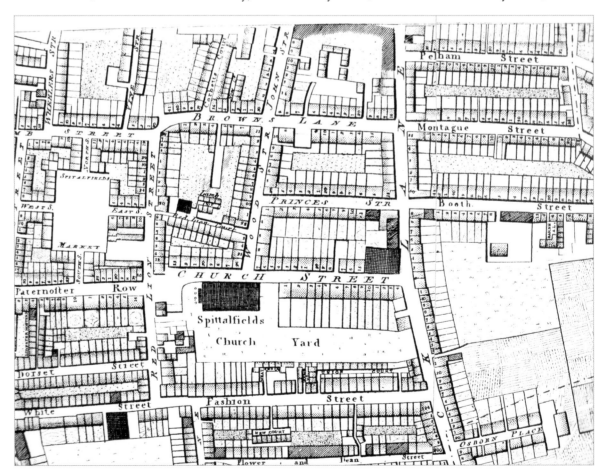

Clerks & Jewellers

The local directories in the 1840s and the 1841 census show that 23 Princes Street was the home of a 30-year-old clerk, Andrew Marr Esq., and his wife Janet. However, at the same time the house was also home to another young clerk, George Hay, and a Mary Ann Western. By 1850 the house had become the home of 49-year-old Jacob Finsterer, a 'dealer in jewellery', his wife Mabette and their three children, Matilda, Lonnie and Isaac, all from Germany. At a time when Spitalfields was known for its lower economic status and poverty-stricken residents, it is noteworthy that the Finsterers appear to have occupied the whole house and had one live-in servant. As a result of his business, the exterior was re-fronted during the middle of the nineteenth century and changes were made to the carriageway to the left of the house.

the south of Princelet Street, was open land known as 'Joyce's Gardens'. The area south of Princelet Street, along Fournier Street, was used as tenter ground – cloth being stretched out on 'tenter hooks' to dry in the open.

The land in this area was acquired by Charles Wood and Simon Mitchell of Lincoln's Inn during the early 1700s, and by 1717 they had begun to build houses. The estate's most prominent builder, Samuel Worrall, completed 9 Princelet Street and its neighbours in 1718. At this time the street was named Princesse Street, later becoming Princes Street. Wood and Mitchell requested permission to construct sewers from houses in Princes Street, which at the time was not normal practice and gives an indication of the high quality of the homes they built. Worrall still held the lease for No 9 in 1724, when it passed to Simon Mitchell's son and heir, Richard Mitchell.

EARLY HOUSE-NUMBERING SYSTEM

During this early period the houses were not actually numbered, and it was only in 1772 that the house officially became 23 Princes Street, brought about by a local act for the management and organisation of 'paving, cleansing, lighting, watching [security] and regulating'. At this time, Princes Street was in fact the area's third most popular street, behind Spital Square and Wilkes Street.

With very few properties numbered clearly it is difficult to identify individual houses within records, but it has been established that during the 1750s the house was home to a silk broker and dealer, Peter Lewis Saubergue, of Huguenot origins. Saubergue was also one of the fifty-nine church wardens who took responsibility for carrying out the management of the Act of 1772. However, by 1775 he appeared in the *London Gazette* bankruptcy listings, and in 1778 he was recorded as an inmate of London's infamous King's Bench debtors' prison.

By the early nineteenth century the Spitalfields silk-weaving industry had deteriorated due to improvements in machine production and imports from France and Italy. This decline led to rising poverty and disruption amongst the weavers. Riots became more frequent and in the 1770s resulted in the 'Spitalfields Acts' which allowed for the regulation of the industry. However, these acts brought in such restrictions that they contributed to the demise of a once prosperous trade.

The land tax records reveal that by the 1790s the ownership of the house had passed to the Sherwood family, who retained it until the 1840s.

1881 Census with the earlier numbers and showing jeweller Morris Barkman.

JEWISH SETTLERS

During the mid nineteenth century fewer Huguenot weavers remained in Spitalfields and the area welcomed a new community of refugees. A large number of Jews moved into the area fleeing persecution from Russia and Poland. Statistics show that by the 1880s, 60–70,000 Jews had moved to the East End.

By 1860, 23 Princes Street had seen new residents arrive: a Polish jeweller, Morris Barkman, and his wife Catherine. At the time of the 1861 census Morris was not recorded at home and it appears he was travelling (he was also listed as 'hawker' or travelling salesman). But Catherine was at home with their six children, including 22-year-old machinist, Elizabeth; 16-year-old mercantile clerk, Matthew; and 15-year-old apprentice watchmaker, Abraham. The Barkman family remained in the house throughout the late nineteenth century, with Morris and Catherine being recorded there at the 1891 census. Their children, however, had left home by this time and the couple were living with just one live-in servant. The London Directory shows that Morris remained in the house until 1897, by which time the street had been renamed Princelet Street, but the house was still numbered No 23.

CIGAR MANUFACTURERS

The 1901 census shows the house was home to another Jewish family, this time cigar manufacturers. Aaron Solomon, his wife Sarah, their four children and a niece. The eldest daughter, Rebecca, and younger son, Harris, were both recorded as cigar makers, while the eldest son, Sepman, was recorded as a painter.

The house was officially renumbered as No 7–9 in the mid 1920s. Around 1955 the house became the offices for a printing firm and remained as commercial property for many years. Today it is a fine Grade II listed residential house retaining many historical features.

The Oldest Synagogues in England

Princelet Street was central to the thriving Jewish community and remnants of this history still survive today, most notably at No 19, one of the oldest synagogues in England. The front of No 19 is an original eighteenth-century weavers' house, but the synagogue was built at the back of the property in 1869. Today, this is a Museum of Immigration.

Documents show that while the Barkman family were living at 23 Princes Street, it was owned by a Mr Henry Pige Leschallas from Surrey (he also owned other Princelet Street houses). He was a successful businessman whose Huguenot family first came to Spitalfields in the 1700s. He inherited a large estate from his cousin, John Leschallas, in 1874, but it is unclear as to whether 23 Princes Street was part of this inheritance.

NORTH FRITH PARK

For Sale

In 1842 the North Frith Estate was for sale and was advertised in *The Times* as having 840 acres of land, 'which includes 540 [acres] of the finest underwood in the country and in a beautiful situation for a residence'. The estate was purchased by Jasper Atkinson, who was still living at North Frith at the time of the 1851 census. Atkinson was recorded as 'provost of the royal mint', from Dulwich, aged 61. John Marsh was also still recorded as living on the estate in 1851, listed as agricultural labourer with his wife Eliza and six children.

North Frith Park is a large country house completed in 1899 and situated in 65 acres of Kentish countryside near Hadlow. The woods and grounds of North Frith were formerly attached to the manor of Hadlow and populated with deer and goshawks for hunting. This was originally in the hands of the dukes of Buckingham, but was later confiscated by Henry VIII during the sixteenth century. By the nineteenth century, North Frith was still predominately woodlands, but the land was also being used for farming. Along with a hunting lodge, a 'homestead' had been built – not the house that stands today – with accompanying farm buildings and outhouses. By the time of the tithe survey in 1840, the homestead was owned by Christopher Idle and occupied by farmer and gamekeeper John Marsh.

By 1856 North Frith had become the home of Edward Hales, a gentleman farmer, who at the time of the 1861 census was responsible for 430 acres and employing twenty men. He was living in a house on the estate with his wife Caroline and three daughters, Sarah, Elizabeth and Mary. Along with the running of North Frith, Edward Hales was also a company speculator, and through the 1850s and '60s was listed as Director of the National Discount Company Ltd; Managing Director of the Oilseed Crushing Company; and by 1865, Director of Britannia Life Assurance Company.

THE ESTATE

The freehold of North Frith was put up for auction in 1862, at which time the estate had 'a commodious residence, placed upon a fine eminence, commanding most extensive views'. However, it appears that the estate did not sell at this time; in fact, Edward Hales seems to have extended it, as by the 1880s it had grown by a further 35 acres.

By the time of the 1881 census the house was still home to Edward Hales, listed as a widower, aged 70, living with his unmarried daughter Mary and one servant, Martha Williams. He was farming 465 acres and employed fifteen men and four boys. In 1885 the North Frith Estate was once again for sale, advertised in *The Times* as 'an important freehold manorial estate … comprising an old fashioned residence, with pleasure grounds' and a number of additional buildings. It continued: 'This property has been in the occupation of the present owner for upwards 30 years … and since 1858 kept on the estate a large herd of pure-bred shorthorn cattle, which has attained great celebrity.'

1891 Census showing Thomas Boyd at North Frith Mansion.

No. of Schedule	ROAD, STREET, &c., and No. or NAME of HOUSE	Inhabited	NAME and Surname of each Person	RELATION to Head of Family	CONDITION as to Marriage	Age Male	Age Female	PROFESSION or OCCUPATION	Employer	Employed	Own account	WHERE BORN
117	North Frith (Farm House)	1	Robert Mathers	Head	M	58		Farm Bailiff F.B.		X		Lincolns. Scawby
			Sophia Do	Wife	M		54					Kent, Chiddingstone
			Mary Do	Daur.	S		21					Do Penshurst
			Harriet Do	Daur.	S		18					Do Do
			James A. Do	Son	S	20		Gardener (Domestic Serv.)		X		Do Do
			Arthur Do	Son	S	22		Butler (Dom.) Do.		X		Do Do
			George Corke	Lodger	S	24		Gamekeeper		X		N.K.
			Eliza Mathers	Daur. in Law	M		28					Somerset Huntworth
			Sidney A. Do	Grandson		1mo						Middlesex Willesdon
			Edith E. Do	Grand Daur			0					London
118	North Frith	1	George Tester	Head	M	42		Waggoner (Farm Serv.) (Front)		X		Sussex, Fletching
			Maria A. Do	Wife	M		36					Do Rotherfield
			Maria A. Do	Daur.	S		11					Do Lamberhurst
			George Do	Son		10		Scholar				Do Rotherfield
			Henry Do	Son		7		Do.				
			Rowland Do	Son		2						Kent Hadlow
119	Do.	1	Robert G. Phippin	Head	M	32		Coachman (Domestic Serv.) (Front)		X		Somerset Clapton Mallet
			Mary Do	Wife	M		30					Scotland, Wigtown Whithorn
			Edith L. Do	Daur.			2					Kent Edenbridge
			New born Child Phippin	Daur.			0					Do Hadlow
			Eliza Caddel	Visitor	M		41	Midwife Sick				Sussex Olstead
120	North Frith Mansion	1	Thomas le Boyd	Head	M	41		Provision Merchant	X			Ireland Co. Cork, City Cork
			Julia C. Do	Wife	M		29					London Clapton
			Daisy Do	Daur.			7					Do Bayswater
			Thomas R. Do	Son		6						Surrey Addiscombe
			Rupert A. Do	Son		4						Do Do
			Mary E. Do	Daur			3					Do Do
			Irene G. Do	Daur			1					Kent Hadlow
			Maria Mise	Serv.	S		30	Cook. Domestic Servant				Herts. St Albans
			Alice Howard	Serv.	S		21	Housemaid Do.				Berkshire Bisham
			Mary C. Lane	Serv.	S		22	Do. Do.				Somerset Bristol
4	Total of Houses and of Tenements with less than Five Rooms	4			Total of Males and Females	13	18					

Property Tycoon

Thomas Lunham Boyd was described as 'The Bacon King', born in Ireland and part of the Lunham Boyd family, who went on to become successful provision merchants in the American ham and bacon trade. The 1891 census records Boyd living in his newly built home with his wife Julia, five children and six servants. At the time of the 1901 census he was listed as a provision merchant, with three daughters and a son. However, his wife and two elder sons were away from home. By the time of Boyd's death in 1931 he had acquired a large fortune, with property in Canada, America and Britain, and was living in San Remo, Italy.

ARTS & CRAFTS ARCHITECTURE

It was in 1889 that Thomas Lunham Boyd commissioned architect George Friend to build a new house, now known as North Frith Park. North Frith Park was built in an Arts and Crafts red-brick vernacular style and features sandstone detailing, turrets and sections of castellated exterior.

The Lunham Boyds lived here for over twenty years, but by 1913 it had become the home of Thomas Despard Bridges. Bridges resided here with his wife Christina, having spent most of his life in Argentina. Bridges was the son of Reverend Thomas Bridges, a missionary who settled in Ushuaia in 1871 as part of the Patagonia Missionary Society. He was in fact the first recorded white baby to be born in this area of Argentina, in 1872. Thomas and Christina lived at North Frith Park for around ten years before moving to Rhodesia in 1923.

HORNE BROTHERS LTD

In 1924 North Frith Park became the home of Frederick Newman Horne of Horne Brothers Ltd, one of the most familiar gentleman's outfitters in London during the twentieth century. Horne and his family continued here during the war years until he died in 1946. His son, George, lived in the house with his mother, Florence, and other members of the family until the late 1960s.

Horne Brothers Ltd opened in London in 1884 and continued to expand throughout the twentieth century. Frederick Horne was Chairman and Managing Director of the 'Hosiers, hatters, tailors, general outfitters, and clothing manufacturers'. By the 1970s Horne Brothers had thirty-five stores across London, including their head office on Oxford Street. The family-run business was eventually sold to Sears in 1987 for £34 million.

HOTHAM HALL

Hotham Hall is located in the suburban streets of Putney and was originally built as St Mary's Hall in 1913. Despite its apparently unassuming location, this hall hosted The Rolling Stones and The Who during the 1960s and was also the location for political meetings addressed by Prime Ministers Sir Winston Churchill and Sir Anthony Eden during the 1930s.

Hotham Road was laid out during the 1840s and was first known as Hotham Villas Road after the eight large detached villas there at the time, which formerly sat between today's Charlewood Road and Gamlen Road, and where Hotham Hall and Hotham School are today.

The expansion of the Metropolitan District Railway (today's District line), to Putney Bridge in 1880 and East Putney in 1889, encouraged further building development in the area. Building along Hotham Road initially concentrated on the northern section, while on the southern section the new Putney cycling track was becoming ever more popular. The freehold of the land where Hotham Hall is located was donated to St John's Church by Misses Blanche and Elma Grace Miles for the building of a public hall in 1911. Drainage plans show that the building was designed by architect Douglas Wells and constructed by builders William Brown & Sons, and St Mary's Hall was opened by local magistrate Mr Samuel Samuel in 1913.

CELEBRITIES

In May 1933 St Mary's Hall was the location for the annual meeting of the Primrose League (a group supporting conservative politics), addressed by Winston Churchill. He spoke on the future of India, paid tribute to the work of the National Government and declared that 'the nations in their perplexity leaned upon England and found here a strong prop'.

Cycling

The Putney Velodrome was formerly located between today's Earldom and Erpingham Roads and was the first cement cycling track in England. The Putney Velodrome was the headquarters of the Putney Athletic Club and had additional facilities for tennis and bowls. The first meeting was held in August 1891, and during the 1890s the club boasted more records than any other in England. Despite this success, the opportunity for building development was too strong and when the lease expired in 1905 it was not renewed. The last cycle meeting was held in August 1905 and the track relocated to Herne Hill.

Ordnance Survey map, 1894, showing the former Putney Velodrome.

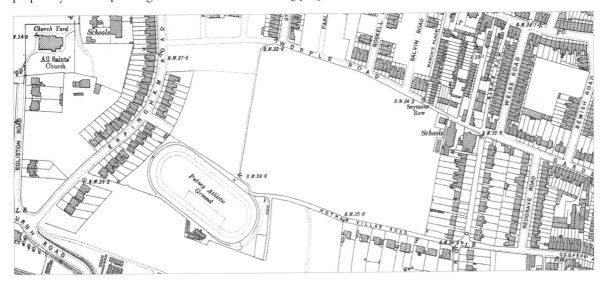

A year later, in November 1934, St Mary's Hall was the venue of another political meeting, this time for the National Conservative candidate, Mr Marcus Samuel (nephew of Mr Samuel Samuel), in the Putney by-election. He was supported by an address from Mr Anthony Eden, who at the time was Lord Privy Seal and Minister for the League of Nations.

In 1963 the hall was the location for a performance by The Rolling Stones as part of their first UK tour. They were supported by The Who, who had recently changed their name from The Detours. The Who returned to St Mary's Hall in 1964 as the support act for The Tremeloes. Very few details of these events survive, but a local resident remembers attending The Tremeloes concert, where the band gave out sweets to promote their new song *Candy Man*.

New Development

During the latter part of the twentieth century St Mary's Hall fell into disrepair and was finally closed in 1986. It was bought for redevelopment in the 1990s and completely redesigned into nine luxury apartments by The Raven Group. The loft-style apartments, renamed Hotham Hall, were first sold in 1997 and described in *The Times* as 'some of the best contemporary design you are likely to come across'.

ELM GROVE

This early seventeenth-century farmhouse is situated in an area known as 'the Marsh', and was the home of the same farming family for almost 150 years. Today, it features a picturesque exterior, added during the 1880s, and still stands amongst open fields in Henstridge, Somerset.

Henstridge was a royal estate held by King Harold during the Anglo-Saxon period and passed to William the Conqueror after the invasion. Throughout the medieval period the lands passed from the king to a number of prominent aristocratic families. By the sixteenth century, the area commonly referred to as 'the Marsh' was in the hands of the Milborne family, but was then divided between two sisters, Elizabeth Titherley and Mabel Ernle.

THE LOVELL FAMILY

During the 1820s, land tax records show the farmhouse was still owned by John Martin and occupied by 'Messrs Lovells', and was known as the 'Marsh Estate'. The census records supported by the electoral registers show Marsh Farm continued to be the home of the Lovell family throughout the nineteenth and into the early twentieth century. In the 1841 census the house was home to Thomas Lovell, his wife Matilda and their three daughters, plus a servant. The 1843 electoral registers also confirm Lovell as the occupier of 'Henstridge Marsh', but the landowner was recorded as Mr William Lambert White, who had acquired the manorial lands originally held by Elizabeth Titherley.

By the 1850s records reveal Marsh Farm had become the home of a relation of Lovell's, William Lovell, who had bought the freehold of the farmhouse and land. The 1861 census shows William living at Marsh Farm, a 'farmer of 120 acres employing 2 men and [was] a cattle dealer'. He was in the farmhouse with his wife Maria, their five children and a general live-in servant. William passed away in 1865 and the farm remained in the hands of his widow. At the time of the 1871 census Maria was away with friends and her children were at home at Marsh Farm, with daughter, Jane, 25 years old, listed as the head of the house, along with her brothers and sisters, George, Francis and Mary. The 1881 census shows that widowed Maria Lovell was still living in

Early Records

The early history of 'the Marsh', and in particular Elm Grove (or Marsh Farm), is difficult to pinpoint. The marshes had been used for farming and grazing since the fourteenth century, but Elm Grove was only constructed in the late Elizabethan period, around the turn of the seventeenth century. Early records for the area attribute the same name – 'marsh' or 'marsh farm' – to a number of different homes and buildings, making it even harder to trace the house's early history. However, sources from the late eighteenth and early nineteenth centuries become a little clearer and start to reveal who was living and working at Elm Grove. During the late eighteenth century, Marsh Farm was owned by Mr John Martin, and by 1818, property deeds show it was still owned by Martin, but was occupied by Mr William Lovell.

War Years

Gillett continued at Marsh Farm into the 1930s, after the death of his mother in 1929. As the country entered the war years, the National Farm Survey reveals a picture of what the farm was like in 1941, with Robert Gillett described as a grazier and the farmhouse was classified as 'good'. He was farming 25 acres of wheat and 10½ acres of oats, and kept 48 cows, over 320 fowl and 65 ducks.

the house aged 67 and receiving an annuity. Her son George was listed as a cattle dealer and her youngest daughter was housekeeper.

After Maria Lovell died in December 1884 her son George appeared in Kelly's Directory for Somerset as farmer at 'Marsh' (1886), and it was during this period that George made great changes to the farmhouse. He added the Victorian decorations and external detailing, and completed the renovations with a new date plaque, clearly seen under the middle gable: 'G.L. 1888'.

ELISHEBA GILLETT

The 1891 census records George Lovell in the farmhouse with his new wife, Elisheba, who it appears was formerly married to a neighbour, Thomas Gillett, who died in 1884. The parish valuation in 1896 lists Lovell as owner/occupier and notes that the farm covered almost 70 acres. The 1901 census shows the couple, aged 53 and 52 respectively, in the house with one live-in servant. The valuation survey described the house as 'in good repair' and 'the buildings are modern and excellent'.

MARSH FARM TO ELM GROVE

George lived at Marsh Farm until the end of the First World War, when he passed away, but Elisheba continued at the farm until the late 1920s. The management of Marsh Farm passed to her son from her first marriage, Robert Gillett, and it was at this point that Marsh Farm was officially renamed 'Elm Grove'.

Robert Gillett passed away in 1947 and for the first time in almost 130 years the farmhouse passed out of the hands of those connected to the Lovell family. By 1950 Elm Grove had become the home of the Warren family, who remained until the early 1960s. It later passed to Herbert and Freda Moody, and then Alfred and Christable Doble, who remained there until the 1980s.

18 LENNOX GARDENS

No 18 Lennox Gardens is situated in the centre of prestigious Knightsbridge and has been the home of many notable residents; but most prominently, it is the former home of Grand Duchess Xenia Alexandrovna Romanova, sister of Nicholas II, the last Tsar of Russia. Prior to building, this area was the site of Prince's Cricket Ground.

From 1836 the area was leased by Mr Cattleugh for market gardens, but by the 1860s and '70s new building was beginning to encroach upon the open fields. Despite this, it was decided to create a cricket ground and, in 1870, Prince's Cricket was established to accompany the other activities of Prince's Club, including tennis and ice skating. Prince's Cricket Ground became the home ground of the prestigious Middlesex County Cricket Club in 1872, though by 1876 the club had relocated to Lord's in St John's Wood.

Military Heroes

The 1885 Boyles Court Guide shows that the first resident at No 18 was Captain Walter George Barttelot, who lived there until the early 1890s, before he became Major Sir Walter Barttelot, 2nd Baronet, and died in 1900 fighting in the Boer War. After 1892, 18 Lennox Gardens became the home of William James Maitland, Most Eminent Order of the Indian Empire (CIE), who appeared in the 1901 census as 'Deputy Governing Director of Indian Guaranteed Railways – Indian Official', aged 53, with his wife Agnes. In 1913 Maitland's daughter, Marjorie, married Lieutenant Arthur Murray Longmore of the Royal Flying Corps. Longmore was one of the first naval officers to be trained in military flying, and went on to carry out some of the first bombing missions in 1914. Maitland remained at 18 Lennox Gardens until 1919 when the house became the home of his daughter and son-in-law, who by that time had been promoted to Colonel Arthur Murray Longmore, Distinguished Service Order (DSO).

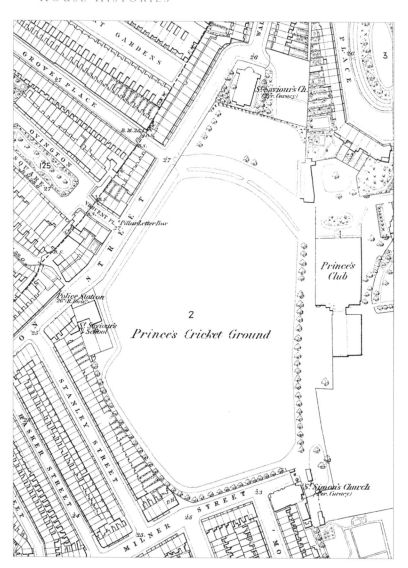

Ordnance Survey map, 1869, showing the former Prince's Cricket Ground.

MARRIAGES.

PRINCE CHAVCHAVADZE AND PRINCESS NINA OF RUSSIA.

Queen Alexandra, in a toque of black *paillettes* and a dress of mauve velvet and gold lace, with Princess Victoria whose grey marocain dress was worn with a black lace hat trimmed with pink roses and a sable stole, and Queen Olga of Greece, in white silk, were present at the marriage yesterday at the Russian Church (St. Philip's), Buckingham Palace road, of Prince Paul Chavchavadze, elder son of Prince and Princess Troubetzkoy, and Princess Nina of Russia, daughter of the Grand Duchess George of Russia. The religious ceremony had been preceded by a civil marriage on August 25 at the St. Pancras Register Office.

A reception was held by the Grand Duchess Xenia at 18, Lennox-gardens, after which the bride and bridegroom left for Warwick Castle, lent by Mrs. Marsh. Owing to the Court mourning, Queen Alexandra did not attend the reception. The large number of guests included, among others :—

Announcement of the reception at 18 Lennox Gardens, *The Times*, 4 September 1922.

The cricket grounds closed in the early 1880s, making way for the 1882–86 building developments such as Lennox Gardens. The name originated from Charles Lennox, 6th Duke of Richmond, politician and former trustee of Smith's Charity Estate. All the houses were designed in variations of the Queen Anne style that dominates much of this area of Knightsbridge. The majority of the houses along the western curve of Lennox Gardens were built by W.H. Willis, with Nos 16 and 18 believed to have been two of the first houses completed in around 1884.

FURTHER FESTIVITIES

By 1925, Geoffrey Reginald Devereux Shaw, MP and his wife Elizabeth moved to Lennox Gardens, and in October 1926 the house once again hosted a wedding reception, this time for Lieutenant W.D. Stephenson of the Royal Navy and Miss Jemima Leveson, daughter of Admiral Sir Arthur Leveson.

Throughout the twentieth century 18 Lennox Gardens continued to be the home of many eminent members of society, including Lieutenant-Colonel Charles Lyon during the 1930s; Lady Averil Tyron from 1954; and Lord Viscount Caldecote from 1977. However, during 1951–52, No 18 Lennox Gardens was also used as the offices for the organisers of the Festival of Britain 1951.

A Royal Wedding

In 1922 No 18 became the home of Grand Duchess Xenia Alexandrovna Romanova of the Russian Imperial family. Xenia only lived here for a short time during 1922, but on 3 September she hosted a wedding reception for Prince Paul Chavchavadze and Princess Nina Georgievna, niece of King George V and Queen Mary. Princess Nina was the daughter of Grand Duke George Mikhailovich of Russia and Princess Marie of Greece. Attending the reception were members of the Greek royal family, as well as many from European and British aristocratic families.

THE PARK ESTATE

Civil War

During the Civil War, Charles I raised the royal standard from Nottingham Castle (giving the south-east area the name 'Standard Hill'), but it wasn't long before the castle was commandeered by the Parliamentarians, led by Colonel John Hutchinson. With the restoration of the monarchy, staunch Royalist William Cavendish, Earl of Newcastle, purchased the by-now ruined castle in 1662 and built a new Renaissance palace. The Estate then passed to Thomas Pelham Holles, the great Whig politician who was twice Prime Minister between 1755 and 1762.

The Park Estate is situated in the heart of Nottingham on the former hunting grounds attached to Nottingham Castle. Today this is one of the most sought-after residential addresses in central Nottingham, with many well-known names having called it home. Prior to the building of houses, the open park was 'used as a promenade by all classes of society, and a most healthy appendage it is to a populous and closely built town'. This city 'lung' was especially popular as an open space for the working classes living in cramped accommodation.

ROYAL CONNECTIONS

William the Conqueror commissioned the first castle to be built on the high rock in Nottingham after the invasion in 1066, and by the time of its mention in Domesday Book (1086) it was complete. The castle was a principal royal residence for the next 400 years, often visited by Henry II during the twelfth century. It was also a favourite dwelling of King John, inspiring the legend of Robin Hood and the Sheriff of Nottingham.

NINETEENTH-CENTURY DEVELOPMENTS

However, by the early nineteenth century, the 4th Duke of Newcastle had grand aspirations for the development of the Park Estate, and in 1825 he

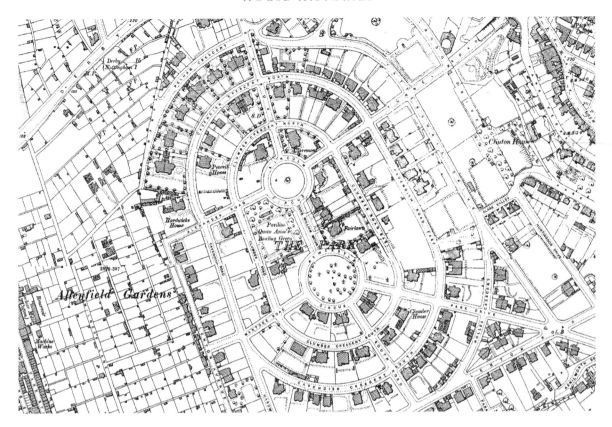

Ordnance Survey map, 1901.

engaged architect Peter Frederick Robinson to draw up plans for an extravagant scheme of impressive buildings. Robinson was to follow the street patterns used by John Nash for his fashionable London terraces comprising squares and wide roads. The first development began along the Park edges, creating The Ropewalk and Park Terrace in 1827, and Derby Terrace in 1829, which exemplified the model Robinson desired. Individual houses on Park Terrace and Park Valley followed in varied designs, including Regency pairs and Italian villas. In 1831, however, locals, angry at the duke's staunch position against the Reform Bill, attacked his palace causing extensive damage.

By this time around forty to fifty houses had been completed, mostly for the new, richer merchant and manufacturing classes who wanted large ornate homes within central Nottingham. The unique feature of a tunnel was at one point incorporated into the design to allow greater access into the Estate, but this was superseded by new roads on the outskirts of the Park, which provided more convenient routes. The duke died in 1851 and his son, Henry Pelham Clinton, continued the development of the Estate by

Watson Fothergill

About twenty-five to thirty houses designed between 1873 and 1900 in the gothic and Queen Anne style are the work of architect Watson Fothergill. He was one of the most flamboyant Nottingham architects. He mixed ornamental brickwork and stonework, soaring chimneystacks and half-timbered gables, turrets and towers.

Portrait of T.C. Hine.

appointing prominent local architect, Thomas Chambers Hine, as Estate Surveyor. This was a significant moment as Hine would act as estate designer, commissioning other architects and ensuring high standards of design and a consistency of architectural vision. Hine took advantage of natural foundations and built many houses with basements down into the original stone. He was also an inventor and created a unique gas lamp in 1874 that functioned both as a light and as a vent for the sewers beneath the Park. The original gas lighting network is still believed to be one of the largest in Europe. Hine launched his new design for the Park in 1855 and was responsible for at least 200 Park Estate houses.

HOUSE DESIGN

The long period (1830s to the early 1900s) in which the Estate was developed led to a broad mix of architectural styles, including classical Regency and gothic Victorian, with Hine repeatedly using unique decorative features and motifs, including Venetian windows, contrasting brickwork and star-shaped vents.

Covenants restricted the density of development, requiring houses to be 'set back from the road among trees, and no house was allowed to be erected which would interfere with the view from the houses'. No businesses were allowed in the Park and it was even illegal for buildings or rooms to be used by any faith other than the Church of England. Once completed, the owners were required to maintain the buildings properly, including painting exterior wood every four years and submitting to a twice-yearly inspection by Hine's office.

STONE CAVES

Hidden in the former garden of No 32, The Ropewalk, is a collection of sandstone caves. The house was the home of Alderman Thomas Herbert, a successful lace manufacturer. His back garden collapsed down the steep slope into the valley and from 1856–72 he had a series of caves cut into the stone. The caves are like a grand folly and feature decorative pillars, stone lions and ornate carvings.

After the 5th Duke of Newcastle died in 1864, the estates were managed by trustees (including former Prime Minister William Gladstone). By 1877 the Park covered 254 acres and had a population of 1,500 residents. Historian Michael Payne stated: 'By 1887 the original scheme was complete; some 650 houses stood in semi-rural splendour on an estate less than half a mile from the centre of town, and Nottingham's merchant aristocracy had a local Belgravia all of their own.'

Famous Residents

By 1900, a Park Estate address indicated that one had definitely 'arrived'. Some noteworthy residents have included: Sir Jesse Boot, founder of Boots the Chemist; Dame Laura Knight, artist and first woman to be elected to the Royal Academy; Sir Jonathan Miller, Director; Albert Ball, a fighter pilot awarded the VC; Sir Frank Bowden, founder of the Raleigh Cycle Company; Sir Paul Smith, fashion designer, and Hugh Grant the actor.

The Twentieth Century to Today

The early twentieth century brought about many alterations and extensions to the Park Estate, with a number of conversions of the larger houses into flats. In 1938, after 280 years, the 8th Duke of Newcastle sold the Estate to Oxford University. Almost fifty years later, in 1986, the Park ended up in the hands of Nottingham Park Estate Ltd, run by a board of directors elected by the residents. It was designated a conservation area in 1969 and over ninety-three of its buildings and features are listed.

6 Church Street

T his small house in the old part of riverside Chiswick was built in the eighteenth century and was formerly the village post office. The house and its occupants were a vital part of the village community; previous residents included the village baker and the grocer. No 6 Church Street is also believed to have once been the home of French philosopher Jean-Jacques Rousseau when he visited England in 1766.

THE EARLY POST OFFICE

When first built, today's Nos 6 and 7 Church Street were in fact three separate properties. This is clearly seen when looking at the upper floors, which show three pairs of windows and three central mansard windows; however, a former chimney that was located on the edge of No 6 has been removed. Although close to the former Lamb Brewery, and behind the Griffin (Fullers) Brewery, it does not appear that these homes were built for the breweries.

Jean-Jacques Rousseau.

The early details of the house are uncertain, with very few documents remaining. However, it appears the original house had long been operating as a shop with accommodation above. The parish rate books for the 1830s and '40s show that all three original homes were owned by Job and Catherine Ives, who also owned other tenements and small cottages along Church Street. The Middlesex Directory in 1837–40 lists Job Ives as the postmaster, as well as the baker, in Church Street, and the 1841 census confirms this, listing him as baker, aged 40, with his wife Catherine, aged 25.

The tithe map of 1847 clearly defines the three separate houses, but by this time Ives had passed away leaving his widow living in one of the homes, while the post office was occupied by new postmaster David Spence. Spence was listed in the 1851 census as a 'master baker' living in Church Street with his wife Mary and their four daughters: Mary, Sarah, Anne and Georgeanna (sic). Also listed in the house at this time were three 'journeyman bakers' – George Dow, James McPhenan and John Bailey – along with two servants.

HAIRDRESSER'S

By the time of the 1896 Ordnance Survey map, the two homes to the north (today's No 6) had been combined to make one larger house labelled as post office, alongside the smaller house to the south (today's No 7). It is also believed that at this time the large double-fronted window was added, which is certainly fitting for the house becoming a grocery store during the late Victorian period.

The 1901 census shows the Spencer family at No 6 Church Street, with William's son, aged 18, working in the shop with his father. Spencer, and his son after him, remained at No 6 as the village grocer and postmaster until around 1930 when the post office relocated down the street towards the church and was operated by Mrs Craig. Spencer continued to run the grocers from No 6 for a short time, but by 1935–36 it had become a hairdresser's, run by Albert Swannell. This new venture operated until 1942, when Mrs Craig revived the post office at No 6A Church Street.

CHANGING FACE OF CHISWICK

It was also during the 1930s that this part of Chiswick saw great change, with the first road developments affecting the layout of the village. The northern section of Church Street, with the buildings that formerly stood to the north and west of the post office, was demolished to make way for the extension of Mawson Lane and Great Chertsey Road – today's A4 and Burlington Lane. Throughout the late twentieth century No 6 Church Street continued to operate as the village post office, as well as a confectioner's and tobacconist's, playing a vital role in the old village of Chiswick.

Rousseau Lodges Here

Rousseau completed his controversial book *Emile* in May 1762 and it was almost immediately banned in both France and Switzerland for its heretical comments relating to the Church in France. He was forced to leave Paris and sought refuge in England. For a short while he lodged upstairs at No 6 Church Street, then the village grocery shop and post office operated by Mr Pulleyn.

Grocer & Cheesemongers

By the 1880s, the shop had changed from a bakery to a 'grocer and cheesemongers' run by Frank Trotman. The 1881 census records he was in the house with his wife Caroline and his cousin Arthur Bevan working as 'grocers assistant', and William Spencer, listed as 'telegraphist'. The 1888 Directory reveals William Spencer followed Trotman as postmaster and grocer, and by the time of the 1891 census he was in the house with his wife Caroline and their three children, along with a boarder, William Sheppard, the grocer's assistant, and a domestic servant, Mary Wood.

16 PERCY CIRCUS

Today, Percy Circus retains only part of the original development built by William Chadwell Mylne during the 1840s. The name of Percy Circus originated from Robert Percy Smith, whose brother, Sydney Smith, was Director of the New River Company. The New River Company formerly purchased this part of Islington for the New River Head.

Large sections of Percy Circus were badly damaged during the Blitz in the Second World War and were redeveloped as apartments in the 1960s. One notable house that does not remain is No 16 Percy Circus, demolished during the 1960s – it was the former home of one of the twentieth century's most significant world leaders: Vladimir Ilyich Lenin.

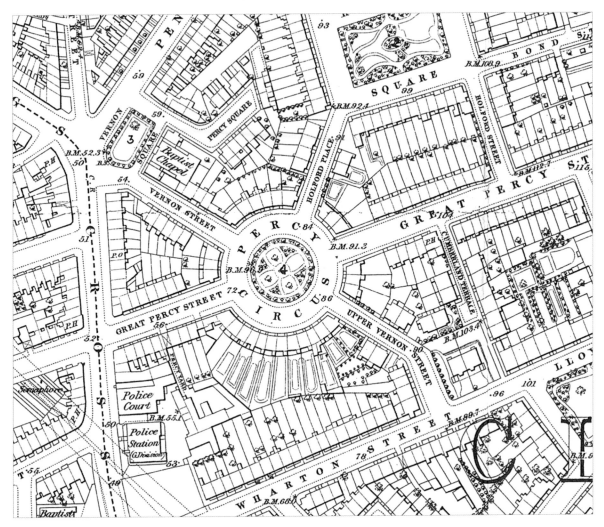

Ordnance Survey map, 1871.

VLADIMIR LENIN

Russian revolutionary and founder of the USSR, Vladimir Lenin visited
London a few times during the early twentieth century, but it was during
his visit in the spring of 1905, when he attended the third congress of the
Russian Social-Democratic Labour Party, that he lived in Percy Circus.
A blue plaque commemorates his residence. The year 1905 was significant
for Lenin and Russian politics, with Bloody Sunday taking place in the
January of that year and the ensuing events culminating in the 1905 revolution. What came to be known as the 'first revolution' was the prequel to the
1917 Russian Revolution which ultimately culminated in the establishment
of the Union of Soviet Socialist Republics (USSR) in 1922.

Vladimir Ilyich Lenin.

40 Lime Tree Walk

New Cottages, Lime Tree Walk, Sevenoaks

House Numbering

When first completed, the houses in Lime Tree Walk were numbered differently and No 40 was No 20. The house was finished by the 1881 census, when it was the home of William Bevan, a 43-year-old carpenter from Stratford-upon-Avon, his wife Katherine, and nine children aged between 1 and 19. Also in the house at this time was Katherine's unmarried aunt, 66-year-old former school teacher Jane King.

In 1929 the house numbers along Lime Tree Walk were reorganised and the house officially became No 40 Lime Tree Walk. By this time the house was home to the Heaths' son, Ernest, along with Rosemary Gray. He remained here during the Second World War and by 1955 he was recorded in the house with his wife, Mary Rose, and their son Nigel. From 1960 the house was solely occupied by Nigel Heath and his wife Mollie, who continued to live at No 40 until the early 1980s.

The houses along Lime Tree Walk were built between 1878–82 by Sir Thomas Graham Jackson and his father. They were built specifically for working-class residents within a high-class residential area that created an 'artisan style' environment within minutes of the busy London Road.

Sir Thomas had trained under Sir George Gilbert Scott and also worked with architect Richard Norman Shaw editing *Architecture: A Profession or an Art*, published in 1892. Sir Thomas worked on many Oxford buildings and was also responsible for restorations and additions to buildings in Eton, Harrow, the Inner Temple, as well as the Bodleian Library and Radley College.

THE HEATH FAMILY

By the time of the 1901 census, the house had become the home of 50-year-old chimney sweep James Heath, his wife, Elizabeth, and their five children, who continued in the house through to 1920. However, by 1922 Elizabeth was in the house with Maud Heath, along with another family, with Frederick and Emily Bowman and Charles Webb also listed as occupants.

HORSESHOE WHARF

This is one of the most historic parts of London, home to the most notorious prison, the stunning Southwark Cathedral and Shakespearean theatre. More recently it has been used for many film and TV locations, including *Dr Who* and *Bridget Jones's Diary*.

An archaeological study conducted by the Museum of London Archaeology Group has shown that the first riverside embankment, by today's Horseshoe Wharf, dates back to the twelfth century. It was at this time, around 1150, that the Bishop of Winchester established his London home by the riverside, and it was here that the bishop would have had a private landing stage providing entry to his palace. The remains of the bishop's fourteenth-century palace are still one of the few hidden gems of London, with the remaining west wall and the partial rose window tucked between the warehouse buildings.

Roman Settlement

This area of Bankside is one of the oldest settled parts of London and has been continuously occupied since the Romans arrived in the first century. The road we know today as Clink Street runs from St Mary Overie Dock, once the site of the Priory of St Mary Overie, down to the Anchor pub, the last remnant of the large former Anchor Brewery, once owned by Samuel Johnson's friends, the Thrales.

Archaeology

The name of 'Horseshoe' originates from an old tavern that formerly sat by Southwark Bridge. The archaeological study of the riverside revealed that a revetment was built in the fourteenth century, but it wasn't until the late sixteenth and early seventeenth centuries that a stone wall was built. This correlates with the time when the area was inundated with people visiting the theatres and taverns. The name of Clink Street first appeared in records during the 1640s and around the same time tenements were built over the site. However, these buildings were demolished between the 1760s and 1790s when a new brick river wall was built.

THE CLINK PRISON

The Bishop of Winchester's presence had a great impact on the history of Bankside as he ruled over the area as lord of the manor. He held his own court and even his own prison – The Clink – which formerly sat to the west of Stoney Street and gave its name to the entire area, known as the manor of the Clink. The Clink was one of the worst prisons in London where prisoners were left to starve or literally rot in their cells. The name 'Clink' is believed to originate from the word for keyhole, but is also thought to be associated with the 'clinking' of keys – either way, the name is now synonymous with the name for prison.

As the area of Bankside was under the jurisdiction of the bishop, and not the City of London, the area became populated with many people who wanted to escape the laws and regulations of the City, including prostitutes and, most famously, actors. During the sixteenth and seventeenth centuries it became known as the 'playground of the City of London' and was the original red light district (with an alley called 'Whores Nest') when Soho was just sheep fields. The area from Clink Street towards today's Blackfriars Bridge became the home of the theatres that made Shakespeare famous, along with bear-baiting arenas and taverns.

VICTORIAN HORSESHOE WHARF

It was during the late eighteenth century that industry began to take over the riverside, permanently changing the image of Bankside and creating the appearance of Clink Street that is recognisable today. After the new river wall was completed in the 1790s, warehouses and wharfs were built, with the first Horseshoe Wharf completed in 1837. The 1838 London Directory confirms that Horseshoe Wharf was first occupied by lighterman John Raymond. Lightermen operated the small flat-bottomed boats known as 'lighters' which transported goods from ships to the quays. John Raymond & Son stayed at Horseshoe Wharf for almost forty years until the 1870s. *The Times* newspaper records an advertisement for the sale of Horseshoe Wharf in 1886, 'with steam power … a 58ft river frontage and consisting of two buildings of four floors'. The lease at this time was still held by the Bishop of Winchester. The trade directory in 1886 shows that it was then occupied by the Doo Brothers, lightermen, and George Doo, wharfinger (or docker), but by 1891 it was occupied by John Muir & Company, corn merchants and grain cleaning company. During the early twentieth century it was occupied by granary keepers, along with Amalgamated Dairies, two packaging material merchants, and rope manufacturers.

TODAY

The 1830s Horseshoe Wharf building was demolished in 1998 in cooperation with English Heritage, and it was at this time the archaeological study took place. Today's Horseshoe Wharf building, featuring twelve luxury apartments, was one of the first apartment blocks with large high-value flats that illustrated the desirability of Bankside as a place to live after the transformation from warehouses and wharfs. The apartment block was completed for Oakmayne Properties in 2000 and is now a sought-after residential location.

THE CHANTRY

The Chantry in Combe Raleigh, Devon, is a rare surviving fifteenth-century priest's house. Now Grade I listed it has survived for over 500 years with many historic features still intact. It was built during the 1490s, after a chantry was established by lords of the manor, William and Joan Dennys. After the Dissolution of the Chantries in 1547, it was owned by the Bonville family, ancestors of the unfortunate Lady Jane Grey, before it came to the Marwood family, physicians to Elizabeth I and James I.

The village of Combe Raleigh took its name from an early lord of the manor, Sir John Ralegh (sic), during the fourteenth century. The manor passed to Ralegh's daughter who married Sir Thomas St Aubyn and was then passed down through a number of generations. By the late fifteenth century it was in the hands of Joan St Aubyn, who married William Dennys. It was during the 1460s, when Joan and William Dennys were lord and lady of the manor, that they founded a chantry with a priest in Combe Raleigh. A chantry house was established as a home for the priest who was employed to 'chant' or sing the mass for the souls of the founders, or for people specified by them. In 1466 William Dennys also became the High Sheriff of Devon.

Architectural Highlights

Architectural studies by English Heritage, along with other Devonshire histories, give the construction of The Chantry at around the 1490s. Today, it contains a chambered upper hall which features moulded beams and three arch braced trusses. There is a newel staircase, which Richard Polwhele in his *History of Devonshire* described as a 'remarkable staircase of heart of oak'. The house also contains a garderobe in a projection at the rear and evidence of the partition that would have originally divided the kitchen and the buttery, along with original door frames and fireplaces, including a large bread oven.

EARLY OWNERS

The Bonville family, through heiress Cecily Bonville, 7th Baroness Harington, were ancestors of Lady Jane Grey, Queen of England for just one week. In 1498 the son of Alice and John Bonville, also named John, was further licensed to found a perpetual chantry at Combe Raleigh, and it is believed that it was at this time that the house was built. It is thought possible that there might have originally been an underground passage between the church and the chantry.

Surviving documents in The National Archives show that the chantry priest in the house during the 1520s and '30s was a John Adams, but it was only a few years later that great change came to the religious structure of England with Henry VIII's Dissolution of the Monasteries, and the national religion turned away from the church in Rome. Although the buildings and lands attached to chantries lasted a little longer, by 1547, in the first Parliament called by Edward VI, The Chantry Act was established which aimed to dissolve the chantries and associated practices.

After this, it appears the lands and house attached to The Chantry of Combe Raleigh were granted to Edward Seymour, 1st Duke of Somerset, who was Lord Protector during Edward VI's minority in 1547–49. A document from the sixteenth century then explains that the 'land and possessions of the late Chantry of Combe Raleigh' were to be conveyed to Sir Thomas Pomeroy, along with other sections of land in Devon and Cornwall.

THE MARWOOD ESTATES

The Marwoods were a prominent Devonshire family who could trace their ancestors back to Eustachius de Merwoode in 1242. It was Thomas Marwood (1512–1619) who brought the family into connection with the royal court. A successful medical practitioner, he was said to be physician to Robert Devereux, 2nd Earl of Essex, the favourite courtier of Elizabeth I, and it was through this connection that he became a royal physician to Elizabeth I. His grandson, another Thomas, also became a successful doctor and rose to become royal physician to both James I and Charles I.

The land and properties of the Marwoods passed to John Marwood, son of Thomas Marwood, physician to Charles I. The property and estates continued to pass through the generations until the late seventeenth century, when we know the house was definitely in the possession of Benedictus Marwood, a grocer of Exeter. One hundred years later, in 1783, a map retained in the Devonshire County Records reveals, 'the estates of the parishes of Beer & Seaton, Honiton & Combrawley … belong[ed] to James Thomas Benedictus Marwood'. From this time, the land tax records also reveal who was actually living in The Chantry. From 1799 we know it was owned by James Marwood, was occupied by Joan Saunders and the annual tax was 12*s*. However, after 300 years, and despite its ornate and historic interiors, the house was deemed 'old fashioned' and only fit for a farmhouse.

James Marwood remained the owner of The Chantry, but he is later recorded as a 'lunatic' and was unable to write a will or continue to manage the estates. He died, childless, in 1813 and the property and estates were

A Tudor Residence

Despite the power struggles in the Tudor court, it appears that after the religious connection to the house was lost, it continued as a respectable gentleman's residence. By the late sixteenth century the house was purchased by John Peter Esq., and by 1603, the year James I came to the throne, he had sold it to merchant of Exeter, Hugh Crossinge.

divided amongst his four sisters, including Mary Marwood, who inherited the Combe Raleigh property with The Chantry.

VICTORIAN LIFE AT THE CHANTRY

From the 1840s we start to see more details about the families living in The Chantry. The tithe map and apportionment in 1840 show that the house and a small area of land was still owned by James Notley (Mary Marwood's son) and occupied by Daniel Pring Jnr. The 1841 census notes that the house was occupied by 30-year-old Daniel, an agricultural labourer, living with Mary Pring, 70 years old and 'independent', and Eliza Colloway, 20 years old and working as a charwoman.

By the 1860s, The Chantry and land had been inherited by James Notley's son, also named James. The 1861 census shows that the house was still occupied by Daniel Pring, now with his brother David, another agricultural labourer, as well as their sister Hannah Lamberton, recorded as 'housekeeper'. The Pring family appear to have continued in The Chantry until the 1870s, but by the early 1880s it had become the home of William Spiller, a 65-year-old gardener, and his wife Eliza.

The Chantry continued as a working-class home into the twentieth century. At the 1901 census it was occupied by the Carnell family from Ottery St Mary, with Richard Carnell, a 52-year-old bricklayer, and his wife Emma, a laundress on her own account, working from home. They had three daughters, Rhoda, Mary and Sarah, all laundresses, as well as a son, Jesse, 16 years old and working as a bricklayer with his father. A diary written by the parish vicar in the early twentieth century records that in 1902–03 the Carnells were regular church goers and that they had another son, Richard, who was a soldier aged 18 and was 'abroad'.

Change at The Chantry

The 1910 valuation survey reveals the Carnell family were still tenants at The Chantry and that it was owned by Marwood Notley, grandson of James Notley. The annual rent for the 'cottage, garden and orchard' at this time was £8 8s. The house was ambiguously described as 'thatch dwelling house 400 or 500 or 600 years old. Contains front passage (oak panelling) [and a] kitchen (very old oak ceiling)'. It is uncertain when the Marwood family sold The Chantry, but the evidence of renovation work on the house during the 1920s and '30s, and an advertisement in *The Times* in 1936 stating the owner as Mrs William Smith Marriott, implies it was likely to have been during the inter-war period.

42–54 VICTORIA STREET

Southwold was recorded in Domesday Book in 1086 when it was part of the lands belonging to the Abbey of Bury St Edmunds. In 1259 it was exchanged for the manor of Mildenhall, owned by the Clare family, but it later became part of the property of the House of York and eventually passed to the Crown. However, the early history of Southwold is a little different to many other areas across the UK, as instead of passing it to a favoured courtier or ally, King Henry VII transferred the lordship of the manor to the inhabitants in 1489.

One of the most significant events in the history of Southwold was a dramatic fire that swept through the village in 1659, destroying much of the town and leaving many families destitute. It took many years for the village to recover and rebuild the hundreds of houses that had been lost.

Only a few years later Southwold was affected by the Dutch Wars of the 1660s, with hundreds of sick and wounded sent to Southwold to be nursed back to health. In 1672 the Duke of York's ships came to Southwold and

on 26 May it was the location for the Battle of Sole Bay against the Dutch, resulting in high loss of life. Throughout this period the threat of press gangs was also a constant problem, when local men were dragged into naval service and forced to leave their families and their own work behind.

INVASION

The threat of invasion caused disruption in Southwold when the Napoleonic Wars arose in the 1790s. In 1796 Southwold was expected to provide twenty-one men for the Navy, and later a land force, known as the Sea Fencibles, which was a naval militia intended to defend against possible invasion. Volunteering also provided protection from impressments into the Navy, and was especially popular amongst smugglers, for whom this was often the punishment. However, the feared invasion by the French never eventuated and by 1813 the volunteers had disbanded.

EAST LANE

Built during the late eighteenth century, Nos 42–54 were the first cottages to be built along this section of Victoria Street, then known as East Lane. Those beyond No 54, towards the coast, were built slightly later, and further building took place on the western stretch during the nineteenth century. Sections of Victoria Street have been known by different names over the centuries, with the upper part near the High Street formerly known as Camel Street (after former residents with the surname 'Camel'). Other sections of Victoria Street have been called Tape Street and Back Lane. However, the lower part of Victoria Street, closest to the sea, was known as East Lane until the mid nineteenth century.

Very little specific information is known about the construction date and landowner, plus few documents have been retained. The lack of a specific address in the early history of the cottages also makes it difficult to be precise, but the ownership does not appear to have been in the hands of the town commissioners.

FISHERMEN & MARINERS

The dominant occupations of the cottage-dwellers involved the sea (and not the nearby brewery), as fishermen and mariners. The 1841 census is the first detailed document to show the type of people living in the cottages, and almost the entire population of the street, recorded as East Lane, were listed as 'mariner' or wife of fisherman or seaman away from home.

The 1851 census gives further details, and while a large proportion were still mariners, there were also 'seaman's widow', 'wife of master mariner', fisherman, fishmonger and 'pauper'. Most households had between two and six residents, although unfortunately, at this time, the cottages are not numbered, so it is unclear as to the exact occupants in each cottage. One typical household was that of Daniel Hurr, 32 years old and a fishmonger, with his wife Charlotte, 30 years old, and their five children under the age of 7.

The May Family

By the time of the 1871 census, East Lane had been officially renamed 'Victoria Street' and it is possible to identify the individual cottages. In particular, No 50 Victoria Street was the home of the May family, with James, 52 years old and a fisherman, and his wife Caroline, both from Lowestoft. They had five children, with the eldest son, 16-year-old Joseph, already working as a fisherman, while the four youngest were still at school. The middle son, 11-year-old Samuel (Sam), is worth noting, as he became one of the heroes of Southwold.

Sam May followed in his father and brother's footsteps to become a fisherman, but at the age of 27 he also became a member of the Southwold lifeboat crew, playing a vital role in protecting people at sea. In particular, he served on the *Alfred Corry*, a famous lifeboat which has been preserved and can still be seen in The Alfred Corry Museum. Sam May crewed the lifeboats for thirty years, and took charge of the *Alfred Corry* in 1898 until 1918. He was involved in many rescues and saved several lives.

Longshore fishing boats on Southwold beach, 1892.

War & Seaside Cottages

Throughout the early twentieth century, the type of occupants in the cottages along Victoria Street remained much the same as those from a century before. Nevertheless, life was beginning to alter as fishing was in decline and Southwold was becoming a fashionable seaside resort. The impact of the First and Second World Wars also greatly affected Victoria Street – and the entire town. In particular, the Second World War meant the evacuation of many residents. It came under direct attack and seventy-seven buildings were destroyed and over 2,000 more damaged, while thirteen people were killed and forty-nine injured.

After the war, the day trippers and sun seekers returned and life turned around. However, the fishing industry further declined and the cottages along Victoria Street changed, too. Today, many are comfortable homes, but some are holiday lets, a fitting development that mirrors the change of the town from fishing village to holiday resort.

EDWARDIAN TIMES

Throughout the late nineteenth century, Nos 42–54 Victoria Street continued to be home to fishermen and mariners, as well as the occasional labourer, bricklayer and charwoman. By the time of the 1901 census, the houses were numbered and show the head of each house: at No 42 was fisherman George Upcroft; at No 44 was seaman Ellis English; at No 46 was grocer Alan Rushbroke; at No 48 was Pearson Newble, recorded as 'foreman – Sea Defence'; at No 50 was fisherman Edward Rogers; at No 52 was mariner Cragie Ashmanall; and at No 54 was fisherman James Peck.

By the turn of the twentieth century, further documents provide a picture of life along Victoria Street in Southwold. The 1910 valuation survey shows that most of the cottages were described as in 'poor repair'; Nos 42–44 were owned by Ernest Naunton and Nos 46–54 were owned by Emma Gayford. We know from other records that Ernest Naunton was a 36-year-old solicitor's clerk living on Stradbroke Road, and Emma Gayford was a 77-year-old spinster living at 54 High Street.

2 HYDE PARK STREET

Built in 1835 as part of a grand nineteenth-century development, the first resident of this Grade II listed grand stucco house was a military hero who fought with the Duke of Wellington at the Battle of Waterloo. Prior to the nineteenth century, the area to the north of Hyde Park was entirely covered in fields and agricultural land. The estate was owned by the Bishop of London and had in fact been in the hands of the Church since the time of Domesday Book in 1086. By the 1790s the Bishop of London had obtained permission to grant leases for building and by 1795 plans were in place for the development of the land. The first estate surveyor, Samuel Pepys Cockerell (great-great-nephew

The Lutyens Family

During the mid twentieth century, No 2 became the home of Lady Emily Lutyens, wife of architect Edwin Lutyens and daughter of diplomat and poet Edward Bulwer-Lytton. Lady Emily is best known for her involvement with theosophy, a form of eastern mysticism, and in particular for her connection with the spiritual leader, Krishnamurti. Lady Emily Lutyens remained in the house until 1964, but her daughter, writer Mary Lutyens, continued to live there until the 1980s with her husband, art historian J.G. Links.

In the 1980s the house was divided into flats, with the first-floor flat retaining many Georgian features.

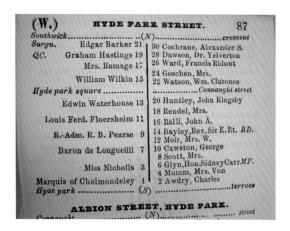

Above: Paddington Estate Design, George Gutch, 1838.

Below: Royal Blue Book, 1884.

of diarist Samuel Pepys), initiated the development, but by the 1820s he had been replaced by George Gutch. Gutch drew up building plans for this area in 1827, making some alterations to what Cockerell had planned. The first resident, Sir Andrew Francis Barnard, was recorded in the 1836 Boyles Court Guide and was a distinguished army officer who had fought at the Battle of Waterloo in 1815. The Duke of Wellington personally appointed him to be commander of the British division in Paris in 1815. By 1849 he was Lieutenant-Governor of the Royal Hospital Chelsea.

Other distinguished residents include Lieutenant-General Skelton in the 1840s, and solicitor and treasurer to Kings College Hospital, Charles Selwyn Awdry, from the 1880s to around 1905. After Awdry left the house it became the home of Mr and Mrs George S.C. Swinton, who were noted for the concerts they held there. In the 1920s the house was occupied by Lieutenant-Colonel Splender Clay, MP.

THE HARRODS DEPOSITORY

Harrods Village is a collection of imposing buildings, situated on the banks of the River Thames, which were formerly the Harrods Depository. The most prominent of the three buildings, William Hunt Mansions, has long been a landmark for the Oxford and Cambridge Boat Race. It was specifically designed to mirror the renowned Harrods department store in Knightsbridge.

The site was originally owned by the West Middlesex Waterworks Company until it was acquired by Lewis, Henry, John and Phineas Cowan, in 1856, to build a new soap factory. Their first factory building of 1858 was altered a number of times through the late nineteenth and early twentieth centuries and was also used as a sugar refinery from the 1880s. The second factory building on the site was constructed during the 1860s and became a candle manufactory.

The site of the soap factory was taken by Harrods in 1894 and was first used for stabling, storing food and even as a slaughterhouse. It was Richard Burbidge, former Harrods managing director, who first realised the need

Kahn System

The most significant element of the former Harrods Depository building is its innovative use of the 'Kahn system' of reinforced concrete, one of the first forms of reinforced concrete created by Albert Kahn. The former warehouse building also retains its original reinforced cantilevers, either side of the lift shaft, which have been preserved, and ultimately contributed to it gaining Grade II listed status in 1990.

Aerial photograph showing the allotments during the Second World War.

for a depository to hold furniture and possessions for people on imperial postings abroad. The former soap and candle factories were both renovated and rebuilt by William Hunt for the Harrods Depository during the late nineteenth and early twentieth centuries.

UNIQUE ARCHITECTURAL FEATURES

William George Hunt was a successful architect who frequently exhibited at the Royal Academy. He was not only responsible for a large number of the Harrods buildings, but also a number of municipal buildings in south London, along with houses in Old Bond Street and Great Portland Street.

William Hunt Mansions was completed in 1913 and designed using red brick and terracotta, featuring baroque-style themes with strong horizontal lines and the prominent cupolas. An additional long wing was added in 1920, with a similar wing planned for the north side, but this was never finished.

Recent History

All three historic Harrods buildings were converted into apartments in 1997–99, with the old soap factory renamed Charles Harrod Building after the founder of Harrods department store. The former candle factory was renamed Richard Burbidge Mansions, while the riverside building was named in honour of the architect and became William Hunt Mansions.

5 BRUNSWICK SQUARE

Brunswick Square epitomises the idyllic Regency town square typical of the fashionable seaside town of Brighton. It was built during the reign of George IV shortly after his own palace, Brighton Pavilion, was redesigned by John Nash.

BRUNSWICK TOWN

Brunswick Square was built as part of Brunswick Town, on land belonging to the Wick Estate, which had been in the hands of the Scutt family since 1701. Charles Augustin Busby (sometimes incorrectly named Augustus Busby) and Amon Henry Wilds were responsible for much Georgian and Regency building in Brighton, including Kemp Town to the east and Brunswick Town. It is understood that Busby was the prime designer of Brunswick Square,

Heroic History

The Grade I listed square was constructed in 1825–27 to the designs of Charles Augustin Busby, using a classic Georgian style with stucco exterior. No 5 Brunswick Square has been the home of many members of the aristocracy and gentry, including Lady Scarlett; Henrietta Toler, daughter of the 2nd Baron Abinger; and a number of residents with heroic links, including brigadier-generals, rear-admirals and heroes of the Boer War and First World War.

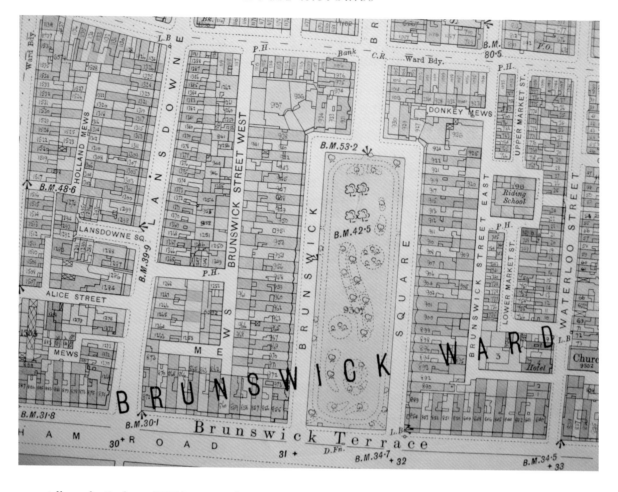

1910 Valuation map.

especially as the Busby and Wilds partnership dissolved in 1824, the very year of the agreement to commence building Brunswick Square.

The layout and design of Brunswick Town aimed to create a separate enclave with wealthy residents at the centre, providing high-quality homes, stables for horses and carriages, and facilities and amenities suited to a high-class resident. The surrounding streets offered housing for the middle and working classes and Busby provided the new residents with a chapel, public baths and local pubs.

DESIGN & CONSTRUCTION

Building plots were sold to individual builders and speculators by land-owner Reverend Thomas Scutt. Busby then stepped in to oversee the construction based on his grand plan which started in 1825. He provided the designs for the facades of each house and even specified the types of building materials that were required. However, when looking closely, the exteriors have slightly different designs, while offering a uniform appearance as an entire square. The interiors were also designed with an upper-class resident in mind, offering the latest household luxuries, including piped water supplies, the latest flushable water closets, and a layout that optimised light and space.

The First Residents

Pigot's 1840 Directory for Sussex records that No 5 was the home of Francis Skurray, Esq. However, within a few years the occupant had become 'Mrs Atkins-Bowyer', who appears to have been the widow of Brevet Major William Atkins-Bowyer from the 59th Regiment and former Brigade Major of the Forces of Halifax, Nova Scotia.

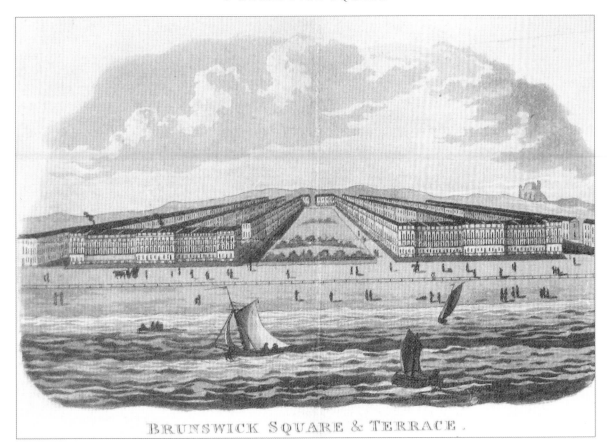

BRUNSWICK SQUARE & TERRACE.

Illustration from the New Plan, 1830.

Famous Residents

Brunswick Square has been the home of many notable residents throughout the last 180 years, including composer Roger Quilter, born at No 4 in 1877; another composer, Sir Hamilton Harty, at No 33; and author and poet Edward Carpenter, who was born at No 45 in 1844. No 2 was the home of Admiral Sir George Westphal, who fought with Nelson at the Battle of Trafalgar and witnessed his death. Westphal died at No 2 in 1875. The Earl of Cardigan, famous as the general involved with the Charge of the Light Brigade, lived at No 45 Brunswick Square while No 17, his grandfather's house, was the birthplace of artist Robert Bevan.

The first houses to be completed were those facing the promenade along Brunswick Terrace and by 1834 all houses had been completed. During the 1820s and the early Victorian period, Brunswick Square was one of the most popular addresses in Brighton. The houses in Brunswick Square were mostly taken as private homes, whereas Brunswick Terrace was predominately furnished apartments for much of its early history.

Brunswick Town was unique in having its own commissioners, established by a private act in April 1830. They were responsible for the management of the area and had their own police, fire engine and firemen, lighting, drainage and roads. Commissioners even monitored the painting of the houses, which had to be painted a uniform colour every three years.

ARISTOCRATIC LINKS

By the time of the 1851 census, No 5 was occupied by Mrs Caroline Mayers, who was recorded as widowed and 'land and fund holder'. She was listed in the house with four unmarried daughters, Clara, Margarette, Anne and Maria, along with grandson Hugh and three granddaughters. This large household of women was supported by five servants, including a footman and a lady's maid.

Mrs Mayers continued to be recorded in the house until 1856, but at the time of the 1861 census the house was rented by Henrietta Toler. The census records her in the house without her husband and described simply as 'peers daughter', aged 35 with six children: Hector, later Captain Toler; James, later Lieutenant-Colonel Toler; George; Francis; Rosamond and

Violet. At this time, there were also eight live-in servants in the house. Mrs Henrietta Toler was the wife of the Honourable Otway Fortescue Graham-Toler, youngest son of Hector Graham-Toler, 2nd Earl of Norbury. The earl had been murdered in his home in Durrow Abbey in Ireland, and to this day the culprit remains a mystery, although speculation has placed the blame on a disgruntled tenant.

Within a few years it appears the house had once again become home to members of the Mayers family, with Miss Margarette Mayers, as well as Lieutenant-Colonel George D'Albiac, who married Anne Mayers. D'Albiac passed away in the house in 1867 and his widow, Anne, continued there with her sister Margarette until moving to Putney a few years later.

By the mid 1870s, the Sussex directories record that a Lady Scarlett had moved in. Earlier resident, Henrietta Toler, was the daughter of Robert Campbell Scarlett, 2nd Baron Abinger, and it is possible that this was Henrietta's mother, Sarah Baroness Abinger. However, it could also refer to Henrietta's aunt, Charlotte Scarlett, the wife of Sir James Yorke Scarlett, second son of 2nd Baron Abinger, a national hero who led the Charge of the Heavy Brigade during the Crimean War.

TURN OF THE CENTURY

Between 1890 and 1894, the house was home to Edward Parker, who was recorded in the 1891 census as 38 years old and as 'J.P. Cumberland', along with his wife Mary, 30 years old, and their three young children: Edward aged 6, Frederick aged 3 and Thomas 'under eight months'.

At the turn of the twentieth century, 5 Brunswick Square became the home of Mrs Judith Hughes-Onslow, former wife of landed proprietor Henry Hughes-Onslow. The 1901 census shows Judith, a widow, 68 years old and 'living on own means', along with her daughter-in-law Ann and six live-in servants. Her eldest sons, Arthur and Denzil, both rose to the rank of major, but both died fighting in France during the First World War; while her middle son, Constantine Hughes-Onslow, rose to become rear-admiral in the Royal Navy. Judith's youngest son, Henry Douglas Hughes-Onslow, was a successful solicitor and became master/chief clerk in the Chancery Division of the High Court.

THE SEYMOURS

In 1906 the Reverend Henry Seymour moved to No 5. The 1911 census reveals he was a retired clergyman of the Church of England, 84 years old, living with his second wife, Emmeline, and two unmarried daughters, Emily and Julia. The family also had five live-in servants and the census shows that the house was made up of seventeen rooms. The 1910 valuation survey reveals Henry's wife as the owner. However, Henry and Emmeline passed away shortly after this time and the house passed to spinster sisters Emily and Julia Seymour, who remained until the 1950s. Like many large Georgian houses, No 5 was then divided into apartments during the 1960s.

War Heroes

By the end of the 1870s, No 5 Brunswick Square was the home of a Mrs Colvin. The census in 1881 shows Emma Colvin was a widow, aged 47, and she was in the house with her 19-year-old daughter Beatrice, along with a visitor, Gertrude Abbot, and three live-in servants. Emma Colvin was the widow of Beale Blackwell Colvin of Monkhams Hall in Essex, who inherited extensive estates from his father, Robert Colvin. Emma's sons all went into the military: the eldest, Richard, fought in the Boer War and later became MP for Epping from 1917–23; Forrester Farnell Colvin also saw action in the Boer War and was made Commander of the Order of the British Empire (CBE); Cecil Hodgson Colvin also fought in the Boer War and was awarded the Distinguished Service Order (DSO). He went on to fight in the First World War and was made a Companion of the Order of the Bath (CB).

12 MORNINGTON TERRACE

This unassuming terraced house in Camden is the former home of science fiction author and socialist, H.G. Wells. Here, he completed one of his best known novels, *The Time Machine*, along with *The Wonderful Visit* (1895), *The Island of Dr Moreau* (1896) and *The Invisible Man* (1897). The name Mornington originates from the brother of the Duke of Wellington, Richard Wellesley, Earl of Mornington. The name was given to a number of surrounding streets, including Mornington Crescent through a family connection with the former landowners, the Fitzroy family.

CHANGING NAMES

When Mornington Terrace was first built it was known as Mornington Road, and when Nos 6–12 were completed in 1841 they were known as Nos 1–6 Ehrenburg Terrace, changing to Mornington Road in 1845. The first occupants of Ehrenburg Terrace were recorded in the poor rate book in March 1842.

The first resident of No 12 Mornington Road (originally No 6 Ehrenburg Terrace) was Mr Leigh Churchill Smyth, a solicitor from Jamaica. He lived here until the late 1840s, when it became the home of John Pinhorn, who was listed in the 1851 census as a clerk in the Admiralty, with his wife Sarah and their 13-year-old son, Edward.

The 1861 census shows the house then became the home of Austrian Albert Lowy, a 'Minister [of the] West London Synagogue', with his wife Gertrude, from Denmark, and their four children: Bella, Julian, Ernest and Lionel. In October 1892, *The Times* described Lowy as 'a leading Jewish minister, who for 50 years had aided many movements affecting the advancement of the Jewish community'.

During the 1850s and '60s the residents at No 12 Mornington Road changed a number of times, but included John Ashby in 1855, F.H. Fiera in 1862 and Henry Charles Trere, Esq. in 1864. By the 1871 census it had become the home of Marian Parker, unmarried, aged 30, from Ireland, along with a visitor, Alfred Hottenbridge, aged 37, and Marian's servant, Elizabeth Brown, also from Ireland.

H.G. Wells.

Herbert George Wells

The electoral register in 1894 and the London Directory in 1895 shows No 12 Mornington Road was then owned by a Mrs Sarah Lewis, a boarding-house keeper. It was at this time that H.G. Wells and his former student – and mistress – Amy Catherine Robbins (known as Jane) moved in, with Wells stating he 'went to live in sin and social rebellion'. Herbert George Wells is often referred to as the 'father of science fiction'. His book, *The Time Machine*, was first published in 1895 shortly after his move to Mornington Road, becoming his first bestseller. *The War of the Worlds* was published shortly after Wells and Amy Catherine, now his wife, moved from Mornington Road to Kent in 1898.

THE BALDRY FAMILY

By 1881 the calibre of residents in Mornington Road had begun to change and No 12 is particularly noteworthy. Compared to ten years earlier, when only three people were listed in the house, the 1880s saw thirteen people residing there. The 1881 census records the house was home to George William Baldry, an artist, aged 46 from Norfolk, with his wife Mary, aged 44, and their ten children, aged between 2 and 21 years old, along with one general servant. Baldry had formerly appeared in *The Times* bankruptcy list twice: first in 1865, listed as a photographer; and again in 1877, listed as an artist from Great Yarmouth.

The 1891 census shows No 12 was the home of George H. Brown, aged 33, a widower, with an occupation of 'Cheesemonger's assistant', along with his sister, appearing simply as A.E. Brown, and his brother, also listed as A.E. Brown, an upholsterer, aged 22. The census also reveals Brown had five children, aged between 3 and 9 years old, and the house was also home to a boarder, Frederick Cookson, a 19-year-old medical student, and a lodger, Florence May, a widow, aged 35, occupying three rooms and 'living on own means'.

EARLY TWENTIETH CENTURY

At the time of the 1901 census 12 Mornington Road was still home to boarding-house keeper Sarah Lewis. This census records that she was a widow, aged 71, living with her nephew, William Evans, aged 26, a 'linotype [early printing machine] operator', and her niece, Alice Rees, aged 20, listed as 'domestic help'. It also reveals No 12 Mornington Road was the home of Katie Stewart, a 39-year-old married actress, occupying one room; Sara Scott, a 51-year-old 'journalist, author', also occupying one room; and, occupying three rooms, was John Turner, married, aged 58, a 'commission agent, Mechanical Engineer'. Mornington Road was renamed Mornington Terrace in 1937.

CHURCH END HOUSE

The land around today's Church End House in Kent was bought in 1882 by lord of the manor William Tipping, and the house was constructed shortly afterwards, appearing in the 1888 Ordnance Survey map. The house has been recorded with a number of variations on its name, including 'Church Cottage' in the 1899 Kent Directory; 'Church House' in the 1901 census; and then 'Church End House' in the 1902 electoral register.

During this time, the house was the home of Charles Victor Benecke. The 1901 census shows Benecke was a retired merchant, widowed, aged 69, and he was living with a large household of women, including his daughters, Else and Margaret, aged 27 and 24 respectively. Also in the house was housekeeper Mary Morrell; house parlour maid Annie Hopkins; cook Sarah Ashby; and housemaid Christina Nunn.

Charles Victor Benecke had married Marie Mendelssohn, the daughter of German composer Felix Mendelssohn, in around 1860. It is also believed that Mendelssohn's second cousin, Arnold Ludwig Mendelssohn, another musician, visited Charles Benecke at Church End House in the early twentieth century. Benecke's son, Paul Victor, went on to become a Senior Fellow of Magdalen College, Oxford, and the Oxford Mendelssohn Collection originates from the family archives and materials left to Paul Benecke.

Charles Benecke lived at Church End House until around 1905, at which time it became the home of 'The Misses Cobb', three sisters – Audrey, Clara and Hester. In 1912 Church End House and grounds, covering over 5 acres, was put on the market by William Tipping and sold to George Alderson. However, with some legal formalities delaying the sale, the house continued to be leased, and in 1913 was occupied by Raymond G. W. Bush, who continued there during the early years of the First World War.

The War Years

Before new owner George Alderson could take possession, Church End House was requisitioned by the War Department during the First World War and became a transit camp for the overseas service. Alderson finally moved in during 1917, establishing a long family association with the house.

G.H. Alderson had created a successful coal and coke merchant company in Brasted in 1898, and during the inter-war years he continued the business from his new home. He also expanded into farming and to a coaching service.

The Second World War saw the house used once again by the military, when airmen from nearby Biggin Hill airfield often visited the house.

After the war the coaching business continued until 1965, while the Alderson coal business was sold by George's son, George Albert Alderson, to local firm Hawksfields in 1957. George Henry Alderson passed Church End House to his son in 1946 and by 1980 it had passed to the niece of George Albert Alderson, continuing the family connection.

10 WELLINGTON PLACE

Music & Poetry

In 1924 until the early 1930s, the house became the home of musical theatre writer Douglas Furber and his wife Peggy. Douglas Furber is best known as the author of *Me and My Girl* (1937), but he also wrote *Limehouse Blues* (1924) and *The Bells of St Mary's*, sung by Bing Crosby in 1945. Furber's music has also been used in a number of soundtracks, including *The Godfather* and *Goodfellas*.

Shortly after the Second World War, No 10 became the home of playwright and poet Louis MacNeice, a contemporary of W.H. Auden. MacNeice's poems include *Holes in the Sky* (1948) and *Star-gazer* (1963). He joined the BBC in 1941 and produced many successful radio shows, such as *Christopher Columbus* (1944) and *The Dark Tower* (1947).

This house is situated in the wide streets of St John's Wood, completed in 1839, and originally known as No 5 Wellington Place. The earliest parish rate records for Wellington Place, in 1840, show the house was owned by John Goodcheap and occupied by 'John Goodcheap's tenants'.

By 1844, the house had become the home of Mrs Elizabeth Beckles, from the island of Barbadoes (sic), and the 1851 census reveals she was a widow, aged 72, living with her three unmarried daughters: 49-year-old Susan, 32-year-old Caroline and 30-year-old Julia. By the 1861 census she was still there and listed as a 'lady', along with three further unmarried daughters – Mary, Frances and Amelia – a married daughter, Maria Hunter, and a granddaughter, Margaret, all listed as 'lady'. Also in the house were three female servants who had travelled with the family, their birthplaces being Trinidad, Dominica and Barbados.

MR & MRS PHELPS

The 1891 census records that the house had become the home of Thomas Phelps, a farrier smith (responsible for fitting horseshoes), his wife Caroline and their children, along with two boarders, James Davies and Walter Parisen, both from Wales. Mrs Phelps continued as the landlady of No 5 until around 1914. The house numbers were reorganised in 1915, when it officially became No 10.

JOHN OLIVER

In 1948 No 10 Wellington Place became the home of John Laurence Oliver, his wife, actress Renee Bourne Webb, and her father, Reverend Charles Bourne Webb. Oliver was the editor of *Tatler* from 1961–65 and is credited with bringing the magazine into the modern era, greatly increasing the circulation. Oliver's wife, Renee, was a stage actress whose performances included *Twelfth Night* at the Savoy Theatre in 1947.

CARLISLE MANSIONS

Carlisle Mansions is just a short walk from the Houses of Parliament and was formerly the home of writer and playwright Somerset Maugham. Other famous residents include the inventor of lawn tennis, Walter Wingfield; peace campaigner, Dame Adelaide Lord Livingstone; and bestselling author, Lady Colin Campbell.

Carlisle Place was first laid out for building during the 1850s and was named after George Howard, Viscount Morpeth and Earl of Carlisle. Carlisle Mansions was designed by George Baines and built in 1885–89. An advertisement for Carlisle Mansions in around 1910 described features such as 'fireproof walls, floors and staircases, Perfect sanitation, Electric Bells and Speaking Tubes and Telephone Cabinets'.

Famous Residents

Carlisle Mansions was formerly the home of Lady Colin Campbell, journalist and art critic, who is most remembered for her notorious divorce case from her husband, Lord Colin Campbell. She later went on to write the bestselling book, *Etiquette and Good Society* (1893). No 63 Carlisle Mansions was the home of Sir Walter Armstrong, art critic and former Director of the National Gallery of Ireland (1892–1914), who wrote extensively on artists such as Joshua Reynolds and J.M.W. Turner.

It was also home of the peace campaigner, Dame Adelaide Lord Livingstone, who, during the First World War, worked on committees for the treatment of British prisoners of war and after the war was appointed to the Army Council. She went on to join the staff of the League of Nations Union and became leader of the United Nations Association.

During the late nineteenth century, Carlisle Mansions was the home of Walter Wingfield, the inventor of lawn tennis. Wingfield patented his version of 'sphairistike' (based on the Greek for 'ball game') in 1874 and it was from this game that we get our modern-day sport of tennis. Living in Carlisle Mansions at the same time was actor and playwright Charles Collette, along with his wife Blanche and daughter Mary, both actresses. Charles Collette was a successful stage actor who performed in *Tame Cats* in 1868 and also played Mr Micawber in *David Copperfield* in 1907.

WILLIAM SOMERSET MAUGHAM

At the time of the 1901 census, Somerset Maugham was listed in flat No 27 as William S. Maugham, a boarder and 'Doctor M.R.C.S.'. He was living with his friend Walter Payne, who was supporting him financially

while he pursued his writing career. He went on to write over thirty plays, including *Lady Frederick* (1907), but he is perhaps most remembered for his novels, including *Of Human Bondage* (1915), *The Moon and Sixpence* (1919) and *The Painted Veil* (1925). Somerset Maugham and Walter Payne remained at Carlisle Mansions for a few years before moving to a house in Mayfair. Bryan Connon, in the *Oxford Dictionary of National Biography*, described Maugham as 'one of the most commercially successful and gifted writers of the 20th century'.

Somerset Maugham.

General Willoughby

Carlisle Mansions was also the home of General Digby Willoughby, after he retired from the foreign services. He fought in the Zulu wars in South Africa in the 1870s and also led a troop of irregulars, named Willoughby's Horse, during the Basuto War in 1880. He was appointed general commander of the Madagascar forces by the last Queen of Madagascar, Queen Ranavalomanjaka III, in 1884, and later fought in Rhodesia and helped in the administration after the peace settlement during the 1890s.

24 VICTORIA TERRACE

The Grade II listed Victoria Terrace is made up of thirty-eight homes and situated on the outskirts of the small village of Hemingford Grey and neighbouring St Ives in Huntingdonshire. Built in 1850, this row of workmen's cottages has hardly changed in the last 160 years, located amongst fields and not far from the River Great Ouse.

THE WATSONS

The stretch of land running behind the terrace towards the river was prone to flooding, so no buildings were constructed here before the nineteenth century. However, with the growing population, increase in industry and the new railway, new housing was required. A plaque on the exterior of Victoria Terrace reads, 'Erected 1850, H.W.', and records reveal this was for Haylock Watson of St Ives and Fenstanton, who was responsible for the building of the terrace.

St Ives

Neighbouring St Ives is most notable for its fifteenth-century stone bridge, which features the Chapel of St Lawrence, or 'Chapel on the Bridge', built on the middle pier of the bridge. It was first consecrated in 1426, but was later converted into a house, then a toll house and later an inn. It has seen many alterations and additions, including an extra two floors (now removed); but today, the chapel is Grade I listed and is one of only four such chapels on a bridge to survive in England.

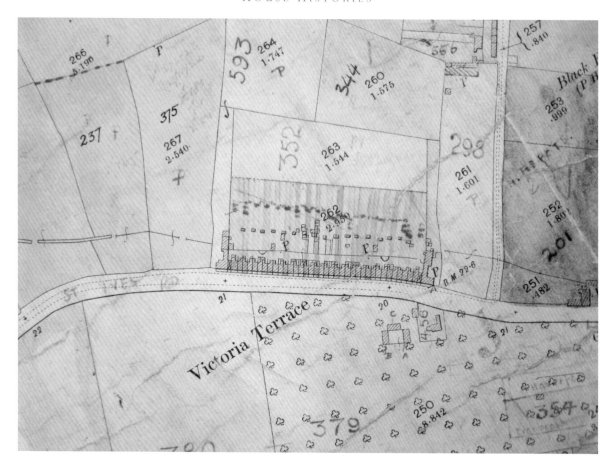

1910 Valuation map.

Sadly, there are very few details known about Watson and his connection with Victoria Terrace. At the time of the 1841 census he was living in Bridge Street, St Ives, as an apprentice tailor to James Ingle, along with James' wife, Catherine, and their daughter Ann. Watson went on to marry Ann Ingle in 1847. By the end of the 1840s, when Victoria Terrace was being constructed, it appears Haylock Watson either inherited the land for building, or was making a substantial enough sum from tailoring to invest in property. Certainly the records for the latter nineteenth century show that he acquired land and wealth enabling him to transform his circumstances.

By the time of the 1851 census, 29-year-old Watson and 36-year-old Ann were still living in Bridge Street, along with Catherine Ingle, now widowed. Watson was recorded as 'master tailor employing 4 men and 2 boys', two apprentices, John Wayman and Henry Baker, and a housemaid, Mary Allsop. By the time of the 1861 census the circumstances of the Watson family had been transformed, and they had moved from St Ives into Grove House in Fenstanton. By this time, he was recorded as a 'landed proprietor' and he was in the house with his wife, his mother-in-law and two live-in servants.

Records reveal that Watson, along with his brother-in-law, George Ingle of Eaton Socon, purchased the manor of Fenstanton in 1890. This had formerly belonged to the famous landscape architect, Lancelot 'Capability' Brown. The Watsons were childless so the manor passed from George Ingle to his son, George Wright Wright Ingle, in 1908, and he held the manor until 1936.

Trade Route

The town of St Ives, originally known as Slepe, has been documented back to the Anglo-Saxon period and is believed to be named after the Persian bishop, Ivo. St Ives has been an important market town since its foundation: records show that in 1110 Henry I granted a charter to Ramsey Abbey for a fair to be held there for eight days during Easter week, and from this it is believed the town was born. The location of St Ives, along the River Great Ouse, meant that it was a vital trade route, with barges transporting goods directly down to London. The later mill on the river further added to the expanding town and its prosperity.

Early History

Hemingford Grey's history has been closely tied to neighbouring village Hemingford Abbots and during the Roman and Anglo-Saxon period both were part of the one estate. The manor house is one of the oldest inhabited buildings in England, with the original structure dating back to the twelfth century. Today, it is still surrounded by its moat on three sides. The name 'Grey' originates from thirteenth-century lords of the manor, the de Grey family, although they had lost the manor by the fifteenth century.

WORKING-CLASS RESIDENTS

Victoria Terrace was built to provide comfortable new homes for working-class occupants, with most of the early residents occupied in trade and industry, ranging from millers and bargemen to railway workers. No 1 Victoria Terrace was originally a pub, appropriately named 'The Queen's Head'.

The first occupants to move into No 24 were 'waterman' James Sanson, who was recorded in the 1851 census as 51 years old, his wife Susannah and their son, 25-year-old William, also a 'waterman'. By the time of the 1861 census, No 24 had become the home of flour miller Thomas Taylor and his wife Elizabeth, both recorded as 27 years old and from Lincolnshire.

Towards the end of the 1860s No 24 became the home of cabinet maker Joseph L. Lawes and the 1871 census records Mr Lawes in the house with his young wife and their 11-month-old daughter, Mary. The occupants of the small terraced house continued to change and by the time of the 1881 census, it was the home of Henry Nayler, a 31-year-old corn miller, who was in the house with his 30-year-old wife, Alice, and their four young children.

By 1891 the house had become the home of another young couple, Walter, a tailor, and Cecilia Hookham, and by the 1901 census it was the home of bargeman William Coulson, his wife Amy and their two young children, 3-year-old Sydney and 2-year-old Nellie. There are a few surviving rate books for Victoria Terrace that clearly show the owner of No 24 from 1897 was still Haylock Watson and the occupant was William Coulson.

By 1910, the valuation survey reveals that No 24 Victoria Terrace was still the home of William Coulson, but the owner was a Mr M.H. Newton from Ely. It also shows that Mr Newton owned the entire stretch of land behind Victoria Terrace, recorded as 'allotments'. At the time of the 1911 census, William Coulson was away from home, but his wife Elizabeth was recorded as 36 years old and 'wife of a waterman'. The census also informs us that she had had six children, but one had died. The five remaining children were all still at home: in addition to Sydney and Nellie were Jennie, aged 9; Harry, aged 7; and Constance, aged 2.

TITCHMARSH & SMITH FAMILIES

The Coulson family appear to have continued at No 24 into the years of the First World War, but by the beginning of 1920, the parish rate books show that the house had become the home of George Titchmarsh. Also by this time, the ownership of the terrace and land had passed to Mrs Newton.

The electoral register reveals the house was the home of George and Florence Titchmarsh, along with Hilda, Winifred and Beatrice Titchmarsh. According to the 1911 census, George and Florence had previously lived in Hemingford Grey, following their marriage in 1907, and George was a farm labourer. After George Titchmarsh passed away in 1942, the house passed to his daughter, Hilda, who had married Herbert Smith. A conveyance shows that the freehold of the house was purchased by Smith in 1948 and they both lived here until the 1980s.

14 LYTTON CLOSE

Hampstead Garden Suburb is one of the most famous of all garden suburbs in England and the inspiration of Dame Henrietta Barnett. No 14 was a later addition, designed by C.G. Winbourne and built in 1935 in the 'Moderne Streamline' style, also described as 'liner architecture'.

Moderne architecture is a unique architectural style of the 1920s and '30s influenced by Egyptian design (following the discovery of Tutankhamen's tomb in 1922), as well as aerodynamics and the appearance of speed through 'streamlining'. It is characterised by curved sections, flat roofs, horizontal bar Crittall windows and art deco details. No 14 was built with many of these characteristics, including the flat roof – for sunbathing and recreation – as well as a glazed stair tower, horizontal bar railings and curved quadrants. It is Grade II listed and sits within the Hampstead Garden Suburb Conservation area.

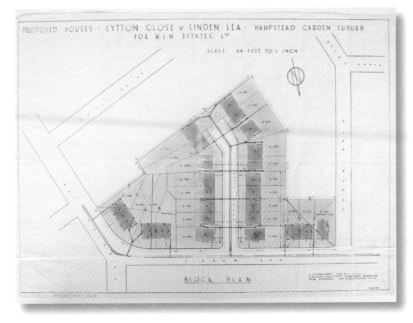

Plans

A map of Hampstead Garden Suburb from 1927 shows Lytton Close laid out for building and was originally planned to extend down to Winnington Road (joining with Winnington Close). However, by 1931 this plan had changed and the street layout appeared as it does today. It was a few years later that the new 'moderne' homes were completed. The first resident of 14 Lytton Close was Hyman Lazarus and his wife Bessie, who remained in the house until the early years of the Second World War. After the war, the house became the home of Richard and Valerie Lehr, who lived there until the late 1950s.

THE LYTTON CONNECTION

The name Lytton originates from Victor Bulwer-Lytton, 2nd Earl of Lytton, who was President of the Hampstead Garden Suburb Trust in 1921. He resigned his post to become Governor of Bengal in 1922, but later returned as Chairman in 1930. Interestingly, Lytton's sister married Edwin Lutyens, former architect of Hampstead Garden Suburb. In 1927–28 Lytton was head of the Indian delegation to the League of Nations; in 1932 he was elected Chairman of the commission to investigate the war in Manchuria, and he later went on to become Chairman of the League of Nations Union in 1938–45.

GREEN & PLEASANT SURROUNDINGS

Hampstead Garden Suburb was the inspiration of Dame Henrietta Barnett, who aspired to create a suburb in which people from all classes (and economic backgrounds) could live happily in green and pleasant surroundings. The area was developed in 1907, with buildings predominately designed by Raymond Unwin and Barry Parker, who were responsible for Letchworth Garden City in 1903. Sir Edwin Lutyens also contributed designs and was the architect behind St Jude's Church.

Dame Barnett aimed to create an area where streets and plots were standardised, boundaries were made from hedges rather than walls, roads were to be tree-lined, noise was to be avoided (including church bells) and houses were built so as not to spoil the neighbours' view. It can be argued that Dame Barnett did not quite achieve her altruistic dreams, but nevertheless, Hampstead Garden Suburb is still noted today for its community spirit, its stylistic architecture and its wide, tree-lined streets.

Samuel and Henrietta Barnett.

PARAMOUR GRANGE

The Paramours

Paramour Grange and Paramour Street were named after a prominent Kentish family, the Paramours. The earliest recorded member of the Paramour family at Ash was a John Paramour, who was buried in the local churchyard in 1497. The most illustrious member of the family, who may have been responsible for the painted room at Paramour Grange, was Thomas Paramour, Mayor of Canterbury from around 1607 to 1619. Thomas Paramour was also the first mayor to commission the making of a sword for the 'Sword Bearer' of Canterbury, granted by James I in 1609.

Paramour Grange in Ash, Kent, may appear to be like any other country house, but behind the front door is an incredible collection of original historic detailing rarely seen elsewhere. It features a rare example of a Jacobean painted room, an original Tudor staircase and inglenook fireplaces.

Large sections of Paramour Grange were built during the late sixteenth century, when Queen Elizabeth I was on the throne; however, there are some doubts and discrepancies as to the date of the original construction of the Grange. It is difficult to be certain, but it is likely that sections of the house actually date back much earlier, to around the early 1400s.

JAMES I & THE PAINTED ROOM

The paintings on the walls at Paramour Grange are very significant, being one of few remaining examples still to be found in situ in a residential home. They were painted in heraldic colours with a bold octagonal design, featuring images of roses, asterisks and ovals. Running along the top is a frieze that depicts inscribed painted verses from the fifth chapter of St Matthews Gospel, commonly known as the Beatitudes. Further decoration includes panels with the crown, the portcullis and the fleur-de-lys, and most

importantly, the date 1603. Above the fireplace are the letters I.R. along with a letter H, but with the crossbar forming a horse's bit, and the letters P.H. The I.R. is understood to stand for James I, and the P.H. for Princeps Henricus (Prince Henry, James I's eldest son who died in 1612).

Unfortunately, very little documentary evidence survives to explain the motivation or reason for the painted room. Various local historians have speculated that it could have been because the house was used as a chapel-at-ease, or it was painted for the newly crowned James I who visited Sandwich

Tracing Ownership

Generations of the Paramour family remained at Paramour Grange throughout the early seventeenth century and are believed to have stayed until around the 1650s. Between the mid and late seventeenth century it is difficult to know what happened to the ownership and occupation of the Grange, with very few surviving documents or details. However, a good collection of land tax records for Ash show that by the 1690s the house had come into the ownership of a Mr Foster and was occupied by a farmer, John Foatt.

shortly after his coronation in 1603. Members of the king's entourage are believed to have occupied the room at this time. Despite the decorative brilliance of the paintings, they are believed to have been covered over only fifty years later, during the Civil War – perhaps understandable if there was fear of recriminations for royal allegiances. The paintings remained hidden for the next 250 years and were only uncovered in 1915.

THE FARMHOUSE

Records show that Mr Foster was the owner from around the 1690s until 1733, but Paramour continued to be the home of farmer John Foatt. In around 1735 Paramour Grange came into the ownership of a Mr Fullagar. The Fullagar family had also lived in Kent for generations, being based nearby in Headcorn since the early seventeenth century.

From around 1747 the house was occupied by Stephen Wood and his family, who remained as residents throughout the eighteenth century. The house passed to his son George in around 1780, who went on to purchase the house and a large portion of surrounding land by 1804. The land tax record in 1805 shows Mr George Wood as the owner and occupier of a section of Paramour Street, and by 1815 he still owned the land, but the running of the farm had passed to his son, George junior, who, by 1830, had taken over the whole farm and house. At the time of the tithe survey in

1840, the Grange had passed into the hands of Lawrence Wood, believed to be George junior's son. The survey shows that Lawrence Wood's property comprised of a house and garden, an orchard and home field, totalling over 18 acres.

DANIEL RALPH

By the time of the 1851 census, the house had become the home of John Bushell and his family, but by 1861 the Grange was the home of 34-year-old Daniel Ralph, a farmer of 230 acres, employing five men and two boys. Daniel resided with his wife Hannah and their two young sons, William and Daniel, along with Daniel's father, 73-year-old Thomas, a retired farmer, and three agricultural servants and one house servant. The Ralph family remained for many years, raising nine children, and Daniel was last recorded at Paramour Grange at the turn of the twentieth century, after which time he retired from farming.

MRS WAKEHAM & THE FULLERS

Within a few years Paramour Grange became the home of Mrs Susan Wakeham. The 1911 census reveals Mrs Wakeham was a widow and 'farmer and market gardener', raising two daughters, Clare and Susie. It was around this time, in 1915, that the unique wall paintings at Paramour Grange were uncovered. It is uncertain if this was during Mrs Wakeham's time in the house; it is more likely to have been when the new occupants, Henry and Ada Fuller, moved in during the early years of the First World War. Apart from a small mention in the Kent Archaeological Society journal, very little is known about the discovery. Despite this grand unveiling in their home, the Fullers continued the farming tradition for the next thirty years. However, they also supplemented their income by renting out the house during the inter-war years. Advertisements in *The Times* from 1929–33 show the house publicised as a 'Spacious Tudor house, historical interest … all conveniences: home comforts: restful: best food: [and with] bountiful table'.

Today

Paramour Grange has been beautifully conserved, highlighting its amazing historic character with the ornate painted walls, outstanding Tudor staircase, inglenook fireplaces, exposed wooden beams and mullion windows. It has also been suggested that a full architectural analysis may in fact find many more historic features that have gone undiscovered for centuries.

SHAFTESBURY PARK ESTATE

Red Brick & Turrets

The houses were predominately built in terraced rows with yellow London brick, and featured red brick and stone details. Some were built with additional detailing, including gables, towers and gothic-style porches, while others have simpler pointed arch door surrounds. Two gothic corner turrets feature on the houses at the entrance to the estate in Grayshott Road.

There were four main types of houses, divided up by classes depending on the number of rooms. The smallest, fourth class, had five rooms, increasing to eight rooms in the first class. The latter was the only class to provide a bathroom inside the house; all the others originally had outside toilets. The details also specified that each house provide sanitary conditions, including drains that did not run through the house. Within the kitchen was a range, a scullery complete with copper, gas stove, a cold water tap and sink, and a ventilated larder.

The Shaftesbury Park Estate in Battersea is a hidden historical treasure and living testimony to the social reformers of the Victorian era. Established in 1867, this housing co-operative was set up to provide affordable and quality housing for the working classes during the mid nineteenth century. Prior to this time, the area was dominated by market gardens and piggeries, and, in fact, it was initially called 'pig hill', but by the nineteenth century the area had become Poupart's Market Garden, owned by Samuel Poupart.

WORKERS' HOUSING

In the nineteenth century the need for housing in London had reached a desperate state, particularly for the working population. The 'Artizans, Labourers and General Dwelling Company' was established by architect and surveyor, William Austin, and supported by the peer and prolific social reformer, Anthony Ashley Cooper, Lord Shaftesbury. In 1872 the Company purchased 40 acres of land from Samuel Poupart and on 3 August Lord Shaftesbury laid the foundation stone for the new development. Close to 1,200 houses were built between 1873 and 1877, and when Prime Minister Benjamin Disraeli opened part of the estate in 1874, he called it a 'social phenomenon'. The houses and cottages were all designed by Robert Austin (no relation to William Austin) as a unified area, but he allowed for unique architectural differences in each home.

On Monday 20 July 1874 *The Times* reported that '8000 people would hereafter be brought from the overcrowded, pestilential centres of London and planted in healthy homes in the pure air, amid pleasant surroundings, with every reasonable provision for happy domestic life and social enjoyment'.

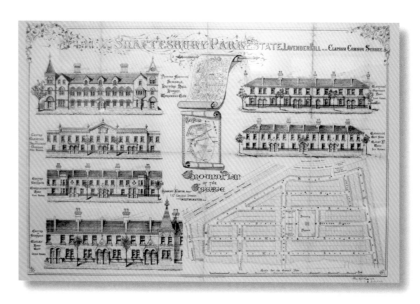

The Estate was built using a 'co-operative' approach, where future residents built their own homes, with some even being shareholders in the Company. Dubbed 'Workman's Town', it aimed to create a community spirit by providing a communal hall, schools and open space, but not a pub, in an effort to curb the social problems of cheap alcohol.

CONSERVATION AREA

In 1963 the Peabody Donation Fund purchased 245 houses on the Estate. The remainder were sold to the Wandsworth Corporation for £776,000. These were subsequently leased to Peabody, allowing for the whole Estate to be maintained and conserved as a group. Designated a Conservation area in 1976, the Shaftesbury Park Estate has seen very few changes over its 130-year history, and maintains its picturesque Victorian terrace rows, gothic architecture and tree-lined streets. Famous residents have included Lydia Russell, Duchess of Bedford, actor Daniel Massey and actress Una Stubbs.

29 NEAL STREET

Change in Classes

When the houses along Neal Street were first built they were occupied by tradesmen, merchants and some from the 'gentleman classes'. However, as the eighteenth century progressed this began to change. The area around Seven Dials became notorious for thieves, vagabonds and extreme poverty, although nearby King Street still managed to continue as a typical shopping street. Businesses listed in the London Directory included grocers, bakers, boot & shoe makers, tailors, butchers, furniture makers, book binders and carpenters, amongst many others.

Neal Street in Covent Garden has had a rather turbulent history, formerly being at the centre of a working-class community and due to its close connection to the former (and notorious) slum of Seven Dials. No 29 Neal Street in Covent Garden was built over 300 years ago and has been the home of labourers, brewers, banana salesmen and police constables. The house has been at the centre of a shifting London, from Georgian and Victorian working-class life through to one of the most fashionable shopping streets in London.

Neal Street and the Seven Dials area of Covent Garden were formerly fields known as the marshland. In 1691 the area was acquired for development by Sir Thomas Neale, the street's namesake. Neale was formerly Master of the Mint from 1678 and a groom-porter from 1684 for James II and William III. Initially, Neal Street was known as King Street and was laid out for building during the 1690s. It is believed that the house was completed between 1700 and 1710, but the earliest retained parish rate books show King Street listed in 1730.

The house numbers along King Street have changed many times over the last 300 years. Richard Horwood's map of 1799 shows the house was No 5, but by the time of the 1841 census it had become No 42. The numbers were again reordered in 1877 when it changed to No 13, until 1908 when the house officially became No 29.

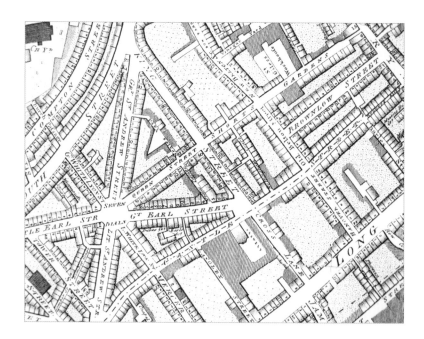

Richard Horwood 1799 map, showing Neal Street with its former name of King Street.

WORKING CLASSES

By the middle of the nineteenth century, the 1851 census records show the house had become the home of five families, including a tailor, a greengrocer and two labourers, and by 1861 it was a similar picture, but with residents from very different occupations. There were two widows – 70-year-old Ann Nightingale, a seamstress, and 76-year-old Elizabeth Hollies, a washerwoman – as well as a police constable, James Brierly, and his wife Catherine. The house was also home to William Huxtable, a tailor, his seamstress wife Mary and their two children, as well as Thomas Parry, a cordwainer (leather shoe maker), his wife Francis and their 18-year-old daughter, Elizabeth.

The 1871 census shows a continuation of working-class occupants in the house, with a plasterer, a brewer, a charwoman, a farrier, three porters and a labourer. By 1881, King Street had been renamed and renumbered, and the house was listed as No 13 Neal Street. It was also at this time that the house was first specifically listed in the London Directory with resident James O'Connor, a lampshade maker. James lived in the house with his wife Rose and their four children, along with a Scottish brass worker, John Ross, his wife Sarah and their six children. There was also another Scot in residence, John Henderson, a type founder (metal caster), with his wife Catherine and their three sons.

Old photograph showing the early shops of Neal Street.

Twentieth Century

Working-class families continued to occupy the house into the twentieth century, particularly those from the nearby Watney Brewery. The 1901 census records that 13 Neal Street was home to a 'cellarman [at] brewery', two brewers' draymen, two labourers, a 'horseman at brewery', a further 'brewer's cellarman' and finally a solicitor's clerk. By 1927, the house had been renumbered No 29 and appeared in the London Directory as dining rooms run by Arthur Slade. The house continued to be used as dining rooms until the Second World War, after which it joined with Nos 31 and 33 to become Forrester & Sons Banana Salesmen.

Holly Lodge

Famous Guests

In the late nineteenth and early twentieth centuries, especially during the inter-war period, St Margaret's at Cliffe was a popular luxury resort. Many illustrious guests chose to stay in the more secluded and exclusive St Margaret's rather than the bigger resorts nearby. During this period, St Margaret's was visited by well-known stars, including Noel Coward, Ian Fleming and Peter Ustinov. It was also popular with royalty, with many of the royal children holidaying here during the 1920s and '30s.

Holly Lodge is located within the coastal village of St Margaret's at Cliffe in Kent. Very few early documents survive for St Margaret's at Cliffe, making it difficult to research the full history of the house, but architectural evidence suggests that the house was originally built during the late seventeenth century. It was rebuilt during the 1730s by the Brett family, with early stonework recording the date 1733 inscribed into the bricks of the house, with the initials 'H.B. and M.B.', along with further lettering, 'H B A B', believed to be attributed to the Brett family when they built Holly Lodge. Sadly, a central plaque has worn away which may have revealed a crest or coat of arms.

The Brett family do not appear to have stayed long, as by the 1750s the ownership of Holly Lodge had reverted to lord of the manor, Richard Solly. The house remained in his hands until the early nineteenth century, when it became the home of a gentleman farmer, Thomas Kingsford Wood. Wood was a prominent figure in the area, owning further land in the village and also doing much to provide relief for the poor in the village. In 1818 he married Maria Lound, who became a renowned socialite in St Margaret's at Cliffe. In fact, Maria wrote a diary describing her life and experiences at Holly Lodge, which has fortunately survived, giving a fascinating insight into life in a Kentish village during the early nineteenth century.

The 1840 tithe apportionment and the 1841 census show the Woods at Holly Lodge. However, by 1845 Thomas had passed away, and eight years later Maria died at the age of 63.

SCHOOLMASTER JAMES TEMPLE

After Maria passed away in 1853, Holly Lodge was purchased by a very distinguished local figure, schoolmaster James Temple, who already owned large sections of land surrounding the house, including the school house, playground, two further houses and an additional ladies school. This seemed an ideal addition to the extensive school grounds. The census returns from 1861 and 1871 reveal around 175 scholars when there were only around 800 residents living in the entire village. The school was so renowned that St Margaret's at Cliffe became known as an educational centre throughout the entire country.

James Temple passed away in 1874, but sadly no one continued with the famed school and it closed. However, by the late 1870s, records show that his unmarried daughter, Maria, continued at the house. In 1891, she was 60, living by her own means, with just a housekeeper and a lady's help in the house, but she died soon after. For a short time, the house was home to Dr John Pollard and his family, recorded in the house in 1899.

WAR COMES

St Margaret's was greatly affected by the start of the Second World War; being so close to the coast, it was not only used by the Allies to house troops, but was under regular attack from the Luftwaffe. The attacks were so bad and so frequent that the area became known as 'Hell-fire corner'. Many regular citizens were evacuated and it appears Holly Lodge was no different. The Woodland family, who had been in the house since around 1919, were no longer listed there after 1939. At the end of the war, the house became the home of what appears to be two sisters, Mabel and Eunice Evens, who continued at the house until the late 1960s, when it became the home of Albert and Evelyn Tatton. Throughout the remainder of the twentieth century, Holly Lodge was a family home, secluded and quiet behind its picturesque gardens, much as it is today.

The Laundry

Around 1907, the Wickenden family arrived and brought about a significant change in the history of Holly Lodge. A public notice in the St Margaret's Visitors' Guide in 1907 advertises 'The Holly Lodge Laundry' operated by Mrs Wickenden, laundress. The advertisement highlights 'High-Class Shirt and Collar Dresser', along with 'Flannels a speciality'. The 1911 census reveals that the house was home to 58-year-old Charles Wickenden, his wife Esther, 42 years old, Charles' mother Charlotte, and two nephews and a niece.

105 BANBURY ROAD

Designs

The building plans, dated 1886, show that No 105 was planned with nine bedrooms and three WCs, and the builder was J.H. Kingerlee. It was to be made of 'red brick with stone dressings' and was being built as the 'New Oxford Residence for Major Adair'. With estate architect William Wilkinson retiring in 1886, this house appears to be mainly the work of his nephew, Harry Wilkinson Moore, who was influenced by the renaissance style of prominent Oxford architect, Sir Thomas Graham Jackson. Nikolaus Pevsner, in his *Oxfordshire Buildings of England*, described the house: '[the] pliant mixing of tile-hanging, leaded windows with mullions and freestone Jacobean ornamentation in the style of Jackson, is adept if a little affected, and quite original.'

Banbury Road has been one of the main roads heading out of Oxford since the eleventh century, and possibly before, but it has only been known by this name since the fourteenth century. For much of its history, the stretch where 105 Banbury Road is located (known as St Giles's Fields) was farming land and part of the estate of St John's College.

NORTH OXFORD

By the 1850s, much of St Giles still remained open land, but St John's College had realised the benefits that could be obtained from establishing high-class housing on the estate. During this period old leases were not

renewed and St John's were able to consider and plan building development and the establishment of a North Oxford suburb. The earliest building development was the Park Town Estate, located on the east side of Banbury Road and on a site that had formerly been chosen for a new workhouse. The homes were constructed in 1853–55 in an Italianate stuccoed mid Victorian style and were reminiscent of the crescents and terraced houses of Bath and Regent's Park in London.

Towards the late 1850s and early 1860s there was once again speculation about a railway line running through North Oxford, but this was averted. Instead, St John's College initiated further developments, selling building leases in what came to be known as the Norham Manor Estate; but building was slow. This time the development and construction was overseen by architect William Wilkinson, who favoured the gothic style rather than the early Victorian Italianate style. A number of the houses in Norham Manor were designed by Wilkinson and were constructed from 1863 to 1870.

By the 1880s, the development of houses in North Oxford was progressing slowly, and by the mid 1880s the threat of the railway coming across the estate loomed once again. In fact, if it had been built, it would have run across the estate north of St Margaret's Road, near 105 Banbury Road. By selling individual building leases, St John's College was able to keep greater control over the estate and could insist on certain building materials being used. The favoured design of the houses was predominately semi-detached and detached villas in the gothic style, with red brick and stone dressings, as well as pointed arches, gables and turrets.

BUILDING NO 105

After the abandonment of the railway development, estate architect William Wilkinson (responsible for the famous Randolph Hotel), along with his nephew, Harry Wilkinson Moore, proposed further building in St Margaret's Road. Although approved, constrained college finances meant they were restricted to houses facing Banbury Road. The financial

Expansion

As Oxford's population increased in the early nineteenth century there was a need for new housing. By the 1840s, land was also needed for expanding colleges and new railways. This part of North Oxford was sought-after for many of these reasons, and St John's College was approached for a new cemetery, an Oxford workhouse and a proposed railway line across North Oxford. None of these proposed works took place.

1891 Census showing Major Henry A. Adair.

Ottoline Morrell

Ottoline Morrell was a renowned literary and artistic socialite; friends with such notable figures as D.H. Lawrence, Siegfried Sassoon, T.S. Eliot and Virginia Woolf, as well as Mark Gertler, Dora Carrington and Gilbert Spencer. Phillip and Ottoline Morrell had an open relationship, with Lady Morrell having relationships with philosopher Bertrand Russell, as well as the artists Augustus John and Henry Lamb. Phillip and Ottoline were at the centre of a lively artistic world, including the Bloomsbury Group, and Lady Morrell is believed to be the inspiration for D.H. Lawrence's Lady Chatterley. She was also the cousin of Lady Elizabeth Bowes-Lyon, the queen's mother and wife of George VI.

implications also influenced the speed of development; rather than houses being constructed as one large estate, they went up piecemeal.

MAJOR ADAIR

No 105 was built for Major Henry Atkinson Adair, youngest son of Alexander Adair of Heatherton Park in Somerset, whose elder brother was Sir Robert Shafto Adair, 1st Baronet (created in 1838). Adair was posted to India as part of the 52nd Oxfordshire Light Infantry at the time of the Indian Mutiny in 1858. In 1885 he transferred to be adjutant to the 3rd Battalion Oxfordshire Light Infantry. This corresponds with his commissioning a new house in Oxford for himself and his family; moving in during 1887. Major Adair retired from the Army in 1894, but continued to serve, most notably volunteering his services during the Boer War.

At the 1891 census Adair was recorded as 59 years old, living with his wife, Charlotte, 44 years old, and their four children, Beatrice, Helen, Alexander and Henry, as well as two live-in servants. On his retirement in 1895 the house became the home of Frances Peel and her sons, John and Charles.

JOHN PEEL

By the early years of the twentieth century, the house was home to Frances' son, solicitor John Douglas Peel, who married Frederica Harriett Morrell, daughter of Frederic Morrell, solicitor and steward of St John's College. Frederica's brother was Phillip Morrell, politician and MP for Henley in 1906–10 and Burnley in 1910–18, but possibly more significantly he married Lady Ottoline Morrell.

John and Frederica Peel appeared to live a quieter life than Phillip and Ottoline Morrell. John was a partner in the solicitor's firm, Morrell, Son and Peel, with his father-in-law, based at No 1 St Giles's, Oxford, from 1902. Peel took over as Oxford University's solicitor after his father-in-law passed away in 1908, a position he held until he retired in 1929. At the time of the 1910 valuation survey, John Douglas Peel was still resident at 105 Banbury Road.

ARCHAEOLOGY PROFESSOR

By the time of the 1911 census, 64-year-old Percy Gardner and his wife Agnes had moved in, along with John Lawson Reid, a clerk in a shipbuilders', and three live-in servants. Gardner was a renowned professor of archaeology at both Oxford and Cambridge universities. He had formerly worked as an assistant in the coins and medals department at the British Museum, where he developed a keen interest in Greek history. Later, he was present at the excavations at Olympia in Greece and saw the recently discovered treasures from Mycenae. In 1880 Gardner became editor of the *Journal of Hellenic Studies*, and in the same year was elected to the Disney chair of archaeology at Cambridge University, a position he held until 1887. He was then appointed professor of classical archaeology at Oxford University, and it was here that he played an influential and vital role in the teaching

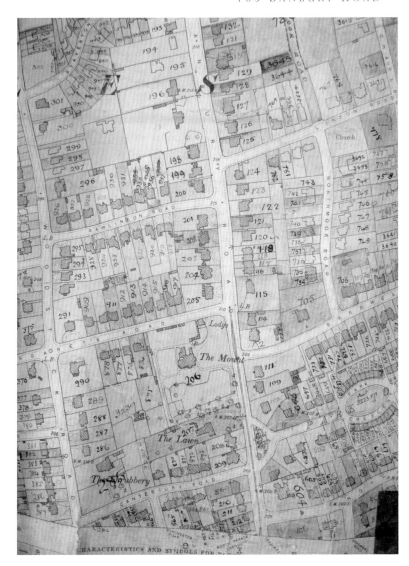

1910 Valuation map.

and studying of archaeology, especially at a time when traditional studies of the Classics was the dominant form of study.

Gardner wrote many books on elements of Greek history, including the first catalogues of coins at the British Museum, as well as *Types of Greek Coins* (1883) and *New Chapters in Greek History* (1892). He was also President of the Hellenic Society. Gardner retired his Oxford chair in 1925.

REV. NUTTALL-SMITH

During the early years of the First World War, No 105 became the home of Rev. George and Maria Nuttall-Smith. Reverend Nuttall-Smith was described as from the high Anglican tradition and he lived in the house with his family until around 1925, when it became the home of Constance Rashdall. The house was subsequently opened up to lodgers, and continued in this way into the 1950s.

Twentieth Century

Lady Knowles, the wife of a renowned Oxford biologist, Sir Francis Gerald Knowles, was recorded at No 105 in the Oxfordshire directories from 1960 to 1962, after which time it appears the house was divided into apartments for single women. In 1970 it became a dental surgery for Symmonds, Williams & Bradshaw, and in 1991 the house was transformed into accommodation for Linacre College. At this time it was named 'Ursula Hicks House' after economist Lady Ursula Hicks, Honorary Fellow of the College.

8 ALWYNE PLACE

lwyne Place in Islington was laid out for building in 1850 on Compton family land. It was named after Lord Alwyne Compton, Bishop of Ely and fourth son of the Marquis of Northampton. Originally it was named Canonbury Place, and No 8, completed in 1852, was first known as No 15 Canonbury Place.

The first resident was lawyer William Skinner, but within a few short years he had left the house to his daughter, Luciana. However, she leased the house so by 1860 it was occupied by John Webb, a soda water manufacturer, with his wife Sarah and their five children. By the early 1870s Luciana Skinner had returned to live in the house and the 1871 census records her as 70 years old and receiving an annuity. She continued there throughout the 1870s and '80s, by which time it had been renumbered No 8 Alwyne Place. Miss Skinner remained in the property until she passed away, at the age of 89, in 1890, and the house passed to Elizabeth Wakefield.

THE HUMPHRIES FAMILY

Elizabeth Wakefield rented the house to her sister and brother-in-law, Agnes and William Humphries. The 1891 census shows William as the head of the house, aged 57, a commission agent, with his wife Agnes and their two daughters: Helen, aged 27, who was already widowed and teaching music privately, and Edith, aged 25. The household income was supplemented by taking in two boarders: firstly, Mary Lister aged 68 and 'living on own means'; and secondly, Joshua Maddington, a 30-year-old civil engineer. At the time of the 1901 census the Humphries family was still living at No 8, with William now working as a wine merchant's manager.

KENNETH GRIFFITH

Between 1972 and 1976 the house was home to actor, writer and filmmaker Kenneth Griffith, who today is familiar as the 'old man' from *Four Weddings and a Funeral*. However, throughout the twentieth century he was seen in many film and television productions, including *I'm All Right Jack* (1959) with Peter Sellers; an adaptation of George Orwell's *Nineteen Eighty-Four* (1954); and *Who Dares Wins* (1982). Yet it is for his documentaries about British imperialism that he is most notoriously remembered. He made a number of films about the Boer War and Northern Ireland, including one of his most controversial, *Hang out the Brightest Colours: the Life and Death of Michael Collins*, in 1972. It was banned by the Independent Broadcasting Authority and was only seen twenty-two years later, in 1994.

Stella Rimington

From 1979 to 1984, No 8 was occupied by Dame Stella Rimington, author and former Director General of MI5 (1992–94). She was the first woman to be head of Britain's secret service and was controversially the first to be publicly named. It was also at this time that elements of MI5 operations were made open to the public. She published her memoirs after leaving the service and is now a successful author, using her knowledge and experience from her former job to write spy novels.

Census showing William Humphries, 1901.

HULME

Two-Up, Two-Downs

The history of the terraced rows of two-up two-down houses across many northern cities, built during the Industrial Revolution, has certainly not been the focus for many looking at the history of houses. Many of the buildings were only associated with poverty and suffering, and were swept away in slum clearances during the mid twentieth century. But despite this sometimes grim past, the style of housing is as much a part of our history as the grand stately homes and vernacular houses across the country.

Hulme, in Manchester, has seen an incredible amount of change throughout its history: from open fields, before the nineteenth-century mill workers' houses were built, through to classic 1970s urban planning and to today, with its redeveloped twenty-first-century housing. Despite its difficult past, Hulme is inextricably connected to the history of its housing. The lives of the residents and the way they have lived are important to the social history of Manchester, as well as to the history of housing across the UK.

INDUSTRIAL REVOLUTION

In the eighteenth century, the area of Hulme was predominately farming land until the introduction of the canal system in the 1760s. This new Bridgewater Canal, attributed with being the first British canal, terminated at nearby Castlefield and allowed for the transport of coal from the mines of the Duke of Bridgewater at Worsley. The introduction of the canals transformed the area, as it became ideal for the cotton mills and factories. This early innovation created the means for Manchester to be at the heart of the cotton industry in Britain during the nineteenth century. It was so much a part of the city that it earned the name of 'Cottonopolis'. As the nineteenth century progressed, many new cotton mills were built, and by 1853 there were 108 mills. Alongside all this industry new homes were needed for the burgeoning working population.

An 1840 study of the area records that in 1773–74 there were only thirty houses in Hulme, but by 1831 this had risen to 1,843. In 1773–74

1960s buildings of Hulme, Manchester.

there were 162 residents recorded in Hulme, rising to 1,677 in 1801 and 9,624 in 1831. Despite this rapid expansion there was very little legislation or any organised plan for housing. The houses that were built for the mill workers and labourers were simply constructed by speculators who were not concerned about standards, just making the most of their investment. This inevitably led to cramped housing, where developers aimed to exploit the land by building as many houses as possible on each plot. These houses were then let to numerous families at once and overcrowding was rife. There are many stories of several families living in the same house; one example being a cellar dwelling where there were eight members of one family and eleven lodgers.

The housing was not only cramped and overcrowded, but very little allowance was made for water supply or sanitation, which led to severe outbreaks of disease. In his work, *The Condition of the Working Class in England* (1845), Fredrich Engels described the housing as 'containing at most two rooms, a garret and perhaps a cellar, on the average [where] twenty human beings live; that in the whole region, for each 120 persons, one usually inaccessible privy is provided'.

Many districts across Manchester had the 'back-to-back' style of small housing with a very narrow space between the backs. This was the most common design of house in Hulme, and back-to-backs were only phased out in 1868. In 1844 the Manchester Police Act specified that no new houses were to be built without a toilet in the yard or in the house, unlike in many other areas where there was one WC between many households. This stipulation, however, did not mean that houses were created with inside toilets, like we know today, but merely meant that outdoor toilets were given a door and a proper covering.

As the nineteenth century progressed, further improvements took place to supply water, to monitor housing standards, including street widths and

Changes in Hulme

It was only after the end of the Second World War that real change began to alter the appearance of Hulme. Up until the 1940s the conditions for residents in Hulme was still below standard. Surveys undertaken during the 1930s and '40s reported that living conditions were extremely poor. In 1945, out of 6,089 houses only 327 had a bath and very few had a hot water supply. It was these studies and the extremity of the deprivation, even into the 1950s, that brought about the grand redevelopment of Hulme.

Manchester housing from the air, 1932.

Typical Manchester back lanes, late nineteenth century.

A New Community

From the time of the redevelopment of Hulme in the 1960s through to the 1980s there was major social and economic decline. After the initial building it was soon evident that poor design, along with bad workmanship and lack of maintenance, had contributed to lowering standards of living. Also, many of the long-established residents of Hulme, who had been at the heart of the old community, moved away, meaning that those who lived in the new Hulme did not have an established community spirit. A large portion of the housing was council housing and many of the new residents were from the poorest and most deprived backgrounds. Hulme soon gained a reputation for violent crime and anti-social behaviour.

The situation in Hulme reached a peak during the 1980s when it became a no-go zone for taxi drivers, and it was decided to rebuild the area once again. During the 1990s new housing was constructed, guided more by traditional housing than alienating grand schemes.

the space between houses, and legislation was passed to ensure owners maintained their properties. Slum clearances also began as early as the 1880s, although there were still vast swathes of terraced housing at the turn of the century. The late nineteenth and early twentieth centuries saw the introduction of a number of housing schemes, and in 1889 the City Council made a way for new housing to replace old through the Artisans' and Labourers' Dwellings Act.

THE 1960S' CLEARANCE

The oldest houses in Hulme, constructed between 1830 and 1870, were finally cleared away during the 1960s and, over an area of 350 acres, new housing with elevated walkways was constructed. The new buildings were a mixture of low-rise houses, as well as three nine-storey blocks. The housing scheme aspired to create an idyllic community environment with green open spaces and the latest interior appliances and amenities, including central heating, double-glazed windows and fully plumbed bathrooms. The scheme planned for the separation of traffic and pedestrian areas, with the entire road system changing and the pedestrianised section linking schools, parks, libraries and shops, becoming known as 'deck-access' apartments. The local facilities would include churches and youth clubs, as well as shopping centres and pubs. A 1966 report from Manchester City Council Planning Department stated: 'the movement of people in their daily life along well-defined routes would encourage social contact and contribute to a sense of community.'

However, history shows that this scheme did not create the community environment so desired, and even as early as 1971 an article by W.S. Fahey, in the *Journal of the National Housing and Town Planning Council*, questioned some of the decisions that had been made.

ORWELL STUDIOS

Orwell Studios is a group of apartments located within the upper floors of the large, early twentieth-century building at No 200 Oxford Street in central London. Situated along one of the world's busiest shopping streets, one would be forgiven for thinking it didn't have much history, but it was in fact the former offices for the BBC Overseas Service during the Second World War. The author George Orwell worked for the BBC during this period, as an Eastern Service Talks producer, and it is understood that it was in this building that he was inspired to create 'Room 101', in his novel *Nineteen Eighty-Four*.

ARCHITECTURAL AWARDS

The BBC left 200 Oxford Street in 1957, at which time it was transformed into one of London's flagship department stores, C&A. However, after almost fifty years in this location C&A closed its doors in the early twenty-first century and a new opportunity arose. A new development of retail and office space on the lower floors and new residential apartments on the upper floors was undertaken by architects ORMS, who won the *Evening Standard* Homes & Property award for 'Best New Apartments' in 2006. The architectural features include giant pilasters and a bronze entrance door, part of the original art deco design. The residential floors of 200 Oxford Street were named Orwell Studios in honour of George Orwell and the building's history as studios for the BBC.

The BBC

No 200 Oxford Street was designed by Herbert Austen Hall with T.P. and E.S. Clarkson in 1923, and when first completed it was the new building for the Peter Robinson department store. By 1942, at the height of the Second World War, the building was taken over by the BBC and used for the Overseas Service's broadcasting. Located in central London, with the constant threat of air raids from the Luftwaffe, BBC broadcasts continued. Today, a plaque at the entrance of the building acknowledges this history, where broadcasts to America during the war often had to be made from the roof during air raids.

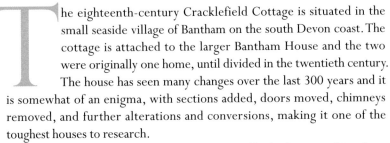

CRACKLEFIELD COTTAGE

Bantham Village

The small village of Bantham was predominately a fishing village, particularly for salmon and pilchard, dating back as far as the Iron Age, with evidence of earthworks on Bantham Ham. Evidence of Roman occupation has also been found, thought to be an ideal location for a Roman trading port. This isolated spot was also perfect for smuggling during the eighteenth and nineteenth centuries, which was so rife that goods were stored in places throughout the parish.

The eighteenth-century Cracklefield Cottage is situated in the small seaside village of Bantham on the south Devon coast. The cottage is attached to the larger Bantham House and the two were originally one home, until divided in the twentieth century. The house has seen many changes over the last 300 years and it is somewhat of an enigma, with sections added, doors moved, chimneys removed, and further alterations and conversions, making it one of the toughest houses to research.

The history of Cracklefield Cottage is actually the history of Bantham House. Despite the fact that both these names only officially came into existence during the twentieth century, for the purposes of this account the property will be referred to as Bantham House.

Surviving documents in the Devon County Record Office reveal that in the mid eighteenth century this section of land close to the Sloop Inn was known as 'Willings' and was in the hands of a local Kingsbridge gentleman, John Square. At this time Bantham only had a few properties, with a row of seventeenth-century cottages running down from the Sloop Inn towards the sea.

CONSTRUCTION & OWNERSHIP

While the ownership of the land continued in the Square family, we know through architectural details and the style of vernacular building in this part of Devon, as well as through surviving documents, that Bantham House opposite the Sloop was built during the mid to late eighteenth century. Originally it appears to have been a substantial house, certainly when compared to the smaller seventeenth-century fishermen's cottages.

Land tax records show that from 1749 to the 1750s, the surrounding land, 'Willings', was owned by John Square, but by the 1780s the land tax was being paid by John Reeve. It appears that it was during this time that the house was first constructed. However, by 1785 it had passed to Mr Thomas Polyblank, who was recorded paying the land tax for Willings through to the turn of the nineteenth century.

From a later indenture of sale, we discover that in the very early years of the 1800s, the house became the home of Hugh Hardy, while the lease-holder was Mr Robert Johnson. The document further provides details about the early history of the house and clearly states that in March 1806 an agreement for the 'messuage or dwelling house, garden and hereditaments' was made between Robert Johnson and Hugh Hardy. The document goes on to say that the 'premises heretofore erected and built on part of a field called Crackell situate near Bantham … [were] formerly in the possession of the said Hugh Hardy as tenant to the said Robert Johnson'.

WEYMOUTH, PRIDEAUX & BRAY

In 1826 the indenture of sale shows that the freehold was sold by descend-ants of John Square, including Henry Roe Square, William Holberton, Henry Richard Roe and John Square. The house was sold to Mr Isaac Weymouth, a gentleman of independent means and a landowner, and by 1839 the house was leased by Weymouth to Charles and Anna Prideaux. In 1840 the tithe map and apportionment clearly identifies the house and surrounding lands, with the house owned by Isaac Weymouth and leased to Charles Prideaux, but by this time the house was occupied by Edmund Moor Bray. Prideaux was a banker based in Plymouth, while Bray was an established farmer who owned over 12 acres of his own land at 'Buckland Parks'.

Meanwhile, the details from the 1840 tithe survey also reveal that the neighbouring land, still recorded as 'Willings', included gardens, fields and small plots of land – including 'Crackhams'. However, by this time the land had been separated from the house and was owned by William Wakenham and occupied by Joseph Hannaford.

EARLY VICTORIAN OCCUPANTS

In 1841 Isaac Weymouth passed away and his property transferred to his wife, Maria Juliana Weymouth. Census records for Bantham during the nineteenth century do not identify streets, houses or give house numbers, so it is not clear as to which house is which. Unfortunately, the details for

'Crackell'

We know from the tithe records that 'Crackell' came under the collection of lands known as 'Willings'; land tax records further support this, as in 1805–07 the leaseholder of Willings was Mr Johnson and the occupant was Hugh Harding. However, the landowners at this time continued to be members of the Square family. These details further confirm that the house had recently been constructed on the field known as Crackell, and was part of the landholdings known as Willings. The connection with Crackell was the inspiration for the later name of Cracklefield Cottage.

Thurlestone tithe map *c*. 1840. Bantham House is numbered 865.

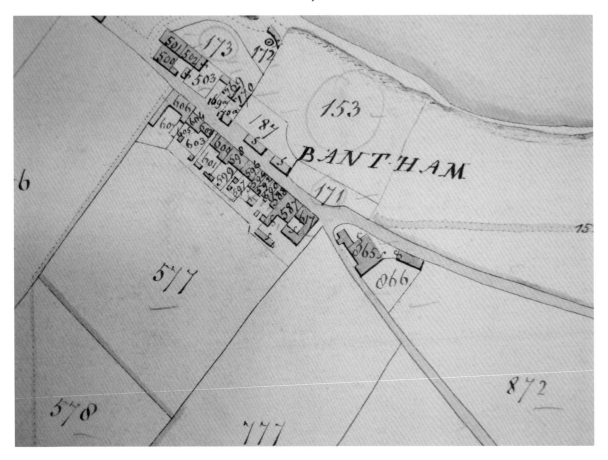

Valuation

The 1910 valuation survey reveals more details of the ownership and occupation, with the main house described as a 'very aged house of stone, timber and slate'. It included three sitting rooms (one large), plus workshop, kitchen, scullery etc. on the ground floor. The first floor had one large sitting room and four bedrooms, and the second floor had two attics. It was described as 'aged but in fair condition'.

Bantham House are uncertain and in some years it appears that the house was in fact unoccupied. However, by 1866 the indenture of sale gives details of the transfer of sale for Bantham House. At this time, Maria, widow of Isaac Weymouth, sold the property to newly qualified barrister Robert Campbell, 'late of 27 Heriot Row, Edinburgh and now of 4 New Square Lincoln's Inn'. His wife, Marian Lucy, was from this area and the couple were married in 1867, just a year after his purchase of the house in Bantham.

BUILDING IN BANTHAM

The Campbells, however, did not live in Bantham House. Records show that they lived in exclusive Campden Hill Square in London; although they continued their connection with Bantham by purchasing neighbouring plots of land, including the field 'Crackhills', in 1872. It was at this time that the house was altered and nearby land built on. To the north, a new building became Sheriffs bakery, apparently famous for its sugary cakes; to the east of that was a separate house, and to the south-east a bake house was built to accompany Sheriffs bakery.

THE CAMPBELLS MOVE

On retirement the Campbells moved permanently to Bantham. The 1911 census records Robert, a 79-year-old 'barrister and advocate of the Scottish bar', his wife Marian, 65 years old, and their eldest son, Ilbert Lewis Campbell, 39 years old and formerly a clerk. The records also show that the Campbells had a cook and a housemaid and the house consisted of nine rooms.

HUGH ELPHINSTONE CAMPBELL

In December 1912, on Robert's death, the property transferred to Marian, who remained there until she passed away, in her nineties, in December 1938. At this time, the property passed to her son, Hugh Elphinstone Campbell, a retired merchant, and his wife Ethel, daughter of Sir Pelham Warren. Hugh Elphinstone, of Combe Royal near Kingsbridge, had been Managing Director of Ilbert & Co. of Shanghai, which was linked with the Ilbert branch of the family. Hugh had fought as a 2nd Lieutenant in the Chinese Labour Corp during the First World War and saw action in France during 1917. Their son, Alan, also had a distinguished diplomatic career. He had served in the Special Operations Executive during the Second World War, and after the war went on to become British Ambassador in Ethiopia in 1969–72 and Ambassador to Italy in 1976–79.

After her husband's death in the early 1940s, Ethel continued in the house until 1949 when she sold it, now officially named 'Bantham House', to Ethel Carter. She remained until the 1960s, and by the 1980s the house was separated into Cracklefield Cottage at the rear and Bantham House at the front.

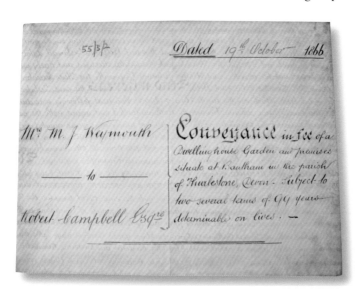

HIGHLANDS HEATH

ighlands Heath flats were built on the site of a large country house called 'Highlands'. It was formerly the home of Colonel Farquharson, who entertained Edward VII there on a number of occasions.

During the late nineteenth and early twentieth centuries, Highlands was the home of Dr George Blundell Longstaff. He was Vice-President of the Royal Statistical and Entomological Societies, was well known for his charitable work, and wrote a number of books, including *Butterfly Hunting in many Lands* (1912). His wife Jane was also an award-winning scientist, who wrote a number of works for scientific journals, was a member of the Geologists' Association and was a Fellow of the Linnean Society (Natural History Society) in 1906.

The Highlands' gardens were a notable feature and were used for fetes and local fairs. One such fair, organised in 1915 to raise money for an ambulance for the Western Front during the First World War, was opened by the Marchioness of Dufferin.

The last resident of Highlands was Egbert Goddard, who sold the house and contents in 1934. The house and land were purchased by Bell Properties for building development and the Highlands Heath flats were built in its place.

Ideal Living in Highlands

Highlands Heath flats were designed by architectural firm H. Toms & Partners, and the sales brochure in 1935 described the residences as 'in the best style of modern English domestic architecture'. Advertisements from *The Times* in 1935 and 1936 listed notable features, including 'electric lifts, uniformed porters, constant softened water and each flat wired for radio and television'. The show flats were also fully fitted by Liberty department store. When first completed there were five types of flat available, with rents ranging from £145 to £330 per annum.

'Nowhere else in London will you find such perfect accommodation so fortunately situated. At Highlands Heath you will live within easy access to town, yet all around is beautiful open country and heathland that makes living sheer delight.' *The Times*, 16 August 1935.

The flats were not the only feature: the brochure explains that the gardens were equally important and that 'every effort has been made in laying out the Estate to preserve the delightful gardens and the old matured timber [of Highlands]'. Facilities also included tennis courts and lawns for bowls.

THE PRIORY

Tithe map for Mansfield Woodhouse.

The Priory has been dated back to the fifteenth century, around the time that the first Tudor king, Henry VII, was on the throne. The house sat within the manor of Mansfield Woodhouse, which by the seventeenth century was in the hands of the Duke of Newcastle of the Cavendish family. The first Duke of Newcastle, William Cavendish, was originally a courtier of James I and eventually rose through the court to be entrusted with the education of Charles II by Charles I. He was Viscount Mansfield from 1620 and the family home was nearby at Welbeck Abbey. At the Restoration, he was created Duke of Newcastle.

The title of Duke of Newcastle passed down through several members of the Cavendish family, but by the early eighteenth century the manor of Mansfield Woodhouse had passed to the Dukes of Portland. It passed to John Holles' daughter, Lady Henrietta Cavendish Holles, who married the 2nd Earl of Oxford and Mortimer, and eventually passed to their daughter, Margaret, Duchess of Portland. Margaret married William Bentinck, 2nd Duke of Portland, in 1734 to become Duchess of Portland. After William's death in 1761 she became Dowager Duchess of Portland, at which time she was the richest woman in Great Britain.

SHERIFF OF NOTTINGHAM

Documentary evidence shows that when the duchess passed away in 1785, the house was purchased by Mr John Coke. His family already had links with Mansfield Woodhouse, as his father, D'Ewes Coke, had been born in the village in 1747. The Coke family played a prominent role in the area and the family can be traced back to the fifteenth century. D'Ewes Coke was rector of Pinxton, as well as a colliery owner and a great philanthropist.

John Coke was living at nearby Debdale Hall, now known as Thistle Hill Hall, but owned large sections of land and property throughout Mansfield Woodhouse. He also had close ties to Pinxton and was instrumental in the development of its railway running to Mansfield, a necessity for transporting coal from the Pinxton colliery. He had a prominent role in Mansfield Woodhouse and Nottinghamshire, rising to become High Sheriff of Nottingham in 1830, as well as magistrate and deputy lieutenant for Nottinghamshire. With no surviving heirs at the time of his death in 1841, his property passed to his nephew, Edward Thomas Coke Esq.

NO RELIGIOUS CONNECTION

The tithe records for Mansfield Woodhouse clearly show that the house was owned by Edward Thomas Coke, but the property was only recorded as a 'croft house'. It appears that at this time Coke initiated the rebuilding of the house, involving the stone refronting. From the records, it is possible to deduce that at this time of rebuilding the house was first named The Priory. The creation of the name appears to be merely reinvention for the house, as there is no evidence of any connection with a priory or any ecclesiastical building or land.

The first evidence of occupants in the newly renovated house appears in the census of 1851, which shows that it was home to Mrs Sarah Sophia Robinson. Her husband, George Robinson Esq., was not at home at this time, but Mrs Robinson was in the house with her five children aged between 2 and 22 years old. Sarah Sophia was the daughter of D'Ewes Coke, but it is unclear if she was the sister or cousin of Edward Thomas Coke. It is possible that the house had been renovated for the new owners, members of the Coke family.

The 1861 census shows George Robinson, officer in the Royal Navy, at home with his wife Sarah and their two daughters, Henrietta and Catherine. At this time, the Robinson family had five live-in servants. Ten years later, in the 1871 census, George was again away from home and Sarah, recorded as Sophia, was in the house with Henrietta and Catherine, as well as her sons, Charles and Henry. Interestingly, the census records the exact birth places of the children (all different), with Henrietta born at Langton Hall; Catherine at Crow Hill Manor; Charles in Paris and Henry at Winthorpe Hall. The status of the family is further confirmed when their occupations were all recorded as receiving 'dividends', except Henry, aged 22, who was recorded as 'landowner'.

Changes Over Time

The Priory in Mansfield Woodhouse is situated close to Sherwood Forest, but a great number of changes through the centuries have created a house that is difficult to unravel. The Priory was at one time owned by the Sheriff of Nottingham, but this was around 600 years after the original sheriff ruled over Nottingham (and Robin Hood). Built over 500 years ago, The Priory has changed from a village cottage, built before Henry VIII came to the throne, to a croft house, to a prominent Victorian gentleman's residence. Today, The Priory is Grade II* listed and features a number of historic features, including exposed timber beams and sixteenth- and seventeenth-century fireplaces.

1891 Census showing bank manager William Abraham Hodges living at The Priory.

New Owners

By the late 1870s and early 1880s, the Robinson family had moved out of The Priory and the house became the home of a bank manager, William Abraham Hodges, and his family. By the early 1890s the house was occupied by Mrs Mary Prance, and the 1901 census records her as widowed, 'living on own means', in the house with her son Cyril, civil engineer, and daughter Edith.

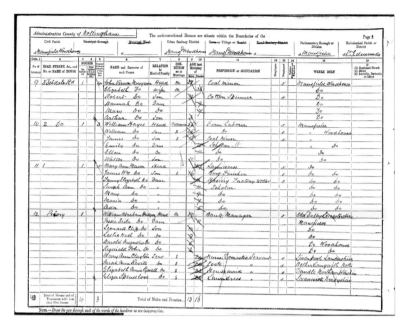

A NEW CENTURY

By the turn of the twentieth century, the ownership of the house had passed to Major-General John Talbot Coke, but in 1907 it was for sale. The sales particulars describe the house as the 'commodious freehold mansion house with garden and outbuildings, known as "The Priory" … sunny and in good repair'. The house was purchased by Mr F.P. Cook on 7 February, but the Nottinghamshire directories show that the house was next occupied by Dr Reginald Anthony Eastmond and his wife Jennie.

The 1911 census shows that The Priory was in fact occupied by two families, and it was at this stage that the house was divided into two homes, The Priory and Western Priory. This census records Jennie Eastmond at home, but her husband was away. Also in the house was the doctor's assistant, Charles Clive from Ireland, along with two live-in servants. Later military records show that Dr Eastmond enlisted in the Royal Army Medical Corp in 1915 and rose to the rank of captain in 1916.

THE WAR YEARS

The remaining records only show Mrs Eastmond at The Priory after 1922 until 1941, but due to the lack of documentation during the Second World War it is unclear what happened after this time. By the end of the war, the house was still divided and the 1947 electoral register shows it was home to Charles and Elizabeth Hill, while Western Priory was home to Michael and Dorothy Royce. The house continued as two separate homes until the 1980s, when the house once again became a single family home.

8 WILTON STREET

ntil the early nineteenth century, Belgravia was still marshland known as 'Five Fields'. The area was dominated by thieves, and without proper drainage it was difficult to establish any substantial building on the swampy land. The name Wilton originated from the Grosvenor family who owned the land: Robert Grosvenor, 1st Marquess of Westminster, married Lady Eleanor Egerton, the daughter of the 1st Earl of Wilton. In 1813 the first plans to develop the land were drawn up by James Wyatt, and building began under the direction of Grosvenor Estate builder, Thomas Cubitt.

SURGEON & ANATOMIST

Grade II listed No 8 Wilton Street is part of a terraced row of simple Georgian town houses, completed in 1817, and has been home to a number of noteworthy residents. In particular, it was home to Henry Gray, author of the famous anatomy textbook, *Gray's Anatomy*, first published in 1858 and, as of 2015, in its 41st edition.

Henry Gray lived at 8 Wilton Street for almost his entire life. He was born in the house in 1827, and he died of smallpox in the same house in 1861. Gray's father was private messenger to Kings George IV and William IV. Henry became a student at St George's Hospital in 1845 and continued there as house surgeon. He became a Fellow of the Royal Society at the age of 25, wrote a number of journals and taught at St George's Hospital. By 1855 Gray had the idea of publishing an inexpensive and easy-to-read anatomy textbook. In co-operation with his colleague, Henry Vandyke Carter (who later became Honorary Surgeon to Queen Victoria), they worked on the contents of the book by dissecting unclaimed bodies from workhouse and hospital mortuaries. After almost two years of work, the book was published in 1858. Gray passed away shortly after the second edition was published in 1860.

Famous Residents

No 8 was also the home of actress and stage performer Miss Ruth Draper during 1936. Draper was a popular stage performer whose famous monologues are still available today, and were revived for a series on BBC Radio 4 in December 2002. In the same year, Valerie Grove described her as 'a theatrical genius. Her comic monologues inspired Joyce Grenfell and her fans included Noel Coward and George Bernard Shaw.'

Wilton Street has also been the residence of former Prime Minister Edward Heath, who moved to No 17 after the loss of the election in 1974.

BALACLAVA COTTAGE

Identification

The occupational records for the village of Lyng during the nineteenth century are not very clear, but fortunately, one of the key features of the village was the pub, The Kings Head, which formerly sat opposite the cottage (now converted into houses). The location of the pub meant that the houses surrounding it were often listed as 'near Kings Head' or even 'Kings Head road', which makes identifying the cottage easier.

B alaclava Cottage is situated in the small village of Lyng, in Norfolk, and was formerly the home of one of the few survivors of the Charge of the Light Brigade, Private James Olley.

The documented history of the small village of Lyng dates back to the twelfth century, although it was most likely settled before then. From the late fourteenth century, through to the early twentieth century, the lords of the manor were the Evans-Lombe family. However, for much of its history, the residents in the village of Lyng continued quietly around the parish church of St Margaret's, formerly named St Michael's and St Clements.

The early history of Balaclava Cottage is unclear as very few documents have been retained, and throughout the history of the village houses were not clearly identified.

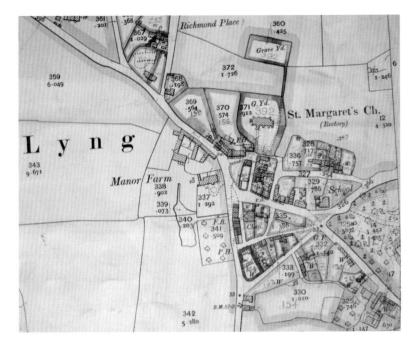

1910 Valuation map.

Using Maps

The 1808 enclosure map, a map outlining land purchased by William Bunn in 1811, and the 1840 tithe map all show the site of the cottage, but on all three maps a different building is shown, perhaps a farm building. It appears that Balaclava Cottage, although not known by that name at the time, was constructed during the 1850s. The lack of documentary evidence makes research difficult, but comparing the early maps and the architectural style of the house, it would appear it was constructed during the mid nineteenth century. Built in brick with a tiled roof, the original building consisted of just four rooms.

A FAMILY HOUSE

The cottage was constructed by the time of the 1861 census, although it is recorded as 'unoccupied'. However, by the time of the 1871 census it was occupied by Edward English, a 47-year-old agricultural labourer, his wife Sarah Ann, 42 years old, and their two young children. By the 1881 census Edward had died and an elderly lodger, Mary Silence, had moved in.

The 1891 census shows that a new family had moved into the cottage, with 46-year-old Noah Skipper, a blacksmith, along with his wife Charlotte and their seven children. The eldest child was 23-year-old general labourer, Frederick Pratt, revealing that this was Charlotte's second marriage. The remaining six children were aged between 4 and 14. The census also records that the family of nine were living in only four rooms. Ten years later, the 1901 census records that only Noah was in the house, while Mrs Skipper was staying away in Swardeston with her daughter Amelia, who had just given birth to her third child. The 1911 census reveals that Noah and Charlotte Skipper, now in their sixties, were still in the cottage after twenty years, with Noah still recorded as a blacksmith. The census tells us that they had had a total of eleven children and two of their sons were still at home. Samuel and Walter Skipper were both recorded as farm labourers, single and in their thirties. We gain further details of the house from the 1910 valuation survey, which describes it as '2/2 brick and tile' freehold and owned by James Olley.

JAMES OLLEY, HERO

The origin of the name Balaclava Cottage becomes clear when looking at James Olley and his history. Renowned as a local character, living in a number of villages in Norfolk, Olley was one of the few survivors of the famous Charge of the Light Brigade in the Battle of Balaclava during the Crimean War in 1854.

Charge of the Light Brigade

The famous charge took place on 25 October 1854 against the Russians and included cavalry from the 4th and 13th Light Dragoons, 17th Lancers, and the 8th and 11th Hussars led by Major-General the Earl of Cardigan. Along with the Heavy Brigade, the overall commander of the campaign was Lieutenant-General the Earl of Lucan, Cardigan's brother. The fateful error in the battle was due to the badly communicated commands from army commander Lord Raglan, which were drafted by Brigadier Richard Airey and carried by Captain Louis Edward Nolan; by the time they reached Lucan, the area given for immediate attack was incorrect. Lucan ordered Cardigan and over 600 cavalry into 'the valley of death' to attack the Russian forces, who had the valley completely surrounded with artillery. There were many casualties, with a total of 156 killed and 122 wounded. The aftermath had the main players pointing the finger of blame at each other, with Raglan and Cardigan both blaming Lucan. The charge was hugely controversial and is still the topic of much debate and study for military historians.

At just 16 he was a member of the 4th Dragoons and took part in the famous charge. His memoirs of this famous military blunder were auctioned in 2008 and sold for £4,500. He recalls the charge with great detail: 'Whilst fighting at the guns, I received two lance wounds, one in the ribs and one in the neck from behind … I was wounded by a sabre across the forehead by a Russian dragoon … I gave him point and stabbed him. The sword fell from his hand and the point penetrated my foot …' He later reveals how on the retreat he 'got a ball from the Russian infantry on my left. It went through my left eye, passed through my nostrils and the roof of my mouth and came out against my right eye.' Incredibly, Olley survived all these wounds and was later nursed by Florence Nightingale. On return to England he was presented to Queen Victoria and Prince Albert at Brompton Barracks.

After his return to civilian life he fell into poverty and was forced to beg in the streets. A local squire, Mr Robinson of Knapton Hall, wrote in the local newspaper of Olley's plight and implored for assistance and donations to put him into 'a little work'. From that time Olley trained horses, including those of Lord Hasting and Sir Alfred Jodrell of Bayfield Hall.

It is unclear when James Olley lived in the cottage, as records do not show him as an occupant. He may have lived there during the First World War years as he was listed as the owner during the early 1900s, with the address of Salthouse, Holt. He ended up in Elsing, where he died aged 82 in 1920. By the 1920s the cottage disappears from the records, until the 1940s when it is recorded (for the first time with the name 'Balaclava Cottage') as the home of Sydney and Laura Rounce, who continued there until the 1960s.

23 ROYAL YORK CRESCENT

Clifton in Bristol is perhaps most famous for Brunel's famous suspension bridge stretching across the Avon Gorge. The late eighteenth century saw the implementation of a number of developments in the area, with the view of reigniting Clifton as a fashionable spa town to compete with nearby Bath.

The development of Royal York Crescent was initiated by renowned developer and builder James Lockier, who was also responsible for Portland Square and other parts of Clifton. The plan was instigated in conjunction with other builders, including John Coles, Ezekiel Evans and Richard Constant. The new grand crescent was laid out over the former gardens of Reverend John Power's Clifton Manor House, which had passed to his grandson, John Beames, in 1743.

UPS & DOWNS

The building of Royal York Crescent began in 1791, but given the steep site and the levelling required for the construction of the basements and vaults – to allow the even level of the terrace and houses behind – it took much longer than planned. This extensive work and the length of time required to dig the foundations also involved a lot more money and soon caused Lockier financial difficulties. By November 1791, Lockier was seeking further finance from investors through subscription. Unfortunately, the investment was not forthcoming and Lockier's company, Lockier, Macauley & Co., were declared bankrupt by 1793. By this time, only a quarter of Royal York Crescent was complete, with over thirty houses left partially finished and without roofs.

The timing was not good, with investment in property in decline due to the outbreak of war with France in 1793. This instability continued into the turn of the nineteenth century with the ongoing Napoleonic Wars, which

William Paty

It is believed that Bath architect John Evesleigh could have initially been responsible for the surveying of the site and planning the building in 1789. The designs for the houses along the crescent have been attributed to William Paty and are similar to the grand crescents and squares of nearby Bath. Paty designed a number of Bristol buildings, including Cornwallis Crescent, and he was also involved with the designs for Harford mansion at Blaise Castle with John Nash.

ROYAL YORK CRESCENT
Construction of Royal York Crescent, reputedly the longest in Europe, began in 1791 to the designs of William Paty. The bankruptcy of the promoter in 1793 brought work to a standstill and in 1801 the Government bought the ground and unfinished portion of the Crescent, intending to build barracks. Local opposition frustrated this plan and the Crescent was completed in 1820 as originally envisaged.

meant very little building work took place. The remaining buildings and neighbouring land at Royal York Crescent were put up for sale in 1800, but it wasn't until 1801 that the War Department came forward to purchase the site for military barracks. However, local opposition was so strong that they abandoned the scheme and the site was once again for sale. In 1809 the completed houses, along with thirty-six unfinished houses and the remaining open ground, were purchased by Isaac Cooke.

FASHIONABLE ROYAL YORK CRESCENT

At this time, between 1810 and 1815, increased confidence in building investment allowed for purchasers to take up the unfinished project of Royal York Crescent. Although it still took some time, the remaining houses were completed by 1820, and Royal York Crescent became a highly sought-after address. The finished crescent consists of forty-six houses in a late Georgian style and when first completed were in red brick with stone dressings. They have since been stuccoed and painted, with most houses in a slightly different pastel colour. One of the key features of the crescent is the first-floor balcony on each facade, although they are not continuous and each has differing ironwork.

COOKSEY YATES, FRAUDSTER

Shortly after the final completion of Royal York Crescent, No 23 was purchased by Henry Chaplin, who was recorded as the owner from 1825 to around 1832, when it was occupied by Charles Cooksey Yates, barrister-at-law. The Bristol directories show that Yates was in the house with a Michael Yates, believed to be his brother, and his chambers were at No 28 Corn Street. Charles had been called to the bar at Inner Temple in 1829 and it seems he continued his practice in Bristol during the early years of the 1830s; but within a few years it had come to an end. It then transpired through a report in *The Gentleman's Magazine* that Charles Cooksey Yates died in Sierra Leone in August 1837. In 1838 *The Times* newspaper reported the story of Yates when it was discovered he had defrauded a client of thousands of pounds. It appears that he fled England for Africa, and although the exact circumstances are unknown, he died unexpectedly while in Sierra Leone. His fraud was only discovered after his death and it is unclear what happened to the money he stole.

MAYOR OF BRISTOL

Charles Cooksey Yates was recorded in the parish poor rate books until 1837, which corresponds with the information we have about his leaving England. After a short break, the records show that in 1838 No 23 Royal York Crescent became the home of a much more auspicious resident, Sir John Kerle Haberfield and his wife Dame Sarah.

Haberfield was a prominent man in Bristol during the mid Victorian period. He began working in Bristol as a solicitor, but soon acquired a notable reputation, being appointed Chief Magistrate in 1837, a year before moving into Royal York Crescent. He became Mayor of Bristol in 1838 and held the position a further five times until 1851. Haberfield and his wife Sarah were also heavily involved in charitable works and John was eventually knighted. The 1851 census records John Haberfield at No 23, listed as Mayor of Bristol and Knight, 65 years old, with Dame Sarah, along with a cousin, Phoebe Haberfield, and three visitors: Mary Cole, Louisa Potts and Sarah Maloney. They had six live-in servants at this time.

Parish Rate Book, 16 November 1844, showing J.K. Haberfield at No 23.

After Haberfield's death in 1857, Sarah continued the charitable works in Bristol; in particular she instigated the building of an almshouse in honour of her husband and for the benefit of the poor in the parish. An insurance certificate from the Phoenix Fire Insurance Company in 1864–65 reveals that Lady Sarah Haberfield continued as the owner of No 23, plus an additional house, No 41 Royal York Crescent. Later records then show that Lady Haberfield did not continue at No 23 and was permanently living at No 41 Royal York Crescent, where she later moved after departing from No 23.

NOBLE LINKS

In 1868 the Bristol directories record that the house was the home of a Mrs Park, but by the early 1870s the occupant of the house was Mrs Julia Parr. She was recorded in the 1871 census as 63 years old, receiving an income from dividends, in the house with her three unmarried daughters (also receiving dividends) and her married daughter, Caroline, as well as her husband Conway, a landed proprietor. The family had five live-in servants. By 1874 the house was home to Mr Anthony Cliffe, who was from an ancient Irish family, and whose family seat was Abbeybraney.

By 1885, the house had become the home of the Honourable Reverend Alfred Francis Algernon Hanbury-Tracy, son of Thomas Charles Hanbury, 2nd Baron Sudeley of Toddington. He later became vicar of St Barnabus in Pimlico, London. During the late 1880s and early 1890s it is uncertain who occupied No 23, but it appears to have been leased by different occupants and been vacant at times. However, by 1897 the house was recorded as the home of Mrs H. Prideaux. The 1901 census records her 'living on own means', a widow, aged 76, in the house with her five grown-up unmarried children, Amy, Edith, Mabel, Henry and Augusta, as well as four live-in servants.

Buckingham's Lodging House

During the early twentieth century No 23 was transformed into rented lodging rooms, appearing the 1907–09 electoral registers and Bristol directories as 'Thomas Buckingham Lodging House'. By 1970 the accommodation that made up Nos 23–25 Royal York Crescent was separated to officially become individual apartments.

47 DOWNSHIRE HILL

Gaetano Meo

It was during the late 1880s that 47 Downshire Hill became the home of Italian artist and mosaicist, Gaetano Meo. He was also one of the most sought-after Italian models for well-known artists such as Dante Gabriel Rosetti and Edward Burne-Jones (who both lived a few doors away). He is remembered mostly for his mosaic work in the dome of St Paul's Cathedral and St Andrew's Chapel in Westminster Cathedral.

A large amount of building along Downshire Hill in Hampstead was undertaken by William Woods between 1813 and 1829, with No 47 Downshire Hill built in around 1820. William Woods was also responsible for constructing St John's Chapel, on the corner of Keats Grove, completed in 1823. Almost as soon as building was completed, Downshire Hill became the home of many prominent residents, particularly artists and writers, including John Constable; Fanny Brawne, the woman who later won the heart of poet John Keats (who at the time was living around the corner); and Dante Gabriel Rosetti.

THE CARLINE FAMILY

It was during the early twentieth century that 47 Downshire Hill became the residence of the Carline family. The Carlines moved into the house in around 1915–16, and included George, his wife Annie and their five children; most prominently Sydney, Richard and Hilda. It is possible to write a book on each member of the Carline family, all achieved great success, especially the children who were painting at a time of revolutionary change within the art world. It is in fact for this very reason that the Carline family and the history of 47 Downshire Hill are so intrinsically linked, as it became an open house for many prominent artists during the inter-war years. They

would come for the friendship and hospitality, but also for the critical debate and inspiration that was found when they gathered together. The artists became known as 'The Hampstead Circle' and exhibited predominately in the New English Art Club and The London Group.

ARTIST GATHERINGS

The list of visitors that gathered at 47 Downshire Hill is full of well-known twentieth-century artists, including Sir Stanley Spencer, who married Hilda Carline in 1925. His paintings appear in many galleries across the world, including the Tate Collection, The Royal Academy and a permanent gallery in his honour, the Stanley Spencer Gallery in Cookham. Other prominent artists included Henry Lamb, Paul Nash and Mark Gertler.

These gatherings featured in a number of paintings, such as 'Gathering on the Terrace at 47 Downshire Hill, Hampstead' by Richard Carline. This depicts Stanley Spencer, James Wood, Kate Foster, Richard Hartley, Henry Lamb, and Annie, Hilda and Sydney Carline, all gathered outside the house. Richard Morphet in the *Oxford Dictionary of National Biography* described them as 'a focal centre, combining hospitality with endless discussion on art and its theory'. All the Carline artists regularly held exhibitions across the country and today their artwork is held in the Tate Collection, the Imperial War Museum, The Ashmolean Museum and many other galleries across the country.

FRED & DIANA UHLMAN

Another connection with artists at No 47 took place during the Second World War. After the Carline family moved to Pond Street in 1936, No 47 became the home of Fred and Diana Uhlman. They set up the Free German League of Culture and the Artists' Refuge Committee with the primary goal of helping artists to escape Nazi-occupied Europe. Fred was a German lawyer and artist, whose own work is held in the Victoria & Albert Museum and the Fitzwilliam Museum in Cambridge. He was of Jewish origin and fled the Nazis in 1936, arriving in England penniless and unable to speak English. The Artists' Refuge Committee helped many to set up a new life in England, including Oskar Kokoshka, Kurt Schwitters, Martin Bloch and John Heartfield.

JOHN HEARTFIELD

John Heartfield stayed with the Uhlmans at 47 Downshire Hill for six years and was commemorated with a blue plaque on the house in 2004. Heartfield is attributed with creating the photomontage style of art that was later made famous by the punk scene in the 1980s. However, it was during the rise of the Nazis in 1930s Berlin that John Heartfield first used his new art form. Due to his anti-Nazi designs he faced heavy persecution and escaped Europe in 1938 for the haven of No 47. After the Second World War the Uhlmans continued to open up their home to artists, including Julian and Mary Trevelyan, Sir Roland Penrose, John Berger, Josef Hermann and Maxwell Fry.

War Artists

Sydney Carline was the eldest of the Carline children and was the first to attend the Slade School of Fine Art. He later went on to study in Paris at a time when post-impressionism and cubism were developing. He was appointed a war artist (along with his brother, Richard) in 1918, and also designed commemorative medals for soldiers. The brothers' artwork from this time constitutes the most comprehensive collection of paintings from the air in the Imperial War Museum. Richard Carline was also involved in working on experiments with camouflage. He later co-founded the International Artists' Association and became Chairman of the UK committee in 1959 and Honorary President from 1968–80. He also co-founded the Hampstead Artists' Council.

'Gathering on the terrace at 47 Downshire Hill, Hampstead' by Richard Carline c. 1924–25.

25 WETHERBY GARDENS

Statue of Thomas Carlyle by Sir J.E. Boehm.

Royal Sculptor

Joseph Boehm was a celebrated sculptor who completed a number of famous works, including sculptures of author William Makepeace Thackeray; artist James McNeill Whistler; Prime Minister William Gladstone; and Benjamin Disraeli. His most famous work is the life-sized sculpture of the writer Thomas Carlyle that still sits prominently in the Chelsea Embankment Gardens. He also completed the sculpture of the Duke of Wellington that sits at Hyde Park Corner.

Boehm was a favourite of Queen Victoria and received over forty royal commissions. He was appointed sculptor-in-ordinary to the queen in 1880 and in 1889 was created a baronet. He was also advisor to Queen Victoria's daughter, Princess Louise, and when Princess Louise was found to be with him in his studio at the time of his death in 1890, rumours spread that the pair were lovers.

Wetherby Gardens is located in an area known as the Gunter Estate, named after the Gunter family, who acquired large sections of land across South Kensington and Earls Court during the eighteenth and nineteenth centuries. The first of the Gunter family was James Gunter, a famous confectioner of Berkeley Square. His son, Robert, continued to buy land across South Kensington, though at this stage the land was almost entirely used for market gardening. Robert Gunter died in 1852 and it was only after this time that his two sons, James and Robert, started to consider that the land held more value for building than for gardening.

Building development began to spread from around the 1860s and the Gunter brothers left a lot of the development in the hands of the estate surveyors, George and Henry Godwin. Wetherby Gardens ('Wetherby' originated from the name of Robert Gunter's home in Yorkshire, Wetherby Grange) was built during the 1870s in the more familiar white stucco Italianate style. By the early 1880s this style had become unpopular and instead the new 'Queen Anne style' was favoured, featuring red brick with terracotta detailing, as well as turrets and more ornate brick and stone decoration.

From 1883, remaining plots in Bolton Gardens and Wetherby Gardens were completed by a selection of builders, including the renowned Kensington builder William Willett. However, the large plot on the corner of Bina Gardens, was uniquely commissioned to be the home of one of the most celebrated sculptors, Joseph Edgar Boehm, who instructed architect Robert William Edis to complete the design. Edis had already designed Boehm's country home, 'Bents Brook', in Surrey in 1881, which has many similarities to 25 Wetherby Gardens. Edis was also responsible for additions to the royal home at Sandringham and the Liverpool Street Railway Hotel. The building of No 25 was completed by 1884, with the portico columns at the entrance featuring sculptural designs by Joseph Boehm himself.

EDGAR BOTELER & GEORGE BIEBER

Boehm moved into his new house along Wetherby Gardens in 1884, but he was not able to enjoy it for very long as he passed away suddenly in 1890. The house passed into the hands of Boehm's son, Edgar Collins Boehm, who took his mother's maiden name of Boteler, but he chose not to live in the house. The next permanent resident at No 25 was Mr George W. Egmont Bieber, who moved with his family from Cadogan Place during the early 1890s. George Bieber was recorded as a 'Merchant to America' in the 1891 census, and ten years later in the 1901 census was recorded as colonial merchant and employer. The 1901 census also reveals that he was only in the house with his youngest daughter, Caroline Francis Bieber, aged 15, along with six live-in servants.

Below: Plans for No 25 Wetherby Gardens, 1883–84.

George remained at Wetherby Gardens until he passed away in 1925. It was at this time that the house was deemed too large for a single family and was divided into separate apartments. The drainage plans from November 1925 detail the plans to convert the house into 'two maisonettes and a flat' by the owner, Sir Edgar Boteler, Fellow of the Royal Geographical Society.

LATER PROMINENT RESIDENTS

After the house was divided it became the home of a number of prominent residents, including Miss Ida Low, granddaughter of the Earl of Denbigh, as well as Major Adrian Dingli, OBE, son of Sir Adrian Dingli, Chief Justice of Malta. In the mid twentieth century William and Catherine Wickham moved in, with their son Glynne Wickham, who went on to be an expert in the history of theatre, writing almost twenty books, and who later advised Sam Wanamaker on the reconstruction of the Globe Theatre.

ORCHARD COURT

'M' & Miss Moneypenny

The 'F' Section was commanded by Maurice Buckmaster, who was assisted by Vera Atkins; these two figures are said to have been the inspiration for Ian Fleming's 'M' and Miss Moneypenny in the James Bond stories. Vera Atkins was responsible for interviewing recruits, as well as organising their training and creating the cover stories for the spies. Atkins has been much praised for her extraordinary work in the SOE. During her time at Orchard Court she sent 470 agents into France, including 39 women, 118 of whom were never to return.

From the exterior, Orchard Court in Portman Square appears to be like many other mansion blocks in central London; however, this simple inter-war building has a fascinating history associated with some of the most heroic men and women of the Second World War. The history of Orchard Court is a good illustration that every home has a story, no matter what the age of the house or what it looks like from the outside.

Portman Square was first laid out for building in 1764 with houses designed by Robert Adam and James 'Athenian' Stuart. Grade I listed 'Home House' on the northern side of the square is one of the few original buildings to survive from this time, completed in 1777 by Robert Adam for the Countess of Home. Most of the eighteenth-century buildings were swept away as part of building redevelopments during the 1920s and '30s, including those on the eastern side, where Orchard Court now stands. It was designed by architectural firm Messrs Joseph and completed in 1929, with residents moving in during 1930. Orchard Court is listed as an 'unlisted building of merit', built with a brick facade and stone detailing, and giant classical columns and pilasters. The name 'Orchard' originates from Orchard Portman, a former country estate belonging to the Portman family, near Taunton in Somerset.

THE 'F' SECTION

The Special Operations Executive (SOE) was created by Prime Minister Winston Churchill in 1940, with the main objective of supporting resistance movements in enemy territory in Europe, including Italy, Poland, Norway and France. The flats within Orchard Court were used by the French or 'F' section (SOE head office was nearby at 64 Baker Street). Here, new spies were recruited and later briefed before being taken into occupied France. Sending women behind enemy lines and training them in espionage, including silent killing, was highly irregular at this time. One former spy, Noor Inayat Khan, said: 'The time the agents spent at Orchard Court was a brief period of luxury before their gruelling, dangerous stints in the field.'

RYTON HOUSE

Today, Ryton House in Lechlade, Gloucestershire, has a genteel Queen Anne exterior featuring sash windows, a moulded stone door case with frieze and segmental pediment, exemplifying early eighteenth-century style. However, closer scrutiny reveals that things are not necessarily as they appear. Old window frames, large stone and brick chimney stacks and, at the rear, earlier mullion windows, blocked-up window frames and wooden beams, show that the house has in fact been converted since its earlier days.

The village of Lechlade is notable for its relationship with the river, being the highest point at which the Thames is navigable. From the thirteenth century it was a busy market town with river traffic, as well as being a major road route from Gloucestershire to London.

A THRIVING PORT TOWN

By the seventeenth century the manor had been granted to Robert Bathurst by James I, and the town was a thriving trade route supported by wharfs and warehouses along the riverside. Goods transported through Lechlade included wool, stone and, in particular, Gloucester cheese. By 1789 the Thames Severn Canal had opened at Lechlade and provided another opportunity for business through the town.

Early History

The manor of Lechlade was first recorded at the time of Edward the Confessor in the eleventh century, and most notably passed to Catherine of Aragon when she married Henry VIII. The medieval history of Lechlade is dominated by the former priory dedicated to the Order of St Augustine and the Hospital of St John the Baptist, both founded during the thirteenth century. The priory was mismanaged throughout its history and by 1472 had closed and the possessions transferred to found a chantry for three chaplains for the parish church. It was Catherine of Aragon who named the church St Lawrence.

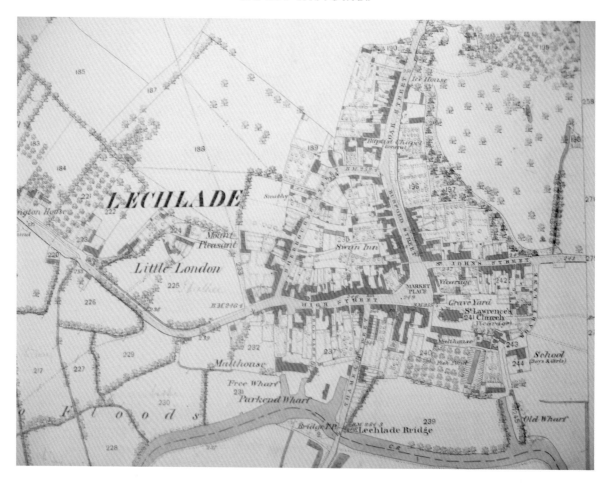

Ordnance Survey map, 1876.

English Heritage

Unfortunately, very few documents survive for the house from the seventeenth century and it has proved difficult to establish specific dates or owners of the property in this early period. However, the architectural evidence and analysis by Nikolaus Pevsner and English Heritage clearly identify that the house was built earlier and rebuilt in the early eighteenth century. The early house was most likely attached to the manor of Lechlade but was sold off by the descendants of lord of the manor, Robert Bathurst, in the mid seventeenth century.

JOHN WARD

In the early 1700s the house was taken by mercer (trader in silks and high-quality fabrics) John Ward, who was responsible for rebuilding the house, including the addition of the striking Queen Anne frontage. Very little is known of John Ward, except that he was a successful and wealthy mercer and was a prominent and trusted local man.

By 1730 Ward's daughter, Letitia, had sold the house to the vicar of Lechlade, John Whitmore, who then sold it to Charles Loder in 1755. Loder was from an important local family who owned large parts of Lechlade, including Sherborne House. A number of areas and streets were named in their honour. In the 1750s, when Charles Loder purchased the house, it was described as 'a Capital Messuage & Garden, Closes, Barn, Lands & hereditaments'.

ROBERT & CATHERINE WACE

In 1803, when Loder passed away, Ryton House transferred into the hands of Robert Wace Esq. and his wife Catherine. Not much is known about Wace, but at his death in February 1820, a notice in *The Times* described him as 'a truly excellent man [in whom] were manifest the practical fruits of the Christian faith without ostentation, for he was ever forward to assist in the mitigation of human suffering'. A tablet in St Lawrence church commemorates Robert, along with his father, William, and his wife, Catherine. After Robert's death, Catherine continued in the house with her family. During the mid 1820s she was joined by her daughter Elizabeth and her husband Captain John William Cole, as well as their children. The 1832 land tax records show Catherine was the owner but her son-in-law, Captain Cole, was the occupier. She passed away in 1837, at the age of 67, and the 1838 tithe map and apportionment records show the 'House, Garden & Pleasure Ground' had passed to Captain Cole. In fact, he was recorded as owning almost 10 acres in Lechlade, including a house and garden in Sherborne Street and further pastureland, cottages and gardens.

HOUSE SURVEY, 1838

In 1838 a survey of Ryton House and the surrounding lands provides an outline of the property, even labelling the dog kennel, the summer house, the privies, and the flag staff, proudly flying the naval ensign in the back garden. It also shows the 'lock up house', later the village fire station (with warning bell on top), sitting adjacent to the house.

The 1841 census shows Ryton House – although at this time it is still not known by this name – occupied by William J. Cole and his wife Elizabeth, along with their four daughters and three live-in servants. The 1842–44 Gloucestershire Directory also records Captain Cole listed under 'Gentry' in Lechlade. Elizabeth Cole passed away in 1849 and, after formally retiring in 1852, Captain Cole passed away at the age of 62 in 1856.

The house passed to the four Cole daughters, of whom only one married. The remaining three sisters were recorded in the house in the census records between 1861 and 1881, only joined by their uncle, Pigott Cole, at the time of the 1871 census. In 1899 Ryton House was sold to Josephine Clementson, wife of local vicar, Reverend Alfred Clementson. She then leased the house to Captain James Robert Lindsay Garrard.

NEW OWNERS

After a successful military career, Captain Garrard retired from the Army in 1905 to set up his own organ-building business from the house, with partners Sidney Spooner and Edward Amphlett. By 1908, the company had changed to Lindsay Garrard Ltd. He was responsible for building a number of church organs across the country, including at Downside Abbey in Stratton-on-the-Fosse; St Mark's Church in Mansfield, Nottinghamshire; and St John's, Boxmoor. Sadly, the organ-building business did not succeed and the company officially dissolved in 1913. By 1916 he had rejoined the 5th Dragoon Guards fighting on the Western Front in France. Garrard's medal card shows that in just over a year he was discharged due to wounds received in battle.

In 1919 Reverend Alfred Clementson sold the house, the Garrard family moved away and it became the home of Robert William Hobbs, owner of an agricultural and farming equipment business, Hobbs & Sons. The business was wound up shortly afterwards and the house sold in October 1926. The sales particulars at this time give a good picture of the house at the beginning of the twentieth century, described as a 'charming old stone-

Captain Cole

John William Cole had joined the Navy in 1802 at the age of 8, and by 1805 had travelled to India and seen the settlement of Van Diemen's Land (Tasmania) in Australia. From an early stage Cole was involved in battle and was wounded fighting in the Napoleonic Wars. He continued active service and was mentioned in despatches in 1815 for transporting the Queen of Wurtenberg to Holland during a severe storm; by 1828 he had attained the rank of commander. In 1837 Cole became a magistrate for the County of Gloucestershire and also received the Knight of Hanover. He was made a captain a year later, exactly at the time that he was settling down to a life on the land in Lechlade.

By direction of Capt. J. Hamilton Stubber.
On the Gloucestershire-Berkshire borders.
*In the upper Thames Valley between the Cotswolds and
the Berkshire Downs.*
RYTON HOUSE, LECHLADE.
EARLY GEORGIAN RESIDENCE, built in the Cotswold style, with well proportioned rooms, and situated in an attractive small town.
The accommodation comprises
Hall, 3 reception rooms (one 22ft. by 14ft.), cloak room, domestic offices and cellar.
Four first-floor bed rooms, 2 bath. and 2 w.c.s, 4 bed rooms and bath room on the second floor (which could be used as a flat).
Central heating ; main electricity ; gas, water and drainage ; attractive simply laid out garden ; garage ; 2 loose boxes.
VACANT POSSESSION. PRICE, £6,250.
Illustrated particulars from
MOORE, ALLEN & INNOCENT, Lechlade, Glos.

Clipping from *The Times*, 12 April 1957.

built freehold residence', with three reception rooms, nine bedrooms and a billiard room. The grounds included a dog kennel, knife room, a large garage and 'lawns with herbaceous borders, privet-bordered tennis court and flower gardens, and ample shade is afforded by well grown ornamental trees and shrubs'.

SECOND WORLD WAR

The house was bought in November 1926 by Robert and Mary Anderson, who remained there until shortly before the Second World War. There are a few gaps in the records during the war years but it is understood that the house was in fact used as an Officers' Mess for nearby Fairford RAF base. This base was used by British and American airmen, in particular for the Special Operations Executive and the SAS. It was also used to support the D-Day landings in 1944.

MAJOR HAMILTON-STUBBER

In 1951 Ryton House became the residence of retired Major Robert Hamilton-Stubber. He had joined the 1st Life Guards (now part of the Household Cavalry) during the 1890s and saw active service in the Boer War, where he was promoted to lieutenant in 1899 and to captain while serving in South Africa in 1901. He was nominated to the Zoological Society in 1910 and took part in a number of honorary events, including commanding the Guard of Honour for the king and queen at the State Opening of Parliament in 1911. At the outbreak of the First World War in 1914 he returned to the Army and was awarded the Distinguished Service Order in 1916 and promoted to major in June 1918. The house passed to his son, Captain John Hamilton-Stubber, in 1952.

Fosters Farm

Tracing the early history of Fosters Farm in Kent has proven quite a challenge, with a lack of documents and continuous changes in the way it was recorded. It has formerly been listed as part of Bidborough, Leigh and Tonbridge, and without a specific house name or address (only officially named Fosters Farm in the late twentieth century). However, despite these hindrances it has been established that the farm was formerly attached to the manor of Bidborough until the eighteenth century.

The manor of Bidborough dates back to the time of Edward I in the thirteenth century, when it was in the hands of George le Chaun. By the time Fosters Farm was being built during the late 1400s, the manor had changed hands and passed to the Palmer family. It remained with the Palmers from the time of Henry VII to Henry VIII, when it was alienated to the Vane family. However, Sir Ralph Vane was found guilty of high treason and was hung on Tower Hill in 1552, at which time the manor returned to the Crown.

Thomas Constable

We know from the land tax records that by 1780, Fosters Farm was owned by distinguished landowner Thomas Constable. His family had been prominent landowners in the Weald area since the late seventeenth and early eighteenth centuries. Records show the family owned sections of land in Withyham and Groombridge, reaching the Bidborough area during the eighteenth century. Land tax records for Upper Hayesden only date back to 1780, but it is possible the Constable family owned the farm before this time.

Deacons of Mabledon

The 1910 Inland Revenue valuation shows that the farmland in Upper Hayesden continued to be in the ownership of the Deacons. John Francis William Deacon (known as Frank) had inherited the lands from his father, John Deacon II, the son of the John Deacon first mentioned in the indenture of 1847. J.F.W. Deacon was also a banker, but along with his father and grandfather he was known for his charitable works. The Deacons contributed to many charities in Surrey and Kent through the nineteenth and twentieth centuries; they helped build a number of churches, gave to the poor, and all three men were involved with the Church Pastoral Aid Society.

Frank Deacon died in 1941 and his estate was in the hands of trustees at the end of the Second World War. Fosters Farm disappeared from records after the war and only reappeared at the beginning of the 1950s. It was at this time that the Vizard family moved into the farmhouse. Robert and Patricia Vizard were recorded at Fosters Farm in the early 1950s and it continued in the same family through to the twenty-first century.

ILLEGITIMATE SON OF HENRY VIII?

Elizabeth I granted the manor to Henry Carey, Lord Hunsdon, the son of Mary Boleyn. (Henry was Anne Boleyn's nephew, Elizabeth's cousin, and was also thought to be Henry VIII's illegitimate son.) The manor eventually passed to the Smythe family in the seventeenth century, and by the eighteenth century was held by Sir Sydney Stafford Smythe, Lord Chief Baron of the Exchequer. He died in 1778, leaving the estate in the hands of his widow, Lady Smythe, who passed away in 1790.

THE CRUNDELLS

Fosters Farm continued in the hands of Thomas Constable until 1789, during which time it was occupied by Thomas Pack, and by 1790 it was owned by William Crundell and occupied by James Godwin. William Crundell (sometimes Crundwell) passed the farm on to his son Henry in 1797, at which time the farm was occupied by Richard Miles. The tithe records from 1838–40 reveal that the entirety of the farmland, farmhouse and outbuildings were owned by Henry's son, Thomas Crundwell, and occupied by Lawrence Foster. The 1841 census shows Lawrence Foster, aged 72, as 'farmer of 53 acres employing 4 labourers'. He was living in the house with his 63-year-old wife Elizabeth and 25-year-old unmarried daughter Jane. This is also where the name 'Fosters Farm' originated. Although not recorded in official documents, it is understood that the farmhouse was known locally as Fosters Farm from the time of Lawrence and Elizabeth Foster.

CHANGING HANDS

A rare surviving indenture from 1847 shows the transfer of the land and farmhouse, now amounting to over 56 acres, at the death of Thomas Crundell. 'Upper Hayesden Farm', which covered a more extensive area around today's Fosters Farm, was broken up and given in trust to Thomas' sons, Thomas, Henry and George, 'with the exception of the said cottages and gardens now in the occupation of Lawrence Foster'; these went to John Deacon of Mabledon in Southborough. Further details show that the farmland was also taken by others, including John Labouchere. This is significant, as both John Deacon and John Labouchere were partners in the London and Manchester bank, Williams, Deacon, Labouchere & Co. The bank is commonly referred to as 'Deacon's Bank' or 'William Deacon's Bank' and was a prominent high street bank both in London and the north-east. Later records show that today's Fosters Farm and the surrounding land were also ultimately acquired by John Deacon.

ROGERS & HEWITT FAMILIES

By the time of the 1851 census, the farmhouse had become the home of the young John Rogers, 30 years old, who lived there with his 31-year-old wife, Anna, and their four young children: James, Emily, Ruth and 4-month-old Louisa. The Rogers family also had two live-in servants. However, by 1861, the farmhouse was occupied by Jabez Rogers, a 34-year-old 'farmer employing 3 men & 1 boy', along with his sister Mary Ann Rogers, also

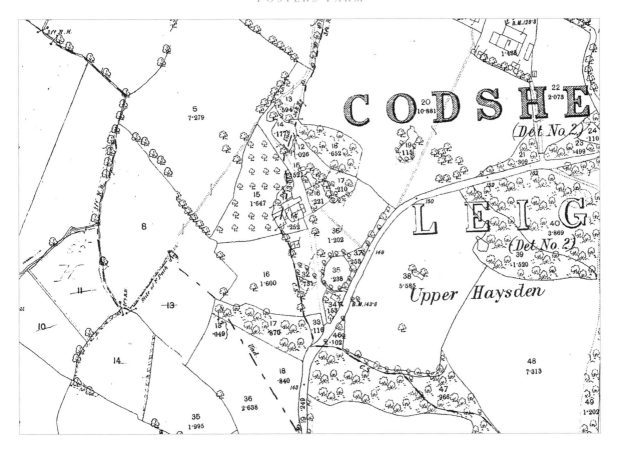

Ordnance Survey map, 1885–91.

34 years old. The relationship between Jabez, Mary and John is unclear, but from their similar ages, and their birthplace in Wadhurst, it appears they were siblings. During the 1870s, Jabez and Mary Ann continued to live in Fosters Farm, which covered over 100 acres.

By the late 1800s the farmhouse was the residence of George Hewitt. The 1901 census is the first document to officially name the house 'Fosters Farm' and records George Hewitt, aged 45, a house painter, with his wife Eliza and their three children: 20-year-old Frank, a clerk in the Gas Co. Office; 17-year-old Herbert, a builder's clerk; and 14-year-old Nora. Also in the house at this time was an Irish boarder, John Brown, a 'Well Sinker' (a well digger). The Hewitt family were still in the house at the time of the 1911 census, but by now Thomas Dealey, a proof reader, was boarding with the family.

THE ROYAL ARSENAL

Marlborough Road

Marlborough Road was named after
the Duke of Marlborough, who was
responsible for creating the first official
royal gunners artillerymen in 1716; and
Argyll Road was named after the
2nd Duke of Argyll, who was also the
1st Duke of Greenwich and Master
General of the Ordnance from 1725–40.

The Royal Arsenal in Woolwich has played a vital part in British military history and the buildings that make up the old Arsenal were designed by some of the country's most renowned architects. Until 1671 the site of the Royal Arsenal belonged to William Pritchard, before he exchanged 31 acres by the banks of the Thames with Charles II. At this time, it was known as the Woolwich Warren, as it was near to the old manor house where Pritchard had kept a large rabbit warren. Charles II used the site to establish the Ordnance Storage depot where military weapons and ammunition, including naval cannons, were made and stored. Today, there are twenty-two listed buildings that make up the Royal Arsenal and the area is being carefully regenerated to maintain its historic character.

VALUABLE HISTORIC BUILDINGS

There are many valuable historic buildings that make up the Arsenal; here are just a few: the Grade II listed Grand Store buildings, constructed in 1806–13, have been attributed to James and Lewis Wyatt. They were originally part of a grand quadrangle that looked out over the river, but now make up part of the new housing development.

The Grade I listed Royal Brass Foundry was built by Sir John Vanbrugh in 1717 and is often compared with the design of a church. It was one of the first buildings at the Arsenal, along with Dial Square and the Board Room, and was built for casting brass cannons. The main entrance, facing

the River Thames, features large double doors in a round arched doorway, with large pilasters of alternate brick and stone either side. It contains the arms of the Duke of Marlborough above the fanlight on the keystone and an impressive coat of arms of George I above the doorway. On the roof is a round lead cupola which was added in 1722. The foundry was extended in 1771–74 by master founder Jan Verbruggen.

The Grade II* listed Dial Square was built for the gun boring and smithy, and has also been attributed to John Vanbrugh, along with Nicholas Hawksmoor. Built in 1717–20, it is a single-storey brick building with large square piers in the entrance way, but most particularly, the top of each pier is topped with a pyramid of cannon balls. In the centre of the gateway is the sundial, dated to 1764, which gives the building its name.

Nicholas Hawksmoor is also believed to be the architect of the Grade II listed Royal Laboratory Model Room, built around 1720. This building was used for the first Royal Military Academy in 1741, an academy even more prestigious than Sandhurst. Hawksmoor was also responsible for Verbruggens House, built in 1773 for the joint master founders, Jan and Pieter Verbruggen. By 1777 the Warren covered 104 acres, and in 1805 George III renamed it the Royal Arsenal.

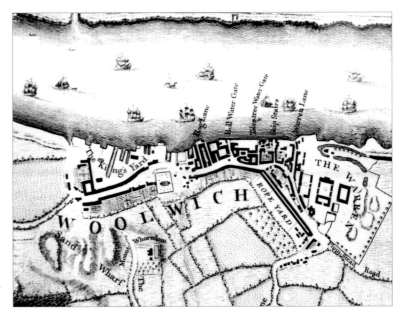

Map of Woolwich by John Rocque, 1746.

Football History

The Royal Arsenal has another significant historic association, as the original home of Arsenal Football Club. The club was first established in 1886 as 'Dial Square football club' after the workshops where the men worked. Two weeks later they were renamed Royal Arsenal, and then in 1893 the team entered the professional football league as Woolwich Arsenal, shortened to Arsenal FC. They moved to Highbury in north London in 1913.

The Royal Arsenal, Woolwich.

11 CHESTERFIELD HILL

Charles Newton-Robinson

Along with publishing a number of books, Charles Newton-Robinson was an avid swordsman and yachtsman. He founded the Epée Club of London and at the age of 50 was part of the Olympic fencing team at Athens in 1906. He was an avid art collector; in particular he formed several collections of Old Masters, but he also admired other arts, including engraved gems and bronzes. Mr Newton-Robinson's interest in art may explain the unique decorative exterior of 11 Chesterfield Hill.

No 11 Chesterfield Hill is conspicuous for its cream and white exterior, compared to its earlier eighteenth-century neighbours with predominately plain brick facades. The house is also noteworthy for its unique ornate plasterwork in bands and surrounding bay windows across the facade. The house displays a date plaque in the centre of the plasterwork, although unfortunately, it is unclear who was responsible for these decorative facades. When first built, Chesterfield Hill was known as John Street and was part of the Berkeley Estate first developed during the 1740s.

A MAN OF MANY TALENTS

The first resident to move into the newly built house in 1900 was Charles Edmund Newton-Robinson, an interesting character who has been described as an art collector, poet, writer, sportsman and barrister. In fact, in his obituary he was described as 'remembered among his large circle of friends, not only for his most attractive personality, but also for his excep-

tionally wide range of knowledge and culture and for the many-sidedness of his activities'.

He moved into No 11 John Street in the spring of 1900 and the 1901 census records him in the house, aged 47, as 'barrister', with his wife Jane and her unmarried sisters, Mary and Rachel, both recorded as 'living on own means', along with four live-in servants.

JOHN HEDLEY, SURGEON

Despite the apparent effort taken to create a beautiful arts-and-crafts-inspired Mayfair town house, the Newton-Robinsons did not stay in their London home for long. In 1907, 11 John Street became the home of surgeon John Prescott Hedley. By the time Hedley moved there, he had gained the post of Obstetric Tutor and Registrar at St Thomas' Hospital. He later went on to become Obstetric Physician and ran the department at St Thomas' from 1928 to 1936; he was also President of the Obstetrics Section of the Royal College of Medicine, member of the General Medical Council and Master of the Society of Apothecaries in 1944–45. John Prescott Hedley remained at No 11 until the time of the First World War.

THE GAMAGES

By 1927 the house was occupied by Leslie and Muriel Gamage. Sir Leslie Gamage was the son of Albert Gamage who founded Gamages, the now lost department store that formerly stood on the corner of Holborn Circus, but he is most remembered for his association with the General Electric Company. In 1919 he married Muriel, daughter of Lord Hurst, the founder of the General Electric Company, and he rose to become Chairman in 1957–60. They left their London home during the turbulent war years and at the same time, in January 1940, John Street was officially renamed Chesterfield Hill.

'WHITE MISCHIEF'

After the Second World War, 11 Chesterfield Hill was the home of a number of residents, until in the early 1950s it was purchased by Thomas Pitt Cholmondeley, the fourth Baron Delamere. The Baron Delameres were directly connected to the first Prime Minister, Sir Robert Walpole, and owned a large estate covering almost 7,000 acres in Vale Royal in Chester. However, the Delameres were far more closely linked with colonial Kenya. Thomas' father, Hugh, the third Baron Delamere, was a very influential figure in Kenya and was one of the first of the great white settlers. However, by the time Thomas Cholmondeley inherited the title of Baron Delamere, in 1931, life was a little different in colonial Kenya, with high society antics attracting much attention and a high-profile murder case.

The fourth Baron Delamere made changes to 11 Chesterfield Hill, splitting the large home into two separate flats in 1954. From this time the house was home to a number of different residents, including a Lady Fairweather in 1962–64. However, by the 1990s the house had once again become a complete family home as it is today.

Murder

The murder case in Kenya involved the wife of Sir Henry 'Jock' Delves Broughton, Diana Caldwell, who was having an affair with Joss, Earl of Erroll. In 1941 Joss was murdered and Sir Henry Broughton was charged with the murder, but was later acquitted. A year later, Sir Henry returned to England but died from a drug overdose in the Adelphi Hotel. The scandalous case of the murder of Joss, Earl of Erroll, was recounted in the book *White Mischief* by James Fox, in 1982, and later became a film starring Charles Dance, Greta Scacchi and Hugh Grant, who played the role of the third Baron Delamere.

HIGH CROSS HOUSE

William Lescaze

Architect William Lescaze was at the forefront of the International Modernist Movement. Born in Switzerland, he studied in Zurich before moving to the United States in 1920. Here he became a noted architect of the inter-war period and co-creator of the Philadelphia Savings Fund Society building, believed to be the first International Style skyscraper in the United States. It was in 1929, while working on school buildings for the Oak Lane County Day School in Philadelphia, that Lescaze met its headmaster, William Curry. Later, after his appointment as headmaster at Dartington, Curry persuaded Leonard Elmhirst to commission Lescaze to build High Cross House. Lescaze went on to design a number of other buildings for Dartington.

High Cross House in Dartington is Grade II* listed and is believed to be one of the best, if not *the* best, example of a home in the International Modern Style in the United Kingdom. The unique modernist home situated in the rolling Devonshire hills and part of the Dartington Estate became famous throughout the architectural and design world.

The origins of Dartington Hall date all the way back to the fourteenth century when it was in the hands of John Holand, Earl of Huntingdon, later Duke of Exeter. John Holand was ultimately executed for plotting against Henry IV, but the Estate managed to continue in the family until the late fifteenth century. It eventually became the home of Margaret Beaufort, mother of Henry VII, but in 1559 it was purchased by Sir Arthur Champernowne, in whose family it continued until 1925.

THE ELMHIRSTS

In 1925 the Dartington Estate was purchased by Leonard and Dorothy Elmhirst, who set about transforming the Estate, firstly restoring the old house and initiating a number of new building projects. The Elmhirsts also used their estate for experiments in agriculture and rural management, even though agriculture in Britain during the 1920s was experiencing a period of decline. They aspired to create a utopian-style community with a focus on agriculture, arts and education.

The Elmhirsts were also responsible for establishing Dartington Hall School, which offered a less formal education and more practical experience, with children learning by taking part in activities on the Estate.

Former students have included artist Lucian Freud and his brother, writer and politician, Sir Clement Freud; politician Michael Young, Baron Young of Dartington, the father of author Toby Young; and screenwriter Ivan Moffat.

The first headmistress of the school was Miss Winifred Harley, but by 1930 a new headmaster, Mr William Burnley Curry, was appointed to take her place.

FROM SCHOOL TO GALLERY

William Curry and his wife Marjorie moved into High Cross House in 1932 and lived there until retirement in 1957. By 1987 the school had closed and the house had a number of different uses; much of the interior changed, as well as some external features due to the constant need of repair. In the early 1990s it was restored and converted, by architect John Winter, into an archive space and gallery for the Elmhirsts' art collection. By 1995 it was ready to be opened to the public for the first time.

The Headmaster's House

High Cross House has a strong geometric shape with a largely white rendered exterior. The windows, originally from Messrs Crittall, are predominately horizontal metal casement and the metal door frames were specially imported from the United States. The house also features a flat roof, along with terrace and patio spaces for outdoor entertaining and living. Lescaze was also responsible for the interiors, including fittings and furniture. He chose floor coverings and curtains, as well as light fixtures, with a view to an overall design complementing the exterior.

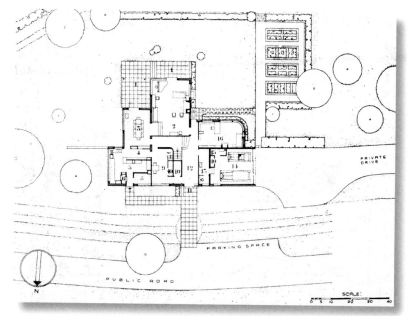

143 TALGARTH ROAD

Sheldon-Williams

By the turn of the twentieth century, 5 St Paul's Studios had become the home of illustrator and artist, Inglis Sheldon-Williams. He moved to Canada for some time during the late nineteenth century, before returning to England to study at the Slade School of Art. He was a war artist during the Boer War (1899–1902) and also became an official Canadian war artist during the First World War. Sheldon-Williams lived at St Paul's Studios between 1901 and 1903.

No 143 Talgarth Road belongs to one of the most recognisable terraced rows in west London, made up of eight uniquely designed artists' studios with large round-headed windows. Originally known as St Paul's Studios and designed for the 'bachelor artist' by Frederick Wheeler, they were completed in 1891 with red brick and terracotta, decorative wrought iron and coloured lead-light windows. The purpose-built studios were constructed with the prominent large window to allow steady natural light for the artists, along with living space and basement accommodation for a housekeeper.

No 143 was first known as 5 St Paul's Studios, and in 1892 the first recorded resident to move in was Jeannie Levick. However, it is more likely the studio was in fact the home of her daughter, Ruby Levick, a sculptor studying at the National Art Training School (later the Royal College of Art) in South Kensington, between 1892 and 1897. Ruby Levick achieved great success, at a time when female artists were less visible. She exhibited at the Royal Academy, the Fine Art Society and was greatly admired by Queen Alexandria. (Jeannie Levick's son, George, was the surgeon and

zoologist on Scott's last expedition to Antarctica in 1910.)

WILLIAM LOGSDAIL

Between 1903 and 1922, 5 St Paul's Studios was the home of prominent and prolific English artist, William Logsdail. He was already exhibiting at the Royal Academy at the age of 18 in 1877 and painted a number of recognisable scenes of London, including *Bank and Royal Exchange* and *St Martin-in-the-Fields*, which was purchased by the Chantry Fund for the Tate Gallery. Queen Victoria purchased one of his works, *The Antwerp Fish Market*. While living here he concentrated on his portrait painting, which included Lord and Lady Halifax and Lord Curzon.

St Paul's Studios, *The Building News*, 1891.

GEORGE KRUGER GRAY

After the departure of William Logsdail, the studio became the home of another successful artist and designer, George Kruger Gray, who was known for his stained-glass windows and in particular his coin designs for British and Commonwealth nations. His designs appeared on many coins in Australia, New Zealand and Canada, as well as Britain, including the shilling, florin, half-crown and sixpence between 1927 and 1952. He also regularly exhibited at the Royal Academy and his works can be seen across the country, including at Eltham Palace. He served with the Artists' Rifles during the First World War, was created a CBE in 1938 and among his many official commissions he created the Great Seal of King George VI and the collar of the Order of the British Empire. Kruger Gray lived in St Paul's Studios from 1922 until 1938.

ERNEST GÉBLER

For a short time during 1949 and 1950 the studio was rented by author and playwright Ernest Gébler, husband of the Irish author Edna O'Brian, and father of author Carlo Gébler. Ernest Gébler wrote a number of books, including *The Voyage of the Mayflower*, which sold five million copies and was made into a film with Spencer Tracy. His play *Hoffman* was made into a film in 1970 with Peter Sellers and Sinead Cusack.

DANCE SCHOOL

The 1950s saw a great shift in the occupation of a number of the studios on Talgarth Road, with many being converted into business space. No 5 became a 'Margaret Morris Movement' school. This was a unique system of dance created by renowned dancer Margaret Morris, later a government advisor on physical education. The dance system was taken up by many children and adults, and eventually spread to several other countries around the world.

Swinging '60s

During the 1960s, the numbers along Talgarth Road were reorganised and No 5 (which had also been known as No 51 Colet Gardens) was renamed No 143 Talgarth Road. It continued to be used as a dance school until the late 1980s, when it was bought by interior designer Allan Day. He set about renovating the studio back to its former glory and creating a living space that emulated the designs of the late nineteenth century, much like it would have been in 1891.

THE BEECHES

The farmhouse in Nottinghamshire now known as 'The Beeches' was first built as a small cottage, called Home Farm Cottage, and was attached to the extensive estate of the Manvers family, of Holme Pierrepont. A survey of the estate taken in 1803 records that the cottage was complete and the earliest occupant was William Richards. Within a few years William Richards' son, George, took over from his father as 'cottager', and a later survey taken during the 1820s shows George Richards living in the house and farming over 6 acres of the Earl of Manvers' land. George continued at the cottage as farmer, and by the time of the 1851 census he was recorded as 'cottager for 8½ acres of land', with his wife Margaret and their granddaughter Ann.

In 1861 a valuation of the Earl of Manvers' estate described the cottage and farm as 'cottage, garden, paddock, orchard and stockyard', and even details the cottage as 'brick and slate stuccoed – 2 rooms and 2 chambers … [and] lean-to kitchen and dairy'. At the same time, the 1861 census shows George widowed, aged 79, and also recorded as blind. He lived in the house with his daughter-in-law, Mary, aged 55, along with a visitor, Sarah Ward, aged 72 and listed as 'formerly cottager'. After being at the farm for almost his entire life, George Richards passed away in 1871 at the age of 89 and Home Farm Cottage was taken over by William Richards (his relationship to George is unclear). The 1871 census records William Richards in the house with his wife Elizabeth and his grandson William, aged 16 and already working as an 'attorney's clerk'.

DAIRYMAN

During the late 1870s, after almost eighty years, the Richards family left Home Farm Cottage. The farm continued as the dairy for the Earl of Manvers and appears to have been run by William Slack, who was recorded in the 1881 and 1891 censuses, as well as in the electoral registers and rate books, as dairy farmer at Holme Pierrepont.

At the turn of the twentieth century, the fourth Earl Manvers spent large sums of money rebuilding and redeveloping his farm buildings, including Home Farm Cottage. It was during the late 1890s that the cottage was renovated and extended and became more like the home of today. In 1897 the building now known as The Beechnut was built to house the earl's herd of pedigree Shorthorn cattle; in fact, the bedrooms in today's home were originally bull boxes.

PRIZED CATTLE

The 1901 census records 'the dairies' as unoccupied, but shortly afterwards the fourth Earl Manvers brought Christopher Dobson from Cumberland to look after his prized cattle. The 1911 census shows Christopher Dobson, aged 38 and 'Cowman on Farm', in the house with his wife Hannah and their three children. At the same time, the 1910 Inland Revenue valuation describes it as a 'good mixed farm' with a number of farm buildings, including cow sheds, engine rooms, stables and a harness room, along with the cottage. Altogether, Home Farm and the surrounding land covered almost 210 acres of Holme Pierrepont.

During the early twentieth century, Christopher Dobson was listed at Home Farm in a number of records as 'herdsman to Manvers'. Dobson and his family remained at the farm until around 1918–19, but by the 1920s it had become the home of William B. Shelton, described as a gentleman farmer, who is remembered locally for working in white gloves. In around 1927 Home Farm Cottage was modernised and it was at this time that it officially became known as 'The Beeches'.

MANVERS ESTATE IN THE 1940S

The late 1930s not only brought change to the nation with the outbreak of the Second World War, but the Manvers Estate, having been in financial trouble for a number of years, was placed on the market. In 1941 the National Farm Survey and the full Estate sales particulars showed a complete picture of the farm and its buildings at this time. The sales catalogue lists The Beeches as 'a very attractive farm, formerly the Home Farm of the Fourth Earl … and used by him for his world-renowned herd of Shorthorns … Together with a delightful house and model farm buildings'. The house was described as conveniently arranged, while the National Farm Survey describes the land as including 20 acres of wheat, 3 acres of turnips and swedes, 8 acres of barley and 4½ acres of potatoes. The farm animals included 39 cows, 97 sheep, 166 fowl and 5 horses. The Farm Survey also reveals that the farm was no longer owned by the Earl of Manvers, but had been sold to five people.

After the war, William Shelton left The Beeches and it became the home of Robert Marsh and his family. Generations of the Marsh family remained at The Beeches for close to forty years and by the late 1980s it was occupied by Robert's grandson, Roy Marsh.

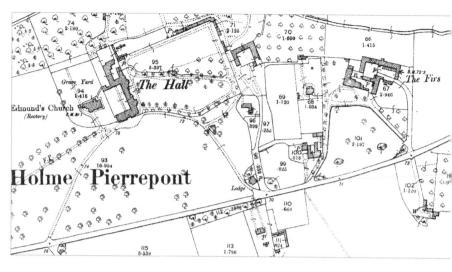

Ordnance Survey map, 1900.

A Royal Visit

During the late 1920s it is believed that Edward Prince of Wales, future King Edward VIII, visited the area. He stayed at nearby Lamcote House (also owned by Earl Manvers) where he visited his mistress, Freda Dudley Ward. He often went to Holme Pierrepont for sport and an old farmer relates that the prince in fact visited the cottage, and in particular popped into the kitchen on a number of his visits.

8 QUEEN ANNE'S GATE

The Architects

James Elmes (1782–1862) was a prominent figure in the arts and architecture in London and was also good friends with the celebrated architect Sir John Soane. However, despite his success in design and architecture, he is often most remembered for his writing. He established the *Annals of Fine Arts* in 1816 and was its editor until 1820, during which time he met John Keats and was the first to publish some of his work, including *Ode to a Nightingale* and *Ode to a Grecian Urn*.

Harvey Lonsdale Elmes (1813–47) was also a well-respected architect, and in 1835, at the age of 22, had already become partner to his father. He is most remembered for his design of the Grade I listed St George's Hall in Liverpool. Lonsdale Elmes passed away seven years before the completion of the hall, which Nikolaus Pevsner called the 'finest neo-Grecian building in the world'.

Many of the homes that stand along Queen Anne's Gate in Westminster date back to the eighteenth century, but before this time the area was covered in orchards and gardens. When building began in the seventeenth century, what is now Queen Anne's Gate was divided into two: Queen Square (to the west) and Park Street (to the east). The two streets were separated by a wall and a statue of Queen Anne, which is now located near today's No 15.

The Royal Cockpit formerly sat on the site of today's Nos 4–12 Queen Anne's Gate, and was built in around 1670–80. Cockfighting was a popular pastime during the eighteenth century, enjoyed by everyone from the upper classes down through the social scale. The Royal Cockpit was said to be the most prestigious of all such venues in London. However, by the early nineteenth century attitudes to the Cockpit had changed and the lease was not renewed. Today, the nearby 'Cockpit Steps' are the only surviving element of the once notorious cockpit.

THE DESIGNS

There were a number of plans and suggestions for new buildings on the site of the Cockpit, but the final designs were by James Elmes and his son

Harvey Lonsdale Elmes. The exterior of 8 Queen Anne's Gate appears as a continuous facade with neighbouring houses, built with brick but few decorative embellishments.

No 8 Queen Anne's Gate was completed the year Queen Victoria came to the throne, in 1837. Today, it is part of Nos 4–12 Queen Anne's Gate, but they have in fact had two earlier numbering systems. When first completed the homes were numbered (west to east) Nos 8, 9, 10 and 11 Park Street, but in 1874 the street was reorganised and given the new name 'Queen Anne's Gate', with house numbers changing to (west to east) Nos 12, 10, 8 and 6.

AN MP & A LORD MAYOR

Residents began to move in almost immediately and one of the first occupants of 8 Queen Anne's Gate was politician and businessman Joshua Scholefield, MP for Birmingham from 1832–44. However, by 1840, the house was home to parliamentary agent Charles Pearson, who campaigned for parliamentary reform, including the freedom of Jews to hold public office and the abolition of capital punishment. The 1851 census records Charles Pearson, 'city solicitor and deputy lieutenant for Middlesex', with his wife Mary, aged 52, and two live-in servants. At the same time, the house was the home of Charles' daughter and son-in-law, Mary and Thomas Gabriel. Thomas is recorded as a timber merchant, 39 years old, and he and Mary had three daughters, Mary, Helen and a newborn 'Infant Gabriel' under a month old. Thomas Gabriel later rose to the position of Sheriff of London and Middlesex in 1859, and Lord Mayor of London in 1866–67, at which time he was also created a baronet.

BIRMINGHAM & MIDLAND BANK

By 1853, No 8 had become the home of a Mr Charles Geach, MP for Coventry from 1851 and the driving force behind the establishment of the Birmingham and Midland Bank (part of today's HSBC bank) in 1836. Mr Geach's political career was short-lived, as he passed away at home in 1854. His widow and children remained in Westminster for a few more years, with Charles S. Geach listed in the house during the late 1850s, at the same time as a colleague at the Midland Bank, Samuel Beale. Samuel Beale was also influential in the foundation of the Birmingham and Midland Bank, of which he later became a director. Beale had been Mayor of Birmingham in 1841 and later became Director and Chairman of the Midland Railway from 1844–64.

In 1874, Park Street and Queens Square were officially reorganised and renumbered and, given their proximity to the Houses of Parliament and Whitehall, No 8 was one of many homes converted into quality apartments for those visiting London. From the 1870s through to the late 1890s, No 8 was occupied by a great many businessmen, artists, engineers and politicians.

Sir Francis Fox

Fox was a civil engineer who was working at the height of development in the new railways. He worked across many parts of the country, building bridges and tunnels, as well as establishing entire train lines. Fox worked on the Great Central, the Liverpool Overhead Railway and the Great Northern and City Railway, these last two with James Greathead (who was also later based at 8 Queen Anne's Gate). In the early years of the twentieth century, Fox worked on the restoration of historic buildings using a unique technique in strengthening masonry. He worked on Winchester Cathedral, Lincoln Cathedral and St Paul's Cathedral. Fox was knighted for his work in restoration in 1912.

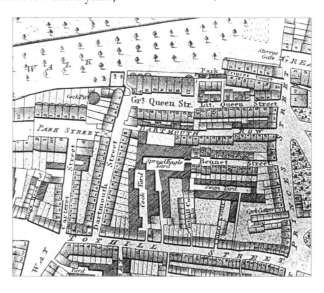

Richard Horwood map, 1799.

Engineering Feats

It was the work of Sir John Fowler and Sir Benjamin Baker on the Forth Rail Bridge in Scotland that is often most noted. Today, the Forth Rail Bridge is still accepted as one of the wonders of the industrial world and an engineering marvel. It was the longest span bridge at the time, using a cantilever design and built entirely of steel. When completed, it was the largest civil engineering structure of the nineteenth century and was opened by the Prince of Wales (later King Edward VII) in March 1890.

NOTABLE VICTORIAN GENTLEMEN

The occupants of 8 Queen Anne's Gate recorded in the 1876 Court Directory included civil engineer Alfred Upward; writer and Fellow of the Royal Geographical Society, Robert Nelson Boyd; and Robert Taylor Pritchett. Pritchett actually had two careers in which he achieved great success and fame. The first was as a gun maker and the second as a landscape artist. He became a gun maker at a young age, working with his father's firm, Enfield Gun Makers. In 1852 Pritchett was working with William Metford, with whom he invented the Pritchett rifle bullet, and he was named 'The Father of the Enfield Rifle'. However, after the abolition of the company's biggest customer, the East India Company, in 1858, Pritchett turned to a completely different career as an artist. He exhibited at the Royal Academy many times from 1851 through to the 1870s, while also working as an illustrator for the celebrated *Punch* magazine during the 1860s. Pritchett was greatly favoured by Queen Victoria and other members of the royal family, who purchased a number of his works. From 1872 the queen commissioned Pritchett to paint over eighty watercolours of ceremonial occasions, which today still remain in the Royal Collection. His sketches, made while retracing Charles Darwin's famous scientific voyage of 1831–36, illustrate the 1890 edition of Darwin's 1839 book, *The Voyage of the Beagle*.

By the early 1880s, 8 Queen Anne's Gate had become the home of a number of other noted gentlemen, including photographer Benjamin Brecknell Turner; barrister and economist David Frederick Schloss; and another civil engineer, Sir Francis Fox.

Benjamin Brecknell Turner was a pioneer of early photography and was one of the first British photographers. He exhibited his photographs regularly, including the first ever purely photographic exhibition with the Society of Arts in 1852, and in the Universal Exhibition in Paris in 1855. Turner was a founding member of the Photographic Society of London and today many of his photographs are retained in the Victoria & Albert Museum.

David Frederick Schloss made a name for himself as both a barrister and a civil servant; in particular he was concerned with the lives of the poor in London. In 1885 his article, 'The Homes of the Poor', was published in *Time*, and he later went on to assist Charles Booth in his *Life and Labour of the People in London*.

Plans for Queen Anne's Gate, 1750s.

DISTINGUISHED ENGINEERS

The number of notable residents who spent time at 8 Queen Anne's Gate continued through the late nineteenth century and by 1896 the house was occupied by three of the country's most noted engineers: James Henry Greathead; Sir John Fowler, 1st Baronet Fowler of

Braemore; and Sir Benjamin Baker. Sir John Fowler and Sir Benjamin Baker were responsible for building one of Scotland's greatest landmarks: the Forth Rail Bridge.

James Henry Greathead was a railway engineer working with companies such as Midland Railway, but today Greathead is most remembered for his work on the Underground railway in London and the creation of the 'Greathead Shield' that made the digging of the 'Tube' a reality. He also worked with Sir John Fowler and Sir Benjamin Baker (during the time they were based at 8 Queen Anne's Gate) on the Central London Railway. James Greathead is honoured with a statue at Bank Underground station for his services to engineering.

Sir John Fowler was a railway engineer, working on the foundation and development of railways across the country during the formative years of rail travel. He worked for the London, Brighton and South Coast Railway during the 1830s, and in the 1860s was appointed engineer for the Metropolitan Railway in London (the first underground railway – part of today's Circle, District and Metropolitan lines). He was also responsible for designing Pimlico Bridge over the River Thames in 1860 and Manchester Central station in the 1870s. In 1865 Fowler was appointed the youngest President of the Institution of Civil Engineers and in 1885 was knighted by Queen Victoria.

Sir Benjamin Baker was another civil engineer who was involved in projects across the country. He worked on the Metropolitan Railway, developments for the Northern line with Sir John Fowler and on the Central London Railway with James Greathead. Baker also worked on the Bakerloo (Baker Street to Waterloo) Railway and the City and South London Railway. He also advised the Egyptian government, in particular on the Aswan Dam. Baker became President of the Institution of Civil Engineers in 1895, Fellow of the Royal Society, as well as honorary associate of the Royal Institute of British Architects.

PREECE & CARDEW MOVE IN

Since the 1870s, the occupants of the house were heavily connected to the engineering profession, and in 1899 it became the permanent home of one of the country's most respected engineering firms, Preece & Cardew, who remained at 8 Queen Anne's Gate for the next seventy years.

The father of the firm was Sir William Henry Preece, who was not only a respected engineer, but also an inventor responsible for developments in electrical transmission and telephone systems in England. He began his career at the Electric Telegraph Company during the 1850s and in 1892 became Engineer in Chief of the British General Post Office. He continued at the Post Office until 1899, at which time he was created KCB and he established the firm with his sons, Arthur and William, in partnership with Major Philip Cardew.

Major Philip Cardew

Cardew began his career as a lieutenant in the Royal Engineers in 1871 and in 1875 he was placed in charge of military telegraphs, responsible for putting electricity to military use. Cardew invented a number of new instruments to assist in the application of electricity, including a galvanometer to measure large currents of electricity and a voltmeter or hot-wire galvanometer. He rose to the rank of major in April 1889 and at the same time was appointed the first electrical advisor to the Board of Trade. He retired from the Royal Engineers in 1894 and then the Board of Trade in 1898, prior to joining Sir William Preece and his sons in the new firm.

Twentieth-Century

The consulting engineering firm Preece & Cardew was very successful. By 1930 they had expanded into 10 Queen Anne's Gate and by 1952 they had expanded again into No 12. The firm only left Queen Anne's Gate during the early 1970s and later merged to form Ewbank Preece, now part of Mott MacDonald. In 1970 Nos 6–12 were listed Grade II*, and by 1998 they had been completely renovated to become Nos 4–12 Queen Anne's Gate as they are today.

2 WILDWOOD TERRACE

Sir Nikolaus Pevsner

In 1936 No 2 Wildwood Terrace became the home of renowned architectural historian, Sir Nikolaus Pevsner. Pevsner's major achievement was the creation of the forty-six-volumed *The Buildings of England* series. He was also editor of the *Architectural Review* and featured regularly on BBC Radio. He edited the *Pelican History of Art* series, was Slade Professor of Fine Art at Cambridge, and in 1969 was knighted 'for services to art and architecture'. An English Heritage blue plaque was unveiled at the house in October 2007 to commemorate the residence of the author. Today, Pevsner is still remembered as a great authority on architecture, as well as commentator and teacher on 'modern' architecture during the twentieth century.

Wildwood Terrace was named after an eighteenth-century farmhouse that formerly stood on the northern edge of Hampstead Heath, which itself gained the name from its association with the 'Wild Wood' on the borders of the Heath. Towards the end of the nineteenth century the four houses in Wildwood Terrace, and those in neighbouring 1–13 Wildwood Grove, were constructed by a local builder, Thomas Clowser. Wildwood Terrace was laid out for building during the mid 1880s, with an official drainage application made in July 1884. It appears that 2 Wildwood Terrace was not occupied until around 1893, when it became the home of Reverend S. Dixon Stubbs.

HOMES FOR THE AGED

The 1894 Hampstead Directory records that the whole terrace was occupied, with No 1 as the Home of Rest for Aged Poor; No 3 as the Convalescents' Cottage Home; and No 4 occupied by artist Edwin J. Lambert, who continued in the house until 1929.

By the turn of the twentieth century, 2 Wildwood Terrace had become linked with No 1 to become the Home of Rest for Aged Poor. The 1901 census records nine 'inmates' living in the care home, including Frederick and Mary Ann Crawford, both aged 75, along with Mary Bathmaker, aged 78, and Anne Bartlett, aged 82. The two homes did not remain connected for long, as by 1907 Nos 1 and 2 Wildwood Terrace had reverted back to private homes. No 2 was now the home of George Clowser, the son of Thomas Clowser, the builder of the terrace. He lived at No 2 with his wife Annie until around 1916, and Annie continued to live in the house until the early 1930s.

Below: Nikolaus Pevsner.

11 THE CIRCUS

The Grade I listed Circus (originally The King's Circus) is a unique example of Georgian building in Bath and considered the masterpiece of architect John Wood the Elder (but constructed by John Wood the Younger). Together with the nearby Royal Crescent, it is one of the top destinations for anyone visiting Bath. It was the centrepiece of John Wood the Elder's plans for transforming Bath into a Rome of Britain, with a circus for sport, as well as a royal forum, parades and even a gymnasium.

BUILDING THE CIRCUS

The foundation stone of the Circus was laid in February 1754, but John Wood the Elder died three months later and his son, also John Wood, took

The Design

The Circus was originally inspired by ideas of an inverted Coliseum and displays a wide range of architectural features. Each level contains paired columns of the different classical order, with Doric on the ground, Ionic on the first, and Corinthian on the third. One of the most striking features is the frieze above the ground floor, decorated with hundreds of pictorial symbols representing science, the arts and industry. On the second floor, capitals are linked by garlands with central female heads. Another key detail is the circle of large stone acorns sitting on top of the parapet. In his *Buildings of Bath*, Walter Ison describes it as being 'in theatrical style … a tour-de-force of external decoration solely contrived to impress the beholder at close quarters'.

'The Circus Bath, 1773' by John Robert Cozens.

'The Circus Bath, 1773' by John Robert Cozens.

William Pitt

The first leaseholder of No 11 was former Prime Minister William Pitt the Elder, 1st Earl of Chatham, and father of William Pitt the Younger, and also later Prime Minister. He was a Whig politician who first entered Parliament as MP for Old Sarum in 1735. During the early 1760s, Pitt was Secretary of State and much praised for his leadership and strategic foreign policy during the Seven Years War. In 1766, after the dismissal of Charles Watson-Wentworth, 2nd Marquess of Rockingham, George III asked Pitt to form a government. However, Pitt struggled with bouts of illness and resigned his post as Prime Minister in 1768, the year the Circus was completed, and Pitt acquired No 11 as his Bath home. Pitt continued in the House of Lords from 1770 until 1778, the year he died.

William Pitt the Elder.

over by following his father's designs. It was constructed in sections, with the south-west section completed first, followed by the south-east and then finally the northern section. Leases were granted in the south-west section from 1755, with one of the first taken by politician William Pitt, and a neighbouring house taken by his cousin, Lady Lucy Stanhope.

There was a lull in building after 1759, until 1762, when work continued on the remaining segments; all sections were completed and occupied by 1768. Leases were granted to individual builders to construct the houses behind Wood's uniform facade, so that the interiors were laid out differently according to the builder and the desires of tenants. No 11 was one of the later houses to be constructed and was part of the sought-after, south-facing northern segment. Andrew Sproule of Bathford bought the building lease for No 11 in 1756, along with Nos 12–14 and the corner house, No 32 Brock Street.

Old prints show that the central area of the Circus was initially an open piazza, with a central reservoir of water for residents. In around 1800 the residents created a railed garden, with the large London plane trees planted in around 1820 (these 'caught' a bomb and saved the Circus from destruction during the 1942 Baedeker bombing of Bath).

ARISTOCRATIC OWNERS

The parish rate books show that William Pitt continued as leaseholder until 1776, when it passed to a Mr William Brimble for a short time, before it became the Bath home of Lord Donegall in 1780. Arthur Chichester, Lord Donegall, was from an Irish aristocratic family dating back to the sixteenth century. He took his seat in the Irish House of Lords in 1757, but became MP for Malmesbury in the British House of Commons between 1768 and 1774. He was created Baron Fisherwick in 1790, as well as becoming Marquess of Donegall and Earl of Belfast in the Peerage of Ireland.

By 1782 George Spencer, 4th Duke of Marlborough, was living in the house. Recorded in the parish rate books as 'His grace the Duke of Marlborough', he kept it as his Bath home until 1788–89. George Spencer had inherited the dukedom when he was only 19 years old. In 1762 he had been made Lord Chamberlain and a Privy Counsellor, and in 1763 had acquired the appointment of Lord Privy Seal. George Spencer's country seat was Blenheim Palace (still retained by the Dukes of Marlborough today).

FRIEND OF JANE AUSTEN

By the late 1790s No 11 had been acquired by Dr Mapleton. At this time, the celebrated author Jane Austen is recorded as having visited Dr Mapleton's daughters at home several times during the early 1800s. After the Mapletons left, the records show a number of women renting the house, including Mary Halsey and Betty Amey, although very little is known about them. Nevertheless, given its location it is not difficult to picture the ladies visiting the Assembly Rooms just minutes away.

By the 1820s, records reveal that No 11 was taken by Lieutenant-General William Neville Cameron and his family, who had returned to England in 1805, after being based in India in the military for over thirty years. He and his wife, Charlotte, the daughter of Sir William Gordon, 7th Baronet, continued at the Circus through the 1820s until Cameron passed away in 1837 at the age of 82.

VICTORIAN BATH

By the early 1850s, the house was transformed into the prestigious Somersetshire College boys' school. There was a particularly notable tutor at the college, scientist and inventor of the telephone, Alexander Graham Bell, who was teaching at the college in 1866–67 while continuing his experiments on telephony and communications. It is believed that Bell, in fact, sent his first telegraph messages while living in Bath, but moved to Canada within a few years. After the departure of the headmaster, Reverend Sweet-Escott, in 1873, William Leonard Courtney took over until 1876 (when he became a tutor in philosophy at New College, Oxford). He wrote a number of books, including *Life of John Stuart Mill* (1889) and *The Idea of Tragedy* (1900).

After 1886, No 11 reverted back to a private home. The Bath Directory records that it now became occupied by a surgeon, Dr Hugh Lane. The 1891 census reveals that he was 31 years old living with his wife, Frances, 35 years old, and three children, Francis, John and Hugh. Unusually, the census shows that the Lane family also had a boarder, 49-year-old Fanny, from Russia, who was recorded as a 'lunatic'. The Lane family had four live-in servants.

In the final years of the nineteenth century and early twentieth century, No 11 became the home of Robert Gordon Rogers, a retired colonel of the Indian Staff Corps, and his wife. He had been awarded a number of medals and in November 1882 was appointed aide-de-camp to Queen Victoria.

Medical Surgery

In 1907 it appears that the house became the medical surgery for Dr J.R. Benson, while other rooms in the house were rented out separately. The 1911 census shows five servants in the property, the doctor, his daughter Alice, from Australia, along with a further four 'guests'. These guests included 50-year-old barrister, William Seddon; a 25-year-old spinster, Bridget, and her 52-year-old mother, also Bridget, who were from St Petersburg; and 24-year-old spinster, May. The Bath Directory records this as the home of Dr Benson until 1912, when dental surgeon Dr Donald Ackland moved in. By 1926 he was joined by Dr Dudley Parsons, and the surgery became Ackland & Parsons. It remained a medical and dental surgery through to the 1960s and '70s.

THE ART HOUSE

Productions

The GPO Film Unit created a number of academy award-winning documentaries and is best known for *Night Mail* (1936), a film about the overnight post train from London to Scotland, which was set to the poetry of W.H. Auden and the music of Benjamin Britten. Other notable writers who worked on films for the GPO included E.M. Forster, J.B. Priestley and Laurie Lee, as well as actors John Gielgud and Laurence Olivier, and director Humphrey Jennings.

The Art House is located in Bennett Park, Blackheath, named after John Bennett, the eighteenth-century landowner, successful watchmaker and 'manufacturer of scientific instruments'. The area began to be developed with new homes during the early 1860s, but the Art House was one of the last buildings to be completed, in 1886.

The Art House was originally built as the Blackheath Art Club, designed by architects John Higgs and Frank Rudkin, to provide artists with a work and display space. It held annual exhibitions from 1886 until 1916 in the style of the Royal Academy. Many notable artists of the time worked at or visited the Art Club, including landscape and marine artist Terrick John Williams, member of the Royal Academy and President of the Royal Institute of Painters in Water Colours.

The Art Club was also used by a number of local societies and clubs, including the Camera Club, the Debating Society and even the Blackheath Badminton Club. The Club continued here until the beginning of the First World War, but in 1916 the building was requisitioned for government use and by 1921 it was put up for auction.

GENERAL POST OFFICE FILM UNIT

During the 1920s and '30s the house had a variety of uses, but in 1933 it became the home of British documentary making, when the General Post Office (GPO) Film Unit moved in. It was first established to explain to the general public the workings of the organisation, which at the time was not only responsible for the postal service but also operated the telephone exchange, the meteorological office and a savings bank. The first Director of the GPO Film Unit was John Grierson, who is regarded as the 'father of British documentary film'.

At the outbreak of the Second World War, the GPO Film Unit became part of the Ministry of Information and was renamed the Crown Film Unit. They continued to use the Art Club building until 1943, making a number of well-known wartime documentaries, including *Target for Tonight* (1941) and *Fires Were Started* (1943). After the Crown Film Unit left, the building was occupied by an engineering firm, a boarding house and even a hat factory.

19 CURZON STREET

Mayfair instantly inspires thoughts of prestige, luxury and elegance, but in fact the early history of the area originated with the notorious May Fair, which was known for its violence, debauchery and crime. The fair was held during the first two weeks of May and was established in the area known as 'Brookfield' in 1688, where Shepherds Market and Curzon Street are today. The fair was closed down in 1708, but only finally ceased when Curzon Street was built during the 1750s. The name 'Curzon' originates from the Curzon family, who owned this area of Mayfair from the seventeenth century. The land passed to Sir Nathaniel Curzon and he set about developing the land from the 1720s. No 19 Curzon Street was completed in around 1758–59, but at this time the houses were numbered differently and No 19 was known as No 17 Curzon Street.

FIRST OCCUPANTS

The parish rate books show that in 1764 the first occupant was politician Hugh Campbell, third Earl of Marchmont. He was a friend of Alexander Pope and Sarah, Duchess of Marlborough, and a prominent landholder in Berwickshire. Shortly before moving to Curzon Street, Marchmont was completing his country home, Marchmont House, in the Scottish borders,

Soane's Alterations

By 1800 the house had changed to No 19, and in 1802 Sir John Seabright commissioned renowned architect Sir John Soane (who had already worked on his country estate, Beechwood, in Hertfordshire) to make alterations to the house. Original drawings show the main addition of a west-facing room on the ground, first and second floors. Architectural historian and Soane expert, Ptolemy Dean, explains: 'This is a very rare and important example of a surviving Soane town house addition.'

Prime Minister Benjamin Disraeli, Earl of Beaconsfield.

which still stands today. He remained in Curzon Street until around 1786 when it became the home of Sir John Seabright, who made a name for himself as an avid scientist, in particular in the area of breeding. In fact, one of the oldest breeds of British chicken is named in his honour – the Seabright Bantam. Charles Darwin called Sir Seabright 'one of the clearest writers on the subject of breeding', and by some he is considered the father of the science.

Benjamin Disraeli

It was in 1880 that 19 Curzon Street became the home of the first and only Jewish Prime Minister, Benjamin Disraeli, Earl of Beaconsfield. Disraeli bought the lease with the proceeds from one of his most successful books, *Endymion*. He first entered Parliament as MP for Maidstone in 1837 and it was the beginning of a long political career. He rose to become Leader of the Commons and Chancellor of the Exchequer in Lord Derby's government in 1852, and after the resignation of Derby in 1868, Queen Victoria invited him to be Prime Minster. He became Prime Minister for the second time in 1874 until 1880 and was created Earl of Beaconsfield in 1879. Disraeli was recorded in the 1881 census as a widower aged 75, with the occupation of 'Ex Prime Minister', and had thirteen live-in servants. A later note was added to the census return: 'died nineteenth April 1881 – R.I.P.' Newspaper reports later claimed that 'in the closing weeks of his life increasing crowds gathered round his house and his passing was followed by a general burst of sorrow'.

POLITICIANS & ARISTOCRACY

Sir John Seabright lived at the house until around 1813, when he leased it firstly to George Ponsonby, and then to Lord King. The Right Honourable George Ponsonby was the grandson of the third Duke of Devonshire of Chatsworth in Derbyshire. He had a long and successful political career culminating in his role as Lord Chancellor of Ireland in 1806 and Leader of the Whig Party in 1808–17. George Ponsonby died at 19 Curzon Street in 1817. Peter King was the seventh Baron King and another politician to grace No 19. Lord King gained the title at the age of 18 and throughout his career published a number of pamphlets and books.

In 1820, 19 Curzon Street became the home of Lord William Vane Powlett, who had become an MP at the age of 20, in 1812, and remained in Parliament until 1857. Powlett was connected to an unusual event in 1847, when he was charged with having stolen two embroidered slippers worth 12s from a shop in Burlington Arcade. The court trial was recorded in *The Times*, giving great detail of the alleged crime, but the charge was thrown out with comments like, 'it was rather singular for a nobleman to carry away slippers in his pocket'. Powlett lived at No 19 for over forty years, and at the time of the 1861 census was recorded as 'landed proprietor' with his wife Lady Caroline and twelve live-in servants. Lord Powlett passed away in 1864, shortly after he inherited the dukedom of Cleveland from his brother.

The next occupant, in 1865, was Charles Bennet, Earl of Tankerville, later Lord Ossulston. Tankerville lived at Curzon Street with his wife, Lady Olivia, until around 1879–80. At the time of the 1871 census, the earl and countess were recorded in the house with their three youngest children and twelve live-in servants. Tankerville was an MP until 1859, when he was called to the House of Lords under the Barony of Ossulston.

COUNTESS OF STAFFORD & LADY BRABOURNE

By 1888, the house had become the home of Dowager Countess of Stafford, widow of George Byng, the 2nd Earl of Stafford. Harriet, Countess of Stafford, was the daughter of Charles Cavendish, 1st Baron Chesham, and was also directly related to the Cavendish family of Chatsworth House. She occupied the house with her children: Lieutenant-Colonel Charles

Byng; Captain Lionel Byng (later Major Byng); Honourable Julian Byng (later Field Marshal Sir Julian Byng, Viscount Byng of Vimy); and her daughters, Susan and Elizabeth. The census also shows that in 1891 the Countess of Stafford had fourteen live-in servants. The countess passed away in 1892 and *The Times* in December of that year revealed some of the contents of the house on sale, including 'valuable plate … Louis XIV tortoiseshell clocks, bronzes … coloured engravings, also a few lots of Havannah [sic] cigars'.

The next occupant was the Honourable Mrs Knatchbull-Hugessen, Lady Brabourne, wife of the 2nd Baron Brabourne. The 1901 census records Lady Brabourne at 19 Curzon Street with her daughters, Margaret and Bettine, along with eight servants, including a governess and a French cook. She remained at No 19 until just after the First World War, when she leased it to Dowager Lady Leven and Melville.

1881 Census recording the residence of former Prime Minister Benjamin Disraeli.

Twentieth-Century

Very little is known about the house during the 1920s and '30s, and by the end of the Second World War the house had been converted into office space for a number of businesses and was known as Disraeli House for a short time. It was during the 1990s that large-scale redevelopment came to the western end of Curzon Street, with the addition of new offices facing Park Lane and the creation of the secluded Curzon Square.

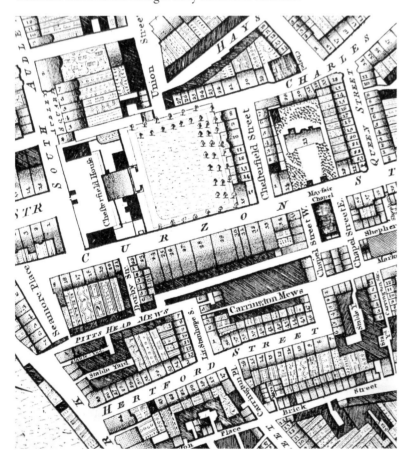

Richard Horwood map, 1799.

THE OLD SWEET SHOP

Early History

This house was formerly part of the Chipstead Place Estate, which can be traced back to the time of Elizabeth I. Before this, the house was most likely part of the Manor of Chepstead, alias Wilkes, which dates back to around the fourteenth century. The Chipstead Place Estate was bought by David Polhill in 1711 and passed through his descendants until it was sold to Frederick Perkins Esq. in 1829. The tithe map from 1840 clearly shows that today's Nos 22, 24 and 26 were one house and labelled 'The Croft House and Garden', and the owner was Frederick Perkins.

The Old Sweet Shop in Chipstead, Kent, is a Grade II listed cottage attached to Nos 24 and 26 the High Street, formerly a complete house built over 500 years ago. The house was constructed in the late fifteenth century as a Medieval Hall house and, although it has been altered many times, it is still possible to see the original foundations and historic features in the stone cellar.

THE COWLAND FAMILY

The census records for Chipstead from 1841 to 1901 do not clearly list house numbers, house names or even street names; however, it appears that all three cottages had a long association with the Cowland family. The 1841 census reveals the house was home to agricultural labourer, William Cowland, and his wife Sophia, both 60 years old, along with 20-year-old Susannah Cowland and 2-year-old Sophia Durling. It seems that the cottages were still connected at the time of the 1851 census and were home to another member of the Cowland family: James, a 60-year-old carpenter. He was listed in the house with his wife, Charlotte, and two grown-up children, Frederick and Harriet.

THE SWEET SHOP

It is uncertain exactly when the house was divided into separate cottages, especially as the house probably changed a number of times. However, it

appears that it was divided sometime during the 1850s and it was also during this time that the large Victorian shop window was added to the front of today's No 22. The 1861 census contains the first reference to the separate cottages and today's No 22 was recorded as the home of bricklayer and grocer Jesse Cowland, his wife Susannah and their three children. It is revealed that James Cowland and his family were still living in the neighbouring part of the house.

It is believed to be during this mid Victorian period that No 22 became the village sweet shop. An old photograph from the late nineteenth century clearly shows the village children spending their pocket money on their favourite sweets and congregating around the shop.

Postcard showing the sweet shop with local children, date unknown.

OLD-FASHIONED COTTAGES

Jesse and Susannah Cowland continued in the cottage shop, known today as No 22, until the 1890s. The 1891 census shows that Jesse had passed away, but 76-year-old Susannah was still in the house with her two unmarried children, Selina and Charles. In 1901 the census records James Cowland's daughter, Isabel, still living next door, but today's No 22 was the home of William Arthur Ford, a 38-year-old 'Prudential Agent' from Surrey. William was in the house with his wife, Emily Jane, and three children, Mabel, Arthur and Ethel.

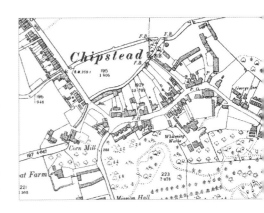

Ordnance Survey map, 1896.

By the turn of the twentieth century, the cottages were still owned by a descendant of Frederick Perkins, but in 1916 the cottages were sold to Edward Cordy. The sales particulars from 1916 tell us that today's No 22 was still occupied by Mrs Ford and she was paying 5s 6d a week. The house was described as 'the end cottage compris[ing] a Shop and Parlour, Kitchen and Cellar ... three good Bed Rooms and an Attic'.

Further property details tell us that in 1925 the house was home to Mrs Ford's daughter, Mabel Alice Ford. The electoral register for 1933 then shows the house was occupied by George and Edith Avis. The Avis' made No 22 the High Street their home for almost fifty years, with George Avis last recorded in the house during the late 1970s, when it became the residence of Mary Glass.

CURRENT NAME

When the current owners heard neighbours and friends referring to their home as 'The Old Sweet Shop', they decided to make the name official and renamed the house, allowing the heritage of the old village sweet shop to be remembered for future generations.

3 PEMBROKE STUDIOS

Early Days

The first reference to a resident at 3 Pembroke Studios was in the electoral register of 1893, which showed a shared occupancy of artists Henry Thackeray Schwabe and Arthur Coleman Behrend. Schwabe and Behrend occupied the studio until around 1896, when it was used by Ernest Oppler until 1899. It then became home to John Young Hunter, who continued in the studio until the turn of the twentieth century when it became a studio for artist Miss Hilda Koe. Unfortunately, the 1901 census records No 3 as unoccupied, but the London Directory in 1902 shows Miss Koe was still using the studio.

Pembroke Studios were built on the site of former nursery gardens in Kensington in 1890–91 by Charles Frederick Kearley. Built as working studios, the first residents were all artists, sculptors and writers. The main feature is the large windows allowing plenty of natural light for the working artists. The 1891 census lists Pembroke Studios but not its residents, and simply records: 'Pembroke Gardens Studios include eleven sets of rooms used as studios only'.

BARON FRANCKENSTEIN

In 1969 No 3 Pembroke Studios became the home of actor Baron Clement G. Franckenstein, descendant of the Franckenstein who was said to have inspired Mary Shelley to write her gothic tale, *Frankenstein*. Franckenstein was the son of Georg Freiherr von und zu Franckenstein, the former Austrian ambassador who became a British citizen and was knighted in 1938, when he refused a call from the Nazis to return to Austria. Georg, now known as Sir George, and his wife were killed in a plane accident in 1953, leaving 9-year-old Clement Franckenstein in the guardianship of an English family. Clement went on to study at Eton and then attempted an opera career in London, but with little success.

Clement lived at 3 Pembroke Studios until he moved to Los Angeles in 1972 to pursue a film career. He went on to feature in a long list of TV programmes and films, including *Star Trek: the Next Generation* with Patrick Stewart, *The American President*, alongside Michael Douglas, and even Mel Brooks' *Young Frankenstein*. His TV credits include *LA Law*, *ER*, *Murder She Wrote* and *The Love Boat*. Baron Clement Franckenstein also appeared in *People* magazine's Fifty Most Eligible Bachelors in the World list in 2001.

Pembroke Studios, 1890–91.

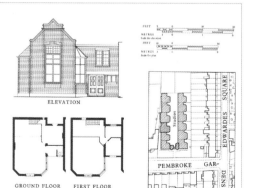

HOME FARM

The village of Colsterworth in Lincolnshire can be traced as far back as the Roman period when a settlement built up along the banks of the River Witham. The name originated from the Anglo-Saxon, meaning 'the settlement of charcoal burners', and the village was recorded in Domesday Book in 1086. Colsterworth formerly had a Priory of St Barbara, based along the banks of the river, but it was suppressed during the Dissolution of the Monasteries. The village is also known for its association with the birthplace of Sir Isaac Newton, at nearby Woolsthorpe Manor, in 1642. Newton lived in Woolsthorpe during his childhood and it is where he allegedly sat under the apple tree and discovered the theory of gravity.

TOLLEMACHE FAMILY

Home Farm was built in 1650 on land connected to the Tollemache family, the Earls of Dysart of nearby Buckminster Park. The early ownership of the house is uncertain as the family had links with two significant aristocratic family lines: firstly, the Tollemache family of Ham House in Surrey;

Design

Home Farm has had many alterations and extensions over the last 360 years. The first part of the house was built as a single range, running east to west, but an additional range was added in 1778 creating an L plan. The interior retains authentic seventeenth-century moulded beams and original roof timbers. The cellar also features original detailing and was initially the storage room for barrels when the house was used as an inn.

Turnpike Trusts

The Grantham to Stamford Turnpike Trust (which allowed for the collection of tolls for the upkeep of the roads) was created in 1738–39, and when the road through Colsterworth was completed in 1752, Colsterworth became a busy post town. This was further boosted in 1756 when the Bourne Colsterworth Turnpike was established linking Lincoln to the Peterborough Turnpike, which in turn linked with the Great North Road Turnpike.

Colsterworth became a bustling coach town for people travelling along the old Great North Road and Home Farm was right in the middle of it. It was formerly The Angel Inn, offering stabling and accommodation for tired travellers at a time when it is believed there were as many as fourteen inns in Colsterworth alone.

and secondly, the Manners family, the Dukes of Rutland of nearby Belvoir Castle. The lands of Home Farm eventually passed to Sir William Manners, Lord Huntingtower, son of John Manners and Lady Louisa Tollemache, 7th Countess of Dysart. From the eighteenth century until the late twentieth century, Home Farm remained in the hands of the Tollemache family, who still own large parts of neighbouring Buckminster today.

FARMHOUSE

Early records for the house are scarce, so it is uncertain if the house was built as an inn or later converted into an inn, but the history of the area suggests that its first use was as a farmhouse. The house was connected to extensive farmland, even into the twentieth century, as well as having a number of farm buildings and stables attached to it. This is further supported when we learn that prior to the establishment of the Turnpike Trusts, in the eighteenth century, Colsterworth was predominately a small agricultural village.

THE ANGEL INN

There are no clear records as to when Home Farm was transformed into The Angel Inn, but it seems likely that it was during the 1760s and '70s, after the completion of the road links. This is supported by the fact that the house was extended in 1778. An additional date plaque clearly shows the date '1778' and 'T.T.' for Thomas Tollemache, second son of Sir Lionel Tollemache and his wife Elizabeth, 2nd Countess of Dysart. In 1808 the lands around Colsterworth were enclosed and at this time the house was described as 'the Angel Inn Homestead', although very little accompanying information is available. Alehouse records do not show an Angel Inn in Colsterworth during the 1830s, by which time it had been converted back to a farmhouse.

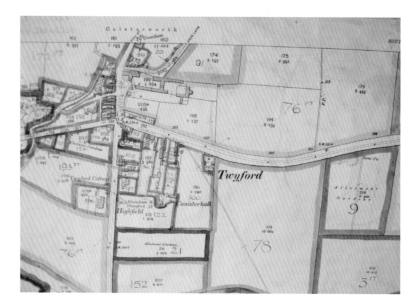

1910 Valuation map.

1910 Valuation field book.

CHARLES DOVE & FAMILY

By the 1870s, the census returns and local directories show that Home Farm was occupied by the Dove family. The 1881 census shows farmer Charles Dove in the house with his wife Elizabeth and their three children, Charles, James and Elizabeth. The Dove family prospered at Home Farm and continued in the house for the remainder of the nineteenth century. Charles' second son, James, took over the family farm and in 1891 and 1901 was recorded there with his wife Susannah and their children, Charles and Annie. It appears that Charles Dove junior moved to his own farm in another part of Colsterworth and Charles senior remained at Home Farm until he passed away in 1905 at the age of 80.

The 1910 Inland Revenue valuation survey records that Home Farm was occupied by James Dove and covered almost 105 acres. The 'Farm House, premises, garden and land' were still owned by the Earl of Dysart of Buckminster Park. The 1911 census shows widowed Elizabeth Dove as the head of the household, 84 years old, with her son James and his wife Susannah, along with their three children, Charles, Annie and George. The Dove family had one servant, 'a waggoner on farm' and there were two visitors, Herbert Bateman, a 'companion', and a female assistant.

MODD'S FARM

James Dove passed away suddenly in 1912 at only 49 years old. His widow, Susannah, continued to manage the farm with her son Charles into the 1920s, but in 1929 the farm passed to William Modd. A valuation survey from 1931 shows the farmhouse and land, by this time over 150 acres, occupied by William Robert Modd and still owned by the Earls of Dysart. The electoral registers during the 1930s also record William Modd, his wife Annie Elizabeth and their son James at Home Farm. Local histories reveal that the farmhouse became known locally as just 'Modd's Farm'. The family continued in the house during the Second World War and were still recorded there up until the 1970s.

Oliver Fiennes

After 320 years of being owned by the Earls of Dysart, Home Farm was sold by the Estate in 1979 and purchased by the Very Reverend, The Honourable Oliver Fiennes, former Dean of Lincoln Cathedral. Oliver Fiennes is connected to the Twisleton-Wykeham-Fiennes family of Broughton Castle and the current baronet, the adventurer Sir Ranulph Fiennes. Oliver Fiennes can trace his family back to the Normans of the 1066 conquest and his ancestor, Lord Saye and Sele, was one of the barons present at the signing of the Magna Carta at Runnymede in 1215. Oliver Fiennes and his family lived at Home Farm until the early years of the twenty-first century.

THE OLD RECTORY

The Manor House

A large section of the land in Thurgarton was acquired by Trinity College at the time of the Dissolution of the Monasteries in 1538, along with a third of the lordship of Thurgarton. The patronage of the curacy of Thurgarton was also in the hands of Trinity College, and with the newly created role came a house. A plan of the house, from 1848, is retained in the Nottinghamshire Archives and shows the original manor house that became the home of Thurgarton's new vicar. It is described as 'Detached from the leasehold in the year 1848 with a view of annexing them to the living of Thurgarton and Hoveringham'.

Above: Plan of Thurgarton Manor House, 1848.

Right: The opening of Whitehouse, 1910, with Rev. Baylay in the centre (with beard).

The Old Rectory sits within the historic village of Thurgarton in Nottinghamshire, in an area described as a typical English Rural Scene. The house can be traced back to the seventeenth century when it was constructed as The Manor House for Mr John Cooper, between 1660–1672.

In 1850 the house was given a new lease of life as the rectory for the newly appointed vicar of Thurgarton. Before this time, the parish of Thurgarton was cared for by the curate based in Southwell, Reverend J.T. Becher, who was curate between 1799–1848.

REV. GUILLEBAUD

The new vicar who moved into the manor house, today's Old Rectory, was Reverend Henry Lea Guillebaud. The 1851 census records the vicar aged 33 and unmarried, with three live-in servants, a groom, a housekeeper and a housemaid. The 1871 census reveals Guillebaud had married Jemima and had five children, Ernest, Alexander, Mary, Lucy and Agnes. In 1872, after twenty years, Rev. Guillebaud moved on from Thurgarton.

REV. BAYLAY

When the Guillebaud family moved from Thurgarton, the curacy passed to Reverend Atwell M.A. Baylay, while the patronage was still retained by the 'Master Fellows and scholars of Trinity College Cambridge'. The 1881 census records Rev. Baylay, 38 years old, in the house with his young wife Alice, 23 years old, and their three children, Charles, Frances and John. They also had three live-in servants, a cook, a housemaid and a nurse. By the time of the 1891 census he had a further three daughters, but had also taken in a boarder, Ruth Mitchell from Scotland.

Reverend Baylay continued as Vicar of Thurgarton for a further thirty years, only moving away in 1920. In fifty years as vicar, he was a central part of village life and was involved in a number of projects, including the opening of a convalescent home for children recovering from tuberculosis, known as The Whitehouse. Baylay was also an avid amateur historian and scholar, and wrote a number of papers on historical subjects, including the history of churches in the area.

REVERENDS COME & GO

In 1920 Rev. Baylay was replaced by Rev. Vincent Taylor Kirby who, like both Baylay and Guillebaud before him, was a former student of Trinity College, Cambridge. However, Rev. Kirby did not stay in Thurgarton long, as by 1928 the curacy was held by Rev. William Basil Evans, who also only remained a few years, and by 1935 the curacy had passed to Rev. George Herbert Halstead. It was at this time that change came to the house. Reverend Halstead requested a new vicarage because the one on Beck Street was deemed too large, so it was sold back to Trinity College and the money was put towards the building of a new rectory.

Second World War

After the sale of the vicarage in 1935, it is unclear as to what happened to the house until after the Second World War. The first reference to the house named 'The Old Rectory' appears in the electoral registers of 1946, where it is recorded as the private home of Norman and Margaret Wigley, along with servant Bertha Sibey. Norman and Margaret Wigley continued at The Old Rectory throughout the post-war period and only moved on during the late 1960s. The house then became the home of Sydney and Jennifer Farr, who also remained there for many years, eventually leaving during the 1990s.

41 OVINGTON SQUARE

Connections

The Comte de Narbonne-Lara, illegitimate son of King Louis XV of France, had been created Minister of War for King Louis XVI, and during the French Revolution had escaped to England and spent a large amount of time with fellow aristocratic émigrés. In particular, he had spent time at Juniper Hall in Surrey with others such as Talleyrand, General D'Arblay, Fanny Burney, and with his mistress, Madame de Stael. The Comte de Narbonne returned to France in 1801 and subsequently became aide-de-camp to Napoleon.

In the early nineteenth century much of the land around Brompton Road, Chelsea, was covered in market gardens and fields. During the 1820s building began to spread rapidly across the area, but the land where Ovington Square is located today was still open for development. It was owned by Baroness Von Zandt, daughter of John Standerwicke of Ovington House in Hampshire. By the 1840s the baroness had begun the development of her lands with the help of architect William Wilmer Pocock, son of William Fuller Pocock, one of the founding members of the Royal Institute of British Architects. William Wilmer became very successful and was responsible for building in Brompton Road and Lowndes Street.

Pocock designed all the grand stucco terraces of Ovington Gardens (first known as Ovington Terrace) and Ovington Square. Building began in 1844 but was not completed until 1852. No 41 Ovington Square was part of the last section to be built during the early 1850s, and was originally named Vincent Street or Vincent Place. The houses were first numbered 1 to 8, with No 41 formerly No 3 Vincent Street.

FRENCH ROYAL FAMILY

By the late 1850s Vincent Street had become a popular address for French émigrés, and in 1860 No 3 Vincent Street was owned by Madam Duchean, but occupied by Mr Van Diepenham. By the time of the 1861 census the house was the home of Louise de Narbonne, Countess de Narbonne, married and 24 years old, with only one servant. The Countess de Narbonne was directly linked to the illegitimate son of King Louis XV, Comte de Narbonne, although the exact connection is not clear. The Countess was most likely the wife of the Comte's grandson, the third Comte du Narbonne and part of the French aristocracy. However, she only stayed in the house for a short time, as by 1871 the census shows the house was home to Joseph Perrin.

RENAMED & RENUMBERED

Vincent Street was officially renamed and renumbered in 1881, when Captain Philip Wynter, aged 41, lived there with his wife Constance, their 1-year-old son Philip, and four live-in servants. The next occupant was James Fortescue Harrison, barrister and MP for Kilmarnock, who moved in between 1874 and 1880. The 1891 census shows James, aged 72 and widowed, with his two daughters – Agnes, aged 51 and also widowed, and Mary, aged 40 – and three live-in servants. Interestingly, at this time James' neighbours in Ovington Square were Lord and Lady Kilmarnock. Alongside his work as a barrister and MP he was a prolific investor. *The Times* newspaper records him as a director and chairman of many companies, including the 'Victoria Hansom Cab Company', 'The Mexican General Land Mortgage & Investment Co.' and 'The Permanent Wall Hangings Company'.

GRANDSON OF WILLIAM IV

By 1895, No 41 had become the home of another notable resident directly linked to the British royal family. Henry Edward Fitz-Clarence was the grandson of King William IV; his father was Lord Augustus Fitz-Clarence, the ninth son of William IV and his mistress, actress Dorothea Bland. Sources show Henry in the house with his wife Mary, their son Augustus and daughter Cynthia for almost forty years, until Henry passed away in 1930 and Mary in 1932. Augustus distinguished himself in both military and sporting pursuits. He took part in the sabre contest in the 1912 Olympic Games and rowed at Henley in 1896–98. He joined the Army at the outbreak of the Boer War in 1899 and was commissioned to the Royal Fusiliers, receiving the Queen's Medal with four clasps. He later served in Nigeria, but died fighting in the Dardanelles during the First World War, in 1915.

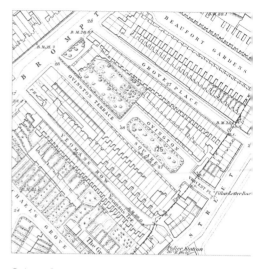

Ordnance Survey map, 1869, showing the earlier name of Vincent Place.

War Heroes

After 1932 the house became the home of more military heroes. Philip Lee-Warner, a pilot with the Royal Air Force Volunteer Reserve during the Second World War, took part in a number of significant operations over Germany during 1944. He was promoted to squadron leader in January 1944, but was shot down over Germany in August that year. By 1948 the house was occupied by Malcolm Romer, whose father was Colonel Nigel Romer, MBE, of the Scots Guards. Malcolm followed his father into the Scots Guards and fought in Italy during the Second World War. He rose to the rank of lieutenant-colonel and was awarded an MBE. The Romers moved out of 41 Ovington Square sometime during the early 1960s, when it became the home of another military man, Major Harold Stanley Cayzer.

HILLES HOUSE

Fire Damage

One of the key features of Hilles House is the large oriel window buttressed from the slope of the hill to the west. The initial L-plan was extended in 1922 and the house was originally thatched, but this was destroyed by fire in 1948 and has now been replaced with stone slate. The rebuilding of the house in 1951–54 was supervised by Detmar Blow's widow and his son-in-law, Philip Warwe-Cornish.

The Grade II* listed Hilles House was designed by Arts and Crafts architect, Detmar Jellings Blow. Construction began in 1914 but was only fully completed in the 1950s. It is situated near Harescombe in Gloucestershire and has views across the Severn Valley to the Malvern Hills; but despite its idyllic location it has been the scene of great family tragedy.

Hilles House was designed by Detmar Blow to reflect the ideals of the Arts and Crafts movement, inspired by William Morris and John Ruskin, which valued the traditional methods of craftsmanship and the focus on natural materials. The house was built with coursed and squared rubble limestone with ashlar dressings and chimneys. Despite the long view reaching across to Wales, the house is placed at a right angle to the view and built with small windows, perhaps again indicative of Blow's approach to a 'natural' style, where the house appears to be part of the landscape. The south front is almost symmetrical and has been described as 'haphazard', while on the north side is a three-storey rectangular gazebo tower with continuous mullioned windows to the lower storeys.

The screen of the Long Room, 1940.

The Design

Pevsner described the interior as 'a curious combination of Jacobean classical detailing with the traditional vernacular style'. Interior features include classical stone fireplaces and timber screen with detached Doric columns, separating the Big Hall and the Long Room, as well as a rare set of seventeenth-century Mortlake tapestries, that were originally in Loudon Castle, and a tapestry of Botticelli's 'Primavera' by Edward Burne-Jones. To correspond with Blow's socialist ideals he specifically designed the house with no servants' quarters and no nursery space for the children. In fact, Neville Lytton explains in his book *English Country Gentleman* that initially the whole household, family and servants combined, all ate together in the kitchen, which did not work out as planned and, 'as the awkward pauses became more and more agonising, was eventually abandoned'.

DETMAR JELLINGS BLOW

Detmar Jellings Blow was fortunate to be taken under the wing of the great John Ruskin, who introduced him to many significant names within the art world, including William Morris, William Holman Hunt, Edward Burne-Jones and Phillip Webb. Through these connections Blow was heavily influenced by the Arts and Crafts movement, which was to dominate his style for the rest of his life. He also became good friends with another notable architect, Edwin Lutyens. However, Blow also had strong aristocratic links, including the Wyndham family of Clouds in Wiltshire, and in 1910 he married Winifred Tollemache, granddaughter of Lord Tollemache.

Detmar Blow was favoured by many of the aristocracy and those in conservative circles, and was commissioned to complete a number of country houses, including Horwood House, the restoration of Bramham Park for the Lane-Fox family, Mill Hill in Yorkshire for Hugh Fairfax-Cholmeley and nearby Holcombe House. He also worked on alterations to Eaton Hall and a hunting lodge in France for Hugh Grosvenor, 2nd Duke of Westminster, known as Bend'Or, with whom he became good friends. In 1916 Blow was appointed to manage the extensive Westminster estate in London and the

Fashion

Detmar the younger and Isabella Blow made Hilles House into an artistic home, where they held glamorous parties to which they invited many notable names from the fashion industry. Isabella Blow was at the heart of the industry and was known for her eccentric outfits, as well as her behaviour. She was best known for having an eye for new and upcoming talent, and played a pivotal role in the careers of Philip Treacy and Sophie Dahl, as well as Alexander McQueen, who often visited the house to gain inspiration for his designs. She formerly worked with *Vogue* editor Anna Wintour in New York and was good friends with actor Rupert Everett. However, the tragic connections with the house were to continue and Isabella Blow also committed suicide in 2007.

connection brought further high-profile links; but in consequence he fell further away from his Arts and Crafts ideals and did very little of his own architectural work. By the 1930s Blow's circumstances had turned and the Duke of Westminster brought an accusation against him which effectively destroyed his career. He was dismissed as the duke's agent, which ultimately led to him having a breakdown from which he never recovered, and he spent the remaining years of his life at Hilles House.

TRAGEDY AT HILLES

Since its construction, this beautiful house has been attached to great sadness for the people who have called it home. The stories associated with Hilles House illustrate how much the history of a house is influenced by the people in it.

After the death of Detmar Blow in 1939, his widow, Winifred, continued in the house with her children and it is through the life of the children that we uncover scandalous stories. It has been suggested by writer Simon Blow, grandson of Detmar Jellings Blow, that his uncle – Detmar's son, Jonathan – was involved in a terrible act as he tried to acquire the full inheritance of Hilles House and all the remaining property of his father. In 1954 Jonathan apparently forced his mother Winifred to change her will to favour him, and when she proposed changing it back, he poisoned her by placing hemlock in her lunch. The will left all the property, apart from a house in London, to Jonathan, leaving the other children, including Simon's father, with virtually nothing. Although Jonathan had got what he wanted, he fell into depression and alcoholism, and committed suicide by drinking weed killer in 1977.

Detmar Blow had aspired to create a house of beauty, but by the 1970s it had been the location of Detmar's mental breakdown, the murder of his

widow and now the suicide of his son. Moreover, the sad associations with the house were to continue in the lives of his grandchildren. After the death of Jonathan Blow, the house passed to his son, named Detmar after his grandfather. Detmar Blow married the fashionista Isabella Delves Broughton, daughter of Sir Evelyn Delves Broughton and granddaughter of Sir Henry 'Jock' Delves Broughton (who was accused of the murder of Josslyn Hay, 22nd Earl of Erroll, in 1941 in the scandalous 'White Mischief' drama in Kenya and committed suicide in 1942).

Today, Hilles House remains with the Blow family and continues as a comfortable family home, much as Detmar Jellings Blow desired when he started the house in 1914.

52–56 ROMNEY STREET

Romney Street was originally named Vine Street due to its association with the vineyard of Westminster Palace that was formerly located by the river. Building slowly began during the seventeenth century as people began to move and work along the banks of the Thames. Up until this time it was not much more than a country track, running from Westminster Palace to fields and the horse ferry. The area belonged to the Marsham family, who were later created the Earls of Romney, and from whom the later name originated.

Larger building development began during the late seventeenth and early eighteenth centuries, with Vine Street first appearing in the parish rate books in 1679. However, it is most likely that today's Nos 52–56 were built during the 1720s, coinciding with the building of St John the Evangelist Church in 1713–28 by Thomas Archer. Nos 52–56 Romney Street were formerly known as Nos 2, 3 and 4 Vine Terrace, and were renumbered 52, 54 and 56 Romney Street in 1869.

NINETEENTH-CENTURY RESIDENTS

By the nineteenth century Vine Street had become predominately a working-class area, with numerous families living in one house. The area was

Eleanor Rathbone.

Women's Rights

From the early 1920s, No 50 Romney Street was the home of social worker Elizabeth Macadam and social reformer Eleanor Rathbone. Eleanor Rathbone has been referred to as 'the most significant feminist thinker and the most effective woman politician of the first half of the twentieth century', but the two women both worked tirelessly during the late nineteenth and early twentieth centuries for the rights of women, refugees, and social and political change in Britain. Rathbone and Macadam remained at Nos 50–52 Romney Street until the latter years of the Second World War, when they moved to nearby Tufton Street.

dominated by industry related to the river and housed a number of warehouses and factories, including a brewery and a sugar-baker. At this time, today's Nos 52–56 Romney Street were home to working-class residents, such as a lawyer's clerk, porters, a blacksmith, a letter carrier, a gun maker's assistant and a warder at nearby Millbank Prison. By the end of the century, the three homes were still shared by numerous families and the mixture of occupations continued with a gas fitter, a lamp lighter, stonemasons, charwomen and needlewomen, as well as a pensioner from the convict colonies, a keeper in St James' Park, a cigar maker, a cheesemonger and an engine driver.

MISS BENGOUGH

In 1918 No 52 Romney Street was bought by Miss Mary George Etheldreda Bengough, who lived in the house until the 1930s. She is remembered for the Bengough Charity, through which she gave funds for the 'relief of women in need, hardship or distress'. By 1935, No 52 appeared listed together with No 50, further confusing the changes in the layout of the houses and the alterations in house numbers. It was at this time that further redevelopment took place in Romney Street.

AIDEN & VIRGINIA CRAWLEY

After the Second World War, Nos 50–52 Romney Street became the home of Aiden and Virginia Crawley. Aiden Crawley was an MP and in 1955 was the first Editor-in-Chief of Independent Television News. Later, from 1967 to 1973, he was Chairman of London Weekend Television. Virginia Crawley was a journalist and author who wrote a number of notable biographies, including *Edward VII and his Circle* (1956) and *The Romanovs* (1971).

BOOTS THE CHEMIST

Nos 54 and 56 Romney Street were first joined in 1918–19 and appeared in the parish rate books for 1924 as one home and owned by John Boot of 32 Smith Square. John Campbell Boot, 2nd Baron Trent, was the son of Jesse Boot, founder of Boots the Chemist. He continued in his father's footsteps and transformed the company into a national brand, as well as instigating many social reforms for his workers, including pension schemes and holiday clubs. His mother, Dowager Lady Trent, was later recorded as living at Nos 54–56 Romney Street during the 1930s.

After the war, 54 Romney Street continued in the Boot family as the home of Rosemary and Alan Burrough. Rosemary was the granddaughter of Jesse Boot, 1st Baron Trent, and Lady Trent, and the niece of John Boot. Rosemary's father was Wilfred Montague Bruce who accompanied his brother-in-law, R.F. Scott, on his Antarctic expedition in 1913 and was awarded the Polar Medal. Rosemary and Alan Burrough remained at No 54 until the late 1950s. Rosemary's sister, Charity Bruce, lived at Nos 50–52 Romney Street with Eleanor Rathbone and Elizabeth Macadam during the late 1930s, at the same time that her grandmother, Lady Trent, was living next door.

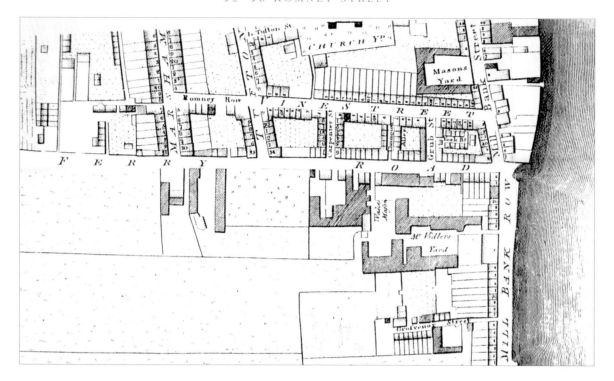

THE VINE HOUSE

It was during the late 1950s and early '60s that the homes along Romney Street changed once again and were renovated to become Vine House, 52–56 Romney Street. After the renovation was completed in 1961, Vine House became the home of Lord and Lady Parker of Waddington. Hubert Parker, Baron Parker of Waddington, was Lord Chief Justice of England from 1958–71. He and his wife remained at Vine House until the late 1960s, when the home was purchased by William Oliver and Marietta Fox-Pitt.

Richard Horwood map, 1799.

Fox-Pitt Family

William Oliver Lane Fox-Pitt was the son of Major-General William Lane Fox-Pitt and the great-grandson of Augustus Lane Fox Pitt-Rivers, notable archaeologist, Vice-President of the Society of Antiquaries and Royal Society Fellow. The Fox-Pitt family are well known in the sports arena, predominately in equestrian sports. The eldest son, William, is an Olympic Eventing rider, who won a silver medal in team eventing at Athens in 2004, and a bronze medal at Beijing in 2008. The two daughters, Alicia and Laurella, were part of The Sisterhood, the first all-female dragon boat crew to row across the English Channel; a fellow crew member was the Duchess of Cambridge.

THE OLD POLICE HOUSE

First Occupants

The architect of the new police house was Mr George Evans, and it cost over £581 to build, including fixtures and fittings, painting and papering. Construction took place during 1860 and, by the time of the 1861 census, the first policemen were living in the house. The census records the first residents as police sergeant George Andrews, 50 years old, with his wife Elizabeth and their 12-year-old son Frederick, along with police constable Charles Bart, 28 years old, and his wife Sarah.

The Old Police House is situated in the village of Cranborne, Dorset, within the Cranborne Chase and West Wiltshire Downs Area of Outstanding Natural Beauty. The village is referenced in Thomas Hardy's *Tess of the D'Urbervilles*, when Tess visits the 'Flower-de-Luce' at 'Chaseborough', otherwise the Fleur de Lys Inn at Cranborne.

The Old Police House was not only the former police house; part of it was the former Methodist chapel, both built during the mid nineteenth century as the village of Cranborne began to expand. However, prior to their construction this section of Salisbury Street was the site of two cottages. Title deeds for the property reveal the ownership of the site back to 1788 when it was in the hands of Anthony Ashley-Cooper, 5th Earl of Shaftesbury. The land contained a small dwelling and garden and was leased by William Liddon, but by 1798 it was all sold to William Miles.

In 1812 William Miles had passed away and the trustees of his estate leased the property to Charles Harbin. On 8 September 1853 the land was purchased by a representative of the Methodist congregation in Cranborne for £160, for 'a chapel or meeting house and school [to] be erected thereon by members of Primitive Methodist Connexion at Cranborne'.

A NEW POLICE FORCE

Within a few years, the church had sold the plot facing Salisbury Street to William Ffooks, clerk of the peace, for the purposes of a police house for the village of Cranborne. This is in line with the 1856 County and Borough Police Act, where every county was required to organise a police force under a chief constable for all rural areas and boroughs. In addition, the new police force needed housing and across Dorset new police houses were built in Beaminster, Sherborne, Cerne Abbas, Blandford and Cranborne. The sale of the land was officially agreed in December 1859 and an agreement of sale shows that local builder Henry Kilford was commissioned with the task of building on the site 'a dwelling house with a police station and strong room for the use of the Dorset County Police'.

SERVING POLICEMEN

The 1871 census shows that the house was home to Sergeant William Webb, 40 years old, along with his wife Lucy and their six children. The police records for Dorset reveal that William Webb moved to Cranborne as acting sergeant in 1869 and by 1870 had been promoted to sergeant. The records also show that in 1875 a prisoner escaped from the station and Webb was demoted. A history of the Dorset Constabulary outlines an incident, believed to involve Webb, in which a PC was sent to the pub to 'fetch 5 pints of beer and half a pint of gin for two prisoners who were in custody at Cranborne on a charge of drunkenness and disorderly conduct', after which Webb released the prisoners from the cells and drank with them.

By the 1880s, the police house was occupied by Sergeant Stephen Stillman, along with his wife and four children. Stillman had been in the police force since 1857 and continued at Cranborne until 1885. The other part of the house was the home of police constable Thomas Johnston, 54 years old, with his wife Susan and their 14-year-old son. It appears that Constable Johnston had experienced a tumultuous career in the police force: he was reprimanded for being 'under the influence of liquor' in 1868; was fined and reprimanded twice for not fulfilling his duty; and was demoted and removed from his station in 1878 for drinking in a pub while on duty at Weymouth.

After the departure of Sergeant Stillman, Cranborne village was protected by Sergeant George Roper, along with his wife Emma. Unlike Thomas Johnston, Roper had a distinguished career; most notably he was rewarded and commended for saving a life during the dramatic shipwreck of the *Royal Adelaide* near Weymouth in 1872. The next policeman was Sergeant Edwin Pike, who was in the house with his wife Mary and their three children. Pike also had a good police career history and was rewarded for 'praiseworthy conduct at a fire at Thorncombe' in 1882. At the turn of the century, the 1910 valuation survey shows that the house was home to Sergeant Ellery and was simply described as 'in fair repair'.

Primitive Methodist Chapel

Meanwhile, the Primitive Methodist Chapel continued to be the meeting place for the congregation in Cranborne. The 1910 valuation described the chapel as in 'fair repair', contained a gallery and seated approximately 100 people.

Throughout the twentieth century, the police house and chapel continued as separate buildings and were central features of the community. It was only in the 1970s and '80s that this began to change, but it wasn't until the end of the twentieth century that these two Victorian buildings were transformed into a single residential home.

Sergeant Stillman and family.

BURGAGE HOUSE

Byron's Poetry

Byron wrote two poems referring to Julia Leacroft. The first was originally entitled *To Julia* and was published in his first collection, *Fugitive Pieces*, but the title was later changed to *To Lesbia*. In the poem he clearly refers to a romance between them, but goes on to say, 'No more we meet in yonder bowers; Absence has made me prone to roving'. The second poem, *To a Lady*, published in *Hours of Idleness* in 1807, talks of an assignation in the garden, and one can only imagine the once-large garden beside Burgage House being the scene of a clandestine meeting between the young Julia and Byron.

Lord Byron.

Burgage House in Southwell, Nottinghamshire, was constructed during the late eighteenth century, and from an early stage was in the hands of the Leacroft family. John Leacroft and his family had a significant connection with the poet Lord Byron, who visited his mother at nearby Burgage Manor from 1803 onwards. During his visits, Byron became close friends with his neighbours, including Elizabeth and John Pigot, who lived a few doors away from Burgage House, and John and Julia Leacroft.

During the summer of 1806, the group of friends decided to amuse themselves by staging amateur dramatics in Burgage House, whose drawing room was apparently perfect for a little theatre. They staged two plays, with Julia Leacroft playing the lead female roles alongside Byron. When Byron stayed in Southwell for the winter, the pair continued their flirtations after the theatricals ceased, and it wasn't long before the gossips of Southwell took notice and they became the

talk of the town. By January 1807 it was generally understood that they would marry – certainly Julia's family believed so. However, Byron had no intention of marrying Julia and the circumstances soon caused a scandal in the quiet village.

It has been suggested that the Leacrofts attempted to entrap Byron in order to make him marry Julia, but Byron made a hasty departure from Southwell just in time. It has also been said that the threat of a duel may have arisen between Bryon and his once friend, Julia's brother, John. Letters between John Leacroft and Byron show the height of animosity that had evolved due to Byron's actions. Byron writes: 'the only effectual method to crash the animadversions of officious malevolence is by my declining all future intercourse with those whom my acquaintance has unintentionally injured'. In a later letter he goes on to say: 'if we must cut each other's throats to please our relations, you will do me the justice to say it is from no personal animosity between us'.

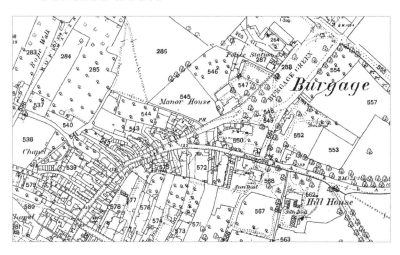

Ordnance Survey map, 1884–85.

GEORGIAN FAMILY HOME

From that time on, Byron never visited the Leacrofts again and soon after he stopped visiting Southwell altogether. Burgage House continued to be the home of the Leacroft family throughout the nineteenth century, with land tax records in 1830 showing that it was occupied by William Leacroft but owned by the Pigot family. However, by 1838 the tithe records reveal that Leacroft had purchased the house and he was recorded as owner and occupier.

Records for the nineteenth century show that 'family magistrate' William Swymmer Leacroft remained at Burgage House until he passed away in 1857, at which time it became the home of his brother, Edward. The 1861 census records Edward, aged 70, a 'gent and landed proprietor', in the house with his sister Caroline, aged 62, a 'fund holder', along with three live-in servants. By 1871 Edward was still in the house, aged 80, with his 8-year-old grandson, also named Edward. Not long afterwards, the elder Edward Leacroft passed away and after almost ninety years as the home of the Leacrofts, the house was sold.

'Potty Roe'

For the remainder of the nineteenth century, Burgage House was home to a corn miller, Edward Caudwell, and his wife Harriet and their six children. Caudwell was still recorded at Burgage House in the 1920s, but by 1925 it was the home of John Chapman Roe, known locally as 'Potty Roe'. The nickname originated from his business in selling pots and pans, as he ran a hardware shop on the corner of King Street, built on a section of the garden where the library now stands.

CHEYNE WALK

Henry VIII's New Manor House

Henry VIII's New Manor House – sometimes called Chelsea Palace – was built as a wedding present for Catherine Parr during the 1540s. It formerly sat along the east side of Oakley Street, approximately where Nos 19–26 Cheyne Walk are today. The Manor House was the home of Elizabeth I when she was a child and later became the home of Lady Jane Grey. John Dudley, the Duke of Northumberland and father-in-law to Lady Jane Grey, also lived in the Manor House, before he was charged with treason and beheaded in 1553. The New Manor House was later occupied by Anne of Cleves, who was the last royal resident, before it became the home of the Duke of Hamilton in 1639. The house was sold to Charles Cheyne in 1660 and the 2nd Lord Cheyne sold it to Sir Hans Sloane in 1742, where he lived until 1753, before it was demolished in 1755.

The early village of Chelsea developed as a small rural community, clustered around All Saints, today's Old Church, along the banks of the River Thames. The river was a vital part of the village, providing a livelihood for the local working people. In the sixteenth and seventeenth centuries, the clean air and fields of Chelsea lured the nobility and aristocracy from dirty central London, and a number of large mansions were built up along the banks of the river. The river also offered a convenient route into the city, which was quicker than travelling along the often dangerous and rough roads by carriage. Chelsea became the home of the great and the good who built large palatial homes, giving it the name 'the village of palaces'.

BEAUFORT HOUSE

One of the most significant early palaces was built for Sir Thomas More in 1520, which later became known as Beaufort House. It formerly sat to the south of the Moravian graveyard, west of Beaufort Street, and had a number of owners including Lord Burghley, his son Lord Salisbury, and the Duke of Buckingham. It was sold to Henry, Marquis of Worcester, who became the Duke of Beaufort in 1682. In 1736, lord of the manor Sir Hans Sloane bought the house, but demolished it three years later. The gateway entrance to the house, designed by Inigo Jones in 1621, did survive but was moved to Chiswick House, where it remains today.

SIR HANS SLOANE

By the early 1700s the isolated palaces that sat by the river were beginning to disappear, either through rebuilding or the development of lands, and in

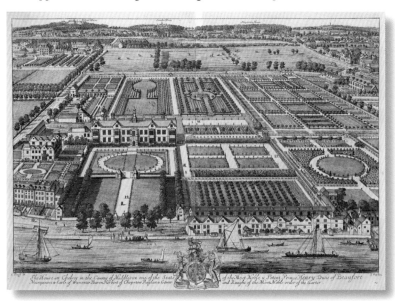

Beaufort House, Chelsea, drawn by J. Kip, 1708.

1717 Sir Hans Sloane leased land in Henry VIII's 'Great Garden' for building, which was the beginning of Cheyne Walk. The village of Chelsea, with its riverside taverns, became a well-established and thriving local community by the banks of the river. Local historian Reginald Blunt confirmed that at one time there was a tavern every 80 yards between Battersea Bridge and the Royal Hospital.

It was during the early eighteenth century that many of the tall Georgian town houses were built along the Chelsea riverside, and these make up some of the oldest houses along Cheyne Walk today. At this time, the street name 'Cheyne Walk' did not extend past the Old Church; it was only after the Embankment was built in the 1870s that the name was applied to the length of the road from Cremorne Road to Royal Hospital Road.

The construction of the embankment of Chelsea Reach, along to Battersea Bridge, began in 1871 under chief engineer of the Metropolitan Board of Works, Joseph Bazalgette, and was completed by 1874. The Chelsea Embankment greatly altered the identity of the village, and the old wharves, streets and waterfront taverns began to close or were demolished to create the Chelsea we know today.

Today, Cheyne Walk has a mixed architectural appearance, as each era has added its own style to this prominent street, while still maintaining elements of earlier domestic building. As Cheyne Walk was the centre of Chelsea village life for many years, it has been the home to many illustrious

Cheyne Walk looking east before the Embankment, 1860s.

Chelsea Old Church

It is believed that there has been a church on the banks of the Thames in Chelsea since Anglo-Saxon times. It was first recorded in Domesday Book in 1086 and the name 'All Saints' first appeared in records in 1175. The parish church of Chelsea came to be known as St Luke's and the first building is believed to have been established during the reign of Edward II in the fourteenth century. The Lawrence and More chapels were added soon afterwards and Sir Thomas More rebuilt the chapel in his name in 1528. By 1667 a large section of the medieval church had deteriorated and was deemed too small. It was subsequently demolished and rebuilt; however, the original chapels were preserved. The church did not significantly alter from the seventeenth to the nineteenth century and retained many of its treasured old monuments and memorials. It became known as Chelsea Old Church when the new St Luke's was built on Sydney Street in 1824. In April 1941 the Old Church was almost completely destroyed by enemy action, but was sympathetically restored in the same style.

residents of the past, including George Eliot, David Lloyd George, William Holman Hunt and James Whistler. Below is an overview of the many notable residents who have called Cheyne Walk home.

NOS 1–6 CHEYNE WALK

No 1 Cheyne Walk was rebuilt in 1887–88 on the site of one of the early eighteenth-century houses and was home to actor-manager Seymour Hicks in 1937. No 2 is an example of one of the remaining eighteenth-century houses, built around 1717 but re-fronted in 1879. It was home to actor John Barrymore in 1924–25. No 3 Cheyne Walk was also built around 1717 and residents have included Admiral William Henry Smith, Vice-President of the Royal Society and a founding member of the Royal Geographical Society; Sir John Goss, organist at Chelsea Old Church and St Paul's Cathedral; and Rolling Stones guitarist Keith Richards.

No 4 was built around 1718 and retains a fine ornate Georgian doorway. It was the home of painters William Dyce in 1846–47 and Daniel Maclise in 1861–70. Author George Eliot also died here in 1880. No 6, like No 4, was built around 1718 and Sir Arthur Sullivan, one half of the famous musical partnership Gilbert & Sullivan, lived here as a boy in the 1840s.

GEORGIAN ARCHITECTURE

Nos 15–18 Cheyne Walk are further examples of early Georgian architecture built around 1717. No 15 was the home of artist Cecil Gordon Lawson, as well as engraver Henry Thomas Ryall. Queens House, No 16, is particularly noteworthy as a beautifully preserved Georgian town house with an additional bay window designed by Edwin Lutyens. The name

'Queens House' is based on a rumour that it was formerly the home of Catherine of Braganza, wife of Charles II. The rumour originated from the initials 'RC' on the gateway in front of the house, thought to be in her honour, but they actually referred to Richard Chapman, for whom the house was originally built in 1717. Dante Gabriel Rossetti lived here with his brother William from 1862–82, alongside his friends, poet Algernon C. Swinburne and writer George Meredith. It was at No 16 that Rossetti annoyed his neighbours by keeping a menagerie of unusual animals, including wombats, parrots, peacocks and an armadillo.

No 17 was home to musician Thomas Atwood, a student of Mozart's, who later became the organist at St Paul's Cathedral. No 18 became the famous Don Saltero's coffee house.

NOS 19–26 CHEYNE WALK

Nos 19–26 are almost a complete terrace, built in 1760, on the site of Henry VIII's Manor House. No 21 was home to author Henry James, and later to artist and writer Percy Wyndham Lewis in 1935–36. Renowned artist James Abbott McNeill Whistler was fond of Chelsea and lived in a number of the homes along Cheyne Walk, including No 21 in 1890, No 101 in 1863–66, No 96 in 1866–78, and finally No 74 in 1902–03. Local artist Walter Greaves was born at No 31 in 1846.

Cheyne Walk with Don Saltero's coffee house, 1850.

Richard Shaw

Nos 7–12 Cheyne Walk are great examples of the late nineteenth-century style of Richard Norman Shaw. No 10 was the home of former Prime Minister David Lloyd George in 1924–25, and later caricaturist Gerald Scarfe. No 13 was the home of composer Ralph Vaughan Williams in 1905–29, and was where he completed his symphony *The Lark Ascending*.

Crosby Hall

Crosby Hall, on the corner of Cheyne Walk and Danvers Street, was built in 1466 for city merchant Sir John Crosby. It features in Shakespeare's *Richard III*, who owned it in real life when he was Duke of Gloucester. It was originally situated in Bishopsgate in the City, but in 1910 it was transferred to Chelsea, brick by brick, to protect it from demolition. At one time, Crosby Hall was in fact owned by Sir Thomas More, the former owner of the gardens on which it was rebuilt. Today, it has been converted into a residential home.

C.R. ASHBEE

Nos 38 and 39 Cheyne Walk were designed by C.R. Ashbee, who was actively involved in the Arts and Crafts movement in the late nineteenth century. These are the only two of the original eight of his houses that remain, with No 38 built initially as a studio house for artist C.L. Christian. No 48 was the home of Mick Jagger and Marianne Faithfull from 1968. Artist William Holman Hunt lived at No 59 from 1850–53. No 72 was home to sculptor Jacob Epstein before the First World War, and architect C.R. Ashbee lived at No 74. Artist Charles Condor lived at No 91 in 1904 and author Elizabeth Gaskell was born at No 93 in 1810, where her mother died a week after the birth. Nos 91–94 Cheyne Walk were all built during the 1770s.

LINDSEY HOUSE

Lindsey House, dating from the seventeenth century, still sits along Cheyne Walk today. The house was built by Robert, Earl of Lindsey, in 1655 and by 1751 was the home of Count Zinzendorf from Saxony, who established a Moravian religious group here. The house was divided up into separate houses in 1775 and became 98–100 Cheyne Walk. There have been a number of famous residents at the house, including Sir Marc Isambard Brunel and his son Isambard Kingdom Brunel, from 1808–25.

Walter Greaves lived at No 104 from 1855–97, where his father owned a boat business. Poet Hillaire Belloc also lived at No 104 from 1901–05. Artist Philip Wilson Steer lived at No 109 from 1898 until his death in 1942, and artist J.M.W. Turner lived at No 119.

12 CHESHAM STREET

hesham Street was laid out for building during the 1830s, as part of the development by William Lowndes, on land that ran adjacent to the Westbourne River (now underground). The name Chesham originated from the family home of the Lowndes', in Chesham, Buckinghamshire. Nos 2–10 Chesham Street were completed during the mid 1830s, with residents that included a viscountess, a baronet and an earl. However, although featuring similar architectural features, No 12 was built almost 100 years after its taller neighbours.

No 12 Chesham Street was built around 1922 and first appeared in the 1923 London Directory as occupied by Mr and Mrs William Riley-Smith. William Riley-Smith later became High Sheriff of Yorkshire. He was an avid polo player and advocate for the game as a member of the County Polo Association Committee. The couple lived at No 12 until 1925, the year that Beryl Riley-Smith sat for a painting by the artist Alfred Munnings. Entitled, 'Snowflake', it depicts Beryl riding the horse Snowflake. The painting was sold at Christie's in 2002 for £1.5 million.

Joyce Carey

In around 1954, 12 Chesham Street became the home of Joyce Carey, actress and good friend of playwright Noel Coward. She was a celebrated English actress who appeared in Coward's films *In Which We Serve* (1942) and *Blithe Spirit* (1945); in many of his stage plays in both London and New York; and in such films as *Brief Encounter* (1945) and *The Way to the Stars* (1945). Joyce Carey often held parties in the house with Noel Coward and his inner circle of friends, and he affectionately nicknamed the house 'the baby grand'. Joyce continued to live at 12 Chesham Street until the late 1970s, while continuing to appear on stage and screen. She went on to appear in *The End of the Affair* (1955), *Libel* (1959) and was still acting at the age of 90, when she appeared in Michael Palin's *No 27*, in 1988.

Ordnance Survey map, 1869, showing early Chesham Street before No 12 was built.

CARLYLE MANSIONS

James Bond

Ian Fleming moved to 24 Carlyle Mansions in August 1950 and it was from here that he began the famous James Bond series of books, completing his first draft of *Casino Royale* in early 1952. Other notable authors at Carlyle Mansions have included Erskine Childers, Irish author of *The Riddle of the Sands* at No 10, and novelist and playwright Somerset Maugham, who briefly lived at No 27 in 1904.

Carlyle Mansions was constructed in 1886, after the building of Chelsea Embankment, by Messrs Sandon Brothers to the designs of Walter Seckham Witherington. The block was named after prominent Chelsea resident, Thomas Carlyle, and features ornate designs and picturesque detailing. It was built in the Queen Anne style with strong red brick and carvings in Portland stone and brick. Most notably it features ten stone relief panels on the western edge depicting birds and flowers, which the architectural and building journal *The Builder*, in 1886, claimed were based on scenes from Aesop's fables. When completed, Carlyle Mansions was described as having fireproofed floors, and the staircase featured 'a wrought-iron grille railing … and a passenger lift by the American Elevator Company had been fitted'.

Carlyle Mansions in the 1970s.

T.S. Eliot.

THE WRITERS' BLOCK

Carlyle Mansions has been popular with many illustrious residents, in particular writers, giving it the nickname of 'the writers' block'. It has been the home of Henry James, author of *Wings of a Dove* and *The Portrait of a Lady*, who lived at 21 Carlyle Mansions from January 1913 until his death in February 1916. The poet T.S. Eliot moved to 19 Carlyle Mansions in 1946, shortly after his Four Quartets was published. Eliot shared the flat with his editor, John Hayward, and during this time completed *Notes towards the Definition of Culture* (1948), and plays *The Cocktail Party* (1949) and *The Confidential Clerk* (1953). Eliot moved out in 1957 after marrying his secretary, Valerie Fletcher.

Other Notable Residents

Other residents have included composer Richard Addinsell, at No 1; actor Gordon Harker, at No 11; historian Arnold Toynbee; and local historian Reginald Blunt, at No 14. Continuing the long list of distinguished residents is political reformer Thomas Hare, during the 1890s; artist Mrs Florence Engelbach, at No 3; medical expert Richard Llewelyn, at No 14; and military heroes Brigadier Henry Hunter of the Queen's Royal Regiment and Major-General William Napier of the Royal Artillery. Lastly, John Singer Sargent often came to Carlyle Mansions when visiting his sisters, Emily and Violet.

Illustration from *The Builder*, 30 October 1885.

LITTLE SWARLING

Pilgrims Rest at Chapel

It is uncertain when the very first building appeared on this site, but it is believed that today's Little Swarling was the site of a chapel as early as 1190. This is only twenty years after the murder of Archbishop Thomas Becket in Canterbury Cathedral, who was killed on 29 December 1170. It is noteworthy that a chapel was constructed here within the early years of pilgrims flocking to Canterbury Cathedral. The chapel is believed to have been administered by the brethren of St John of Jerusalem.

ittle Swarling in Kent is a seventeenth-century timber-framed house surrounded by fields and sitting in the valley below Chatham Downs. It features exposed timber beams, original stone and brickwork, and weatherboarding on the north front. Little Swarling and Swarling Manor have many historic associations; it was at Swerdling Downs that the invading Romans met with the Britons when they came to England in 54 BC, and is believed to be the site of one of the first battles between the Romans and Britons. The next specific reference to Swerdling is in the ninth century, when the King of Mercia sold the manor to Vulshard, a priest belonging to the archbishop's monastery of Christ Church. By the time of the Norman Conquest, the manor of Swerdling was recorded in Domesday Book in 1086 as owned by the Archbishop of Canterbury, Lanfranc. By the end of the eleventh century the manor was in the hands of a prominent family, the Valoigns, who were described as being from 'time to time knights of the shire, and sheriffs of

Changes in Industry

Throughout the twentieth century the farm changed hands a number of times, while the business of farming and agriculture also saw great change across Britain. The hop farmers of Kent had seen much growth in the previous centuries, but with changes to mechanised farming things began to change and it was not the lucrative business it had once been.

Swarling Manor continued as one whole estate throughout the twentieth century, predominately under the ownership of the Collard family. However, by the 1960s the Collard family were selling parts of the farm and in 1967 Little Swarling was sold as a separate home, purchased by James Robert Neville Croft.

this county'. Waretius de Valoigns was recorded as one of the Kentish gentlemen who were at the siege of Acon in Palestine during the third crusade with Richard the Lionheart.

MEDIEVAL SWARLING

During the reign of Richard II in the fourteenth century, the manor of Swerdling was in the hands of Sir Nicholas Haut, and it passed through the Haut family until the time of Henry VII at the turn of the sixteenth century. By the seventeenth century the manor had passed to Edward Hadde Esq. of Canterbury, through his marriage with Margaret, daughter of Thomas Spilman. It was at this time that Little Swarling, known simply as a The Farmhouse or 'Swarling Farm', was first built.

Neighbouring property Swarling Manor, meanwhile, came into the ownership of William Hammond in 1747 and continued in the Hammond family through successive generations until the end of the nineteenth century. It was during the eighteenth and nineteenth centuries that the manor farmlands saw great success as a hop farm, like many farms across Kent. In fact, hop farming was the biggest industry in Kent during the nineteenth century.

THE FARMHOUSE & SWARLING MANOR

It is difficult to be certain who was living in Little Swarling from the time it was built, but by the 1840s the census records show that it was home to agricultural labourer William Stockbridge, his wife Hannah and their five children aged between 6 and 15. William and Hannah Stockbridge were still living in Little Swarling at the time of the 1861 census, by this time recorded as both 71 years old, but none of their children were recorded at this time.

Later census records, between 1871 and 1901, do not clearly identify Little Swarling, but it is clear that the house continued to be occupied by farm labourers. Meanwhile, the Hammond family were still recorded at Swarling Manor. Surviving property deeds from 1885 give further details of the ownership of Swarling Manor and, with it, Little Swarling. In 1898, after 150 years, Charles Hammond, descendant of William Hammond, conveyed the estate to Miss Emily Blake and Thomas Fitzroy Blake.

37 WAPPING WALL

Today

The hydraulic mains from Wapping once spread across London as far as Chelsea, Kensington and Camden. Yet during the twentieth century the use of electricity was becoming more popular and increasingly less expensive, making hydraulic power less viable. The extensive bomb damage in the city during the Second World War and the move of the docks to Tilbury further deprived the LHPC of business during the 1950s and '60s. The power station closed in June 1977 when the company was bought by a subsidiary of Cable & Wireless, which used the pipes as telecommunications ducts. When it closed, the LHPC was the last hydraulic power station in the world. In 2000–13 the former power station housed an artistic space, 'The Wapping Project', but it is now undergoing redevelopment.

This three-storey Victorian house is the former home of the station master for the London Hydraulic Power Company. It features a stepped gable with rounded top to the front, as well as an additional stepped gable to the side.

LONDON HYDRAULIC POWER COMPANY

The London Hydraulic power station was built along Wapping Wall in 1891 for the London Hydraulic Power Company (LHPC), the biggest hydraulic company in London, originally formed in 1883. The power station was responsible for driving the bascules (arms) on Tower Bridge, and the LHPC supplied power to drive the lifts in many buildings and hotels across London, including the Savoy. Numerous London theatres were also powered by the Wapping power station, including the Coliseum; Her Majesty's Theatre; the revolving stage at the Palladium; the safety curtains at the Drury Lane Theatre; and even the organ console lifts of the Leicester Square Theatre.

During the 1920s and '30s, at the height of the company's success, the LHPC supplied 8,000 machines with power and transported 33 million gallons of water a week through 186 miles of cast-iron pipes beneath central London.

STATION MASTERS

No 37 Wapping Wall was constructed in 1891, as the date plaque clearly shows, and the first recorded station master was Charles Loughborough. Loughborough was recorded in the 1901 census as a hydraulic engineer, aged 32, with his wife Laura, aged 31, and a housemaid, Ellen Oram, also aged 31. By 1905, the electoral register shows that 37 Wapping Wall had become the home of Thomas McCreath and his wife Annie. They lived in the house until the early 1920s, at which point it became the home of Charles Henry Tilling and his wife Louisa Ann.

In 1935 the station master Robert Stanley Lister lived in the house with his wife Emily. He remained station master for almost thirty years, handing the job over to Daniel Donnachie in the early 1960s. Donnachie was the last station master for the LHPC, living at No 37 with his wife Ann at the time the power station closed in 1977. Daniel and Ann continued to live at 37 Wapping Wall until the 1990s.

5 LISLE STREET

The name 'Lisle' originated from Viscount Lisle, son of the Earl of Leicester. It was the 2nd Earl of Leicester who built Leicester House in 1631, on the north side of today's Leicester Square. Grade II listed, No 5 Lisle Street is situated behind busy Leicester Square and is the sort of building that is often passed without much attention; on looking up, however, it certainly has a striking appearance. The ornate building was designed by Frank T. Verity and completed for Treadwell and Martin in 1897. The house was designed in a Franco-Flemish renaissance style and includes many ornate architectural features, including the distinct six-step gable with side scrolls and obelisk finial on the peak.

COMPOSERS, HOSPITALS & ACTORS

Once completed, the building became the home of Pathé of France Ltd and was used for residential and business purposes. During the 1900s it was the home of songwriter and composer James William Tate, who remained until 1922. He composed and performed in a number of revues and pantomimes during the early twentieth century and was Musical Director at Wyndham's Theatre. He wrote a number of popular shows, including *The Maid of the Mountains* (1916) and *Aladdin* (1920).

In 1934–35 No 5 Lisle Street became the home of St John's Hospital for Diseases of the Skin, which had formerly been at No 45 and also No 49 Leicester Square. It was officially opened in January 1936 and remained for the next fifty-three years, closing in 1989. After the closing of St John's Hospital, 5 Lisle Street was renovated back to residential and commercial use, while maintaining its ornate decorative facade. Since that time, one of the apartments has been the home of Scottish actor Alan Cumming, who has appeared on stage and screen in both the UK and America, including *Golden Eye*, *X-Men 2* and *The Good Wife*.

Frank T. Verity, Theatre Architect

Frank T. Verity was a prominent architect who was particularly noted for his work on theatres and cinemas, including Scala Theatre in Bloomsbury; a theatre for Lillie Langtry; and his Shepherd's Bush Pavilion cinema, which won the Royal Institute of British Architects bronze medal in 1930. Verity was also surveyor of theatres to Lord Chamberlain in 1891–1900 and along with his business partner, Samuel Beverley, was European advisor to Paramount and the Union Cinema Company.

MICKLEGATE

Prosperous & Fashionable York

It was in the eighteenth century, when York was becoming a vibrant and prosperous town, that new wealthy merchants and gentry built town houses along Micklegate. Along with the new houses, many of the earlier buildings were re-fronted in the latest Georgian style. During this period, York became the centre of fashionable society in the north and attracted many visitors for the social season, with balls, entertainment and horse racing, and many aspiring to live in Micklegate.

Micklegate House and Bathurst House in the early 1900s.

Micklegate is one of York's most prominent streets. Architectural historian Nikolaus Pevsner described it as 'without any doubt the most architecturally rewarding street in York'. Micklegate means literally 'Great Street' and for most of its history it has lived up to its name. It is known to have run this course since Anglo-Saxon times and was the main road running into York from London and the south.

MEDIEVAL MICKLEGATE

Micklegate Bar is the southern gateway into the city of York that has stood on this site for over 800 years. It was first recorded in the twelfth century, with the central archway constructed during the Norman period, although it was rebuilt in the late 1100s. In the early fourteenth century the three-storey building was added, which allowed for the addition of a portcullis. The facade that we see today is predominately from the fourteenth century, but of course since that time it has been altered and restored many times. The stone figures on the top of the bar date from the seventeenth century.

This vital road route meant that Micklegate was populated by wealthy merchants throughout the Middle Ages. The street still features several late medieval timber-framed houses, most particularly near Trinity Lane and

Priory Street towards Micklegate Bar. Nos 85–89 make up a range of tim-ber-framed houses with double-jettied fronts. Believed to be constructed in the fifteenth century, the prominent 'black and white' houses have been altered many times over the last 500 years. However, all three houses still retain original timber beams and detailing.

Blossom Street in front of Micklegate Bar c.1890.

JOHN CARR OF YORK

There are many lovely examples of surviving Georgian town houses along Micklegate, but in particular, there are three believed to have been designed by renowned York architect, John Carr, who was responsible for many of York's prominent Georgian buildings. In fact, he was so renowned in the city that he is often simply described as 'Carr of York'. He was responsible for the interiors of Fairfax House and the designs for the County Court House, along with many private homes along Bootham and Micklegate. He was highly favoured by many of the gentry. He was born the son of a master mason and rose to become very wealthy. He held a number of prominent local positions, including that of Lord Mayor twice.

MICKLEGATE HOUSE

Micklegate House, Nos 88–90 Micklegate, is the largest and most promi-nent of the Georgian town houses along Micklegate. It has been attributed to John Carr and was built for John Bouchier of Beningbrough in 1752. Like many of Carr's York houses, it was constructed with red brick and

Bathurst House

Many houses along Micklegate retain their original Georgian features, including No 86 Micklegate, Bathurst House, built for Charles Bathurst and completed in around 1720. The heads of the drainpipes display the initials of Charles and his wife Frances, and the family crest can be seen on the brackets of the downfall pipes. Charles and Frances' son, also named Charles, went on to become High Sheriff of Yorkshire.

Micklegate remained the most prominent street address during the eighteenth century, but by the nineteenth century, and due to the expansion of the city, many wealthy families began to move out into the 'suburbs'. Micklegate then transformed once again and, while still continuing to be a good address, became occupied by many more businesses and merchants.

stone detailing. It follows the usual style of symmetrical Georgian design, although the door to the east, which appears out of place, is original. By the turn of the nineteenth century, the house had been purchased by Joshua Crompton, in whose family it remained until 1896. It was then converted into business premises and some internal features were removed, including the wood panelling and the fireplace from the best bedroom, which are now in the Treasurer's House. Despite these changes, the house contains a number of original features.

NOS 53–55 MICKLEGATE

Completed in 1755, these two houses were originally one (No 55), and were designed by John Carr for Paul Beilby-Thompson of Escrick, second husband of Lady Dawes. Carr also later designed Escrick Hall for Beilby-Thompson in 1763–65. In the early nineteenth century, No 55 was the home of Countess of Conyngham, widow of the 1st Earl, until 1806. When first completed, the house had a symmetrical front elevation, but by 1813 it had been divided into two to become Nos 53 and 55. At this time, the central Doric doorway was doubled and the original main staircase became part of No 53.

GARFORTH HOUSE

Garforth House, No 54 Micklegate, is also believed to be the work of John Carr and was built in 1757 for the Garforth family of Wiganthorpe. From the time of its construction, the house was the home of Reverend Edmund Garforth and his wife Elizabeth. It later passed to their son, William, who was High Sheriff of Yorkshire in 1815; however, he passed away without an heir and the house was sold. Throughout the nineteenth century it continued as the home of many notable residents, including Barnard Hague and Walter Fawkes of Farnley Hall. The house has a number of original features, including the staircase, with a Corinthian Venetian window in an arched recess; plasterwork ceilings with rococo decoration; and a number of fireplace surrounds. The front of the house is built with red brick and stone detailing, and features the initials of Edmund and Elizabeth Garforth, the date '1757' and the Garforth crest on the lead rainwater pipe.

WESTLANDS FARM

Westlands Farm in West Sussex is believed to be located on the site of a lost medieval village – East Itchenor. The area of Chichester Harbour, and in particular West Itchenor, Birdham and the former East Itchenor, can be traced back to the time of the Romans when it was used as a landing place for travellers heading to Chichester. However, the first occupation of the area was during the Anglo-Saxon period, in the seventh century, when it was occupied by Icca, the son of the ruling Saxon Cissa (who was in the former Roman encampment at Chichester). The peninsula became known as 'Iccen Ora' or 'Icca's landing place', which over time became Itchenor. By the time Domesday Book was recorded in 1086, Itchenor and Birdham were under the lordship of Earl Roger and East Itchenor was recorded with three families. East Itchenor was originally part of the Priory of Boxgrove, and by the thirteenth century both Birdham and East Itchenor had churches.

Census Data

William Gibbs and his family continued as leaseholders of Westlands and the neighbouring land into the 1850s. However, we know from the census returns and Sussex directories that the house was in fact tenanted to agricultural labourers. The 1841 census reveals that the house was shared by William French, agricultural labourer, aged 45, and his wife Annie, with John Hebberden, also an agricultural labourer, aged 55, and his wife Lydia. The 1851 census shows that the farmhouse was occupied by other members of the French family; in one part of the house was William, a labourer, with his wife Elizabeth and their five children (under the age of 9), and James French, agricultural labourer, only 23, with his wife Ruth.

PLAGUE HITS SMALL VILLAGE

It is during the medieval period that East Itchenor's history took a turn. Records show that in 1332 the manor of East Itchenor was tenanted to William de Hunston, while the church and attached lands were still held by Boxgrove Priory. When the Black Death came to England in 1348, East Itchenor was badly affected, although we know that the parish survived until the 1440s, when it was united to Birdham, almost 100 years after the plague had swept across England. It may appear to be a long time, but it is believed the after-effects of the plague ultimately caused the demise of the village. After 1441 the church at East Itchenor became a chapel of ease. The manor of East Itchenor continued through the hands of wealthy owners, but it is clear that there were no longer any people living in a village, but rather the area was relegated to farming land as part of the manor and church lands. Surviving documents give a picture of the history of East Itchenor, but the exact location of the village is uncertain.

At the time of Henry VIII's Dissolution of the Monasteries, the land was acquired by the Crown and in 1557 was granted to Sir Richard Sackville, Under-Treasurer of the Exchequer and Chancellor of the Court of Augmentations. After only seven years Sackville transferred the estate to the Dean and Chapter of Chichester.

WILLIAM GIBBS

Westlands farmhouse was built in the early years of the nineteenth century, with the first reference found in the 1828 land tax records. It records the house and land leased from the Dean and Chapter of Chichester by a Mr William Gibbs, who owned several other sections of old East Itchenor, including part of the old manor. The tithe documents also record Gibbs occupying large parts of the area, amounting to hundreds of acres.

FOR SALE

In 1854 we find the house and farm on the market, promoted as 'the very compact and fertile farm … comprising a double tenanted brick built and thatched cottage, having 4 rooms to each tenement, with detached wash-house, jointly used'. The property details from 1854 also show that it was still owned by the Dean and Chapter of Chichester and the leasehold had passed to William Gibbs' sons, Wyatt, aged 24, and Edward, aged 19.

It appears that Westlands was purchased by the executors of Stephen Farndell Esq. of Chichester, but not much changed at the farmhouse because it continued to be rented by agricultural labourers. The 1861 census records that one part of the house was occupied by James Peters, agricultural labourer, aged 72, with his 70-year-old wife Rebecca. The other part of the house was occupied by labourer James Bowers, aged 33, and his wife Anne and their four children.

THE BOUGHTON FAMILY

The farmhouse continued to be the home of agricultural labourers through to the late nineteenth century, while the leasehold continued in the hands of the executors of Stephen Farndell. However, by the 1890s Westlands had become the home of the Boughton family, who established a family-run farm. The 1901 census shows that the farmhouse had become one single home, with head of the house Henry Thomas Boughton as 'farmer', 39 years old, with his wife Fanny, 38 years old, and their six children between the ages of 6 and 17.

THE MASON FAMILY

In 1935 things began to change, with the house leased to different families, and during the war Mr Antony Mason, who resided at nearby Itchenor House, was asked by the War Office to run the farms attached to his house. In 1945 he permanently moved to Westlands Farm, where his family continued to live into the twenty-first century.

Boughton Brothers

The Boughton family continued to farm at Westlands during the early twentieth century, adding further farm buildings, while the Ecclesiastical Commissioners were lords of the manor and had taken over the leasehold. Even in the twentieth century Westlands Farm was rarely named in records and was simply known for the 'Boughton Brothers'. During the 1920s and '30s the farm was run by three brothers, Henry Thomas (Jnr – known as Harry), Frank and Frederick Boughton.

5 HOLLY VILLAGE

Famous Friends

Angela became good friends with Charles Dickens, who assisted in her philanthropic endeavours and was said to have planned Holly Village with her. She was also a close friend of the Duke of Wellington, even to the point of possible marriage. In 1871 she was created Baroness Burdett-Coutts of Highgate and Brookfield, and was given the freedom of the City of London in 1872. Edward VII said of her that, 'after my mother [Queen Victoria, she is] the most remarkable woman in the country'.

Angela Burdett-Coutts.

Grade II* listed Holly Village in Highgate, London, is a unique group of Victorian cottages created by Baroness Angela Burdett-Coutts. Angela Burdett was the daughter of Sir Francis Burdett and the granddaughter of Thomas Coutts of Coutts bank. With these connections she grew up with diverse associations, such as politicians like William Gladstone and Benjamin Disraeli, and European royalty and nobility, including the French royal family. In 1837, at the age of 23, Angela Burdett inherited a large portion of the Coutts estate, making her one of the wealthiest women in Britain.

Along with being vastly wealthy and having some of the most illustrious connections in Britain, Angela Burdett-Coutts was also extremely generous, and gave large sums of money to charitable causes. Her generosity led to schemes for improvement in sanitation in London slums; Ragged Schools (those for poor and neglected children); homes for prostitutes and homeless women; and she donated huge sums for the building of new churches. She was also involved in the establishment of the NSPCC; the RSPCA; and schemes in Ireland and Scotland, including the token statue of Greyfriars Bobby in Edinburgh.

UNIQUE DESIGNS

There have been many conflicting theories as to the motivation behind the building of Holly Village, the most popular being that the homes were designed for Angela's former estate workers or retired Coutts bank employees. However, the evidence shows that even if this was her initial intention,

the cottages were actually first home to those from the professional middle classes.

Holly Village is unique because of its ornate gothic architecture, which is characterised by highly decorative adornments. Italian craftsmen were even hired specifically for the elaborate wood-carvings. The houses were completed in 1865 by Henry Darbishire, who also produced a number of designs for another Victorian philanthropist, George Peabody.

NO 5 HOLLY VILLAGE

The ornate architectural features of No 5 Holly Village include a projecting medieval-style bay window, with a band of elaborate brickwork along the first floor. The second-floor windows have decorative mouldings and carved bargeboards with finials, and the house also features a central ornate brick chimney.

In 1866, the first occupant at No 5 was Mr Albert Prebble, but by 1868 it had become the home of George Welsh, who was recorded in the 1871 census as a collector for the New River Company. Welsh lived in the cottage with his wife, Elizabeth, and their 9-month-old baby Florence, along with one domestic servant, 15-year-old Mary Collins. By the 1890s No 5 was the home of Louisa Witherby, 'living on her own means' with her two children, Evelyn, aged 21, working as a school governess, and Sydney, aged 18 and working as an accountant's clerk.

By the turn of the twentieth century, 5 Holly Village was the residence of William Carter, a 29-year-old bank clerk. He was living in the house until around 1909–10 with his wife, Marion, their two children, as well as his brother Gerald, also a bank clerk, and one servant, 19-year-old Mary Entwistle. The 1911–12 electoral register reveals No 5 was then occupied by Miss Lucy Alexander, along with a lodger occupying 'one room, first floor, furnished', paying a yearly rent of £12 10s. Just before the start of the First World War, No 5 became the home of Ernest George Buckeridge and his wife Gertrude. Ernest fought on the battlefields of the war with the Honourable Artillery Company, returning to his home at 5 Holly Village in 1918.

Distinct Differences

The twelve cottages that make up Holly Village were built with colour stock brick and stone dressings. The entrance gate features a gabled archway with two stone female statues, one holding a lamb, which is said to represent Baroness Burdett-Coutts, and the other holding a dove. Each home within Holly Village may look similar, but they all have distinct characteristics, including variations of ornate wooden turrets and stone gargoyles. When built, the homes included a unique cleaning system – a dust-shoot below the floor, which took dust directly into the cellar.

47 ALBEMARLE STREET

No 47 Albemarle Street, situated a short distance from Piccadilly in Mayfair, was first constructed in the early years of the eighteenth century. The first occupant moved in during 1715, but a mortgage for both Nos 46 and 47 Albemarle Street, dated 1 September 1716, reveals it became the London residence of Sir John Hales of Kent.

ANCIENT AND NOBLE OWNERS

Sir John Hales was from an ancient family, dating back to the fourteenth century, which included Sir Edward Hales, his grandfather, who attempted to save King Charles I when he was imprisoned on the Isle of Wight in 1648, and his father 'much in favour with King Charles II', who held a number of high-profile positions in the royal court. The house continued in the hands of the Hales family, but by the 1740s it began to be occupied by tenants, and in 1745 it became the home of Mary Sophia Charlotte Howe, Viscountess Howe. Lady Howe was the daughter of Baron von Kielmansegg and Charlotte Sophia von Platen-Hallermund, Countess of Darlington, but it is also believed she could have been the illegitimate daughter of King George I.

During the remaining years of the eighteenth century, No 47 Albemarle Street continued to be the home of several aristocrats and gentry, including Lady Exeter, only daughter and heiress of the Honourable Horatio Townshend, MP and Director of the Bank of England, as well as Sir Thomas Mostyn and Sir Edward Hales, 5th Baronet, grandson of Sir John Hales.

However, by the beginning of the nineteenth century, the ownership passed to John Riley, who continued to rent it to a succession of different tenants. In 1800, No 47 Albemarle Street became the home of John Adey Repton, the son of renowned landscape designer Humphry Repton.

CHANGING FACES

While John Nash's apprentice, John Adey Repton, was taking rooms at the house, the lower floor of No 47 Albemarle Street was transformed into the original French and English Circulating Library, run by 'Earle and Hemet', who offered books for loan for a small fee. However, by 1816, the house was taken by the newly established Royal Naval Institution. They also did not stay long and by 1820 the

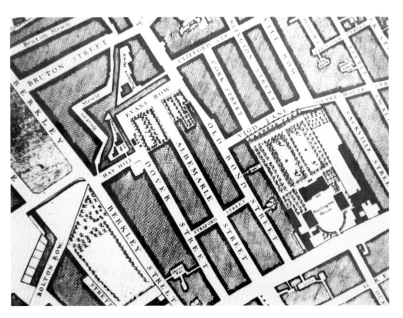

ohn Rocque map, 1746

Repton and Nash, Architects

Perhaps much overshadowed by his famous father, John Adey Repton was a noted architect and antiquarian in his own right, and significantly was completely deaf from infancy. John moved to London to be apprenticed to celebrated architect John Nash, who was already working with his father, but a short time later a disagreement arose, when Humphry Repton accused Nash of denying his son credit for his work on several projects. The collaboration dissolved and John Repton went to work with his father.

John Adey Repton, 1800

ground floor had changed into business premises for tailors George and Benjamin Robertson.

Meanwhile, the upper floors of the house continued to be the home of a range of different tenants, including, in 1825, Algernon Percy, 4th Duke of Northumberland, who at this time was known as Lord Prudhoe. He first served in the navy as a young man, but later acquired degrees from both Oxford and Cambridge universities and became a notable man of intellectual interests, with connections to a long list of institutions, including The Royal Society, The Royal Astronomical Society, The Royal Geographical Society and the Society of Antiquaries. In 1842 he married Lady Eleanor Grosvenor, daughter of Richard Grosvenor, 2nd Marquess of Westminster, and he later became a privy councillor, and in 1853 was made a Knight of the Garter.

NINETEENTH CENTURY

Throughout the early nineteenth century, the house continued as the home of different tenants, including James Graham, 4th Duke of Montrose, MP, who later held several high-profile positions, including Chancellor of the Duchy of Lancaster; George Vivian, esquire, painter, who was one of the competition commissioners responsible for choosing Charles Barry as architect for the new Houses of Parliament in 1835; and Sir William Russell, who rose through the ranks of the army, but later retired as lieutenant-colonel, and MP for Norwich.

Despite this long list of notable residents, newspaper reports in 1844 reveal the house was also connected to some disreputable events. On the morning of 8 May, police raided several properties in the area, including Nos 46 and 47 Albemarle Street, on suspicions they were being run as illegal gambling houses. The reports detail the events, including the examination of prisoners the following day and details of the raid at No 47, believed to be known as the 'New Berkeley', but no evidence of gambling was found. However, money and gambling material was uncovered at neighbouring No 46, known as the 'Old Berkeley'.

By the 1880s, the Robertson tailoring business had been acquired by John Goodman, and in 1882, part of the house became St George's Chess Club, and became the location for several high-profile chess matches, including the annual Oxford and Cambridge chess match.

A NARROW ESCAPE

During the Second World War, the house was under serious threat from bombing and only just escaped on two separate occasions, when high-explosive bombs fell on neighbouring Nos 45 and 46 Albemarle Street in September and November 1940. Both houses were later demolished (and were replaced with a building by Ernö Goldfinger in 1955). After the Second World War, rate books reveal that No 47 Albemarle Street was owned by Dame Evelyn E.M. Fox, who worked tirelessly for the education and treatment of the mentally disabled. She was the first secretary of the Child Guidance Council, which later became part of the National Association for Mental Health (and today forms part of the charity, Mind) and was appointed DBE in 1947.

HOLTOM HOUSE

Holtom House is situated in a small Cotswold village in Gloucestershire, and although it appears to be a large Georgian house, the earliest part dates back to the time of Elizabeth I in the sixteenth century. Records reveal the first part of the building was constructed in around 1586, and by 1588 the house and surrounding land was part of a grant by the bishops of Worcester to Queen Elizabeth I, when it was occupied by the Joyce family. Elizabeth I did not keep the property long as she granted it to her personal physician, Dr Roger (Roderigo) Lopez, who in turn sold it on to others.

Famous Connections

John Wheatcroft turns up in several records at this time, particularly in relation to some very famous historical names. Details are revealed that in September 1789, John Wheatcroft became good friends with the future President of the United States of America, Thomas Jefferson. At this time, Jefferson was heading back to America with his family after almost five years as Minister to France. The references in diaries and letters reveal the Jefferson family spent time with the Wheatcroft family in Le Havre before their departure, and Wheatcroft and Jefferson continued to correspond after the Jeffersons had returned to America.

John Wheatcroft was linked with another famous name at this time, when, in 1794, he rented rooms and became friends with the author Mary Wollstonecraft. When Mary arrived in Le Havre she was pregnant with the child of Gilbert Imlay, but it was during this time she completed, *An Historical and Moral View of the Origin and Progress of the French Revolution*. Several records reveal John Wheatcroft not only assisted her with accommodation, but he was even a witness to the birth of Fanny Imlay on 14 May 1794. He continued to assist Mary Wollstonecraft, even after her departure from Le Havre, when he acted on her behalf in several areas of business.

FROM THE JOYCES TO THE WHEATCROFTS

Throughout the remainder of the sixteenth, seventeenth and into the eighteenth century, parish registers, deeds and estate records reveal Holtom House (although not named this at the time) continued to be occupied by generations of the Joyce family. However, after almost 200 years of being with them, the house passed to the Wheatcroft family during the 1750s. In 1764 the house became the home of John Wheatcroft and it was after this time that the small Elizabethan farmhouse was extended to create a large Georgian country house. By the time of the Enclosure map, in 1773, the house clearly appears as a large gentleman's residence. But, within a few years, John Wheatcroft was leasing the house and land, while he moved to Le Havre in France.

Several sources reveal John Wheatcroft continued to rent the house and land during the 1780s, at which time he was establishing a prosperous business in Le Havre. This was an interesting time to be in France, after the outbreak of the French Revolution in 1789, but the port town of Le Havre continued to thrive.

BECOMING HOLTOM HOUSE

Meanwhile, back at Holtom House, records show that in 1789 it was acquired by farmer Thomas Roberts and continued in the hands of the Roberts family for three generations. By the 1880s, the house and land were held by Joseph Roberts and the house had been named 'The Shrubbery'. However, by 1893 Joseph Roberts had died and the house and farm were for sale, described as '… very valuable and commodious stone-built and slated … villa residence, known as The Shrubbery'. It was a few years later that the house became the home of Dennis and Eliza Holtom, for whom the name 'Holtom House' first originated. The Holtoms continued at the house throughout the early twentieth century, but by 1936 it was again on the market.

Holtom House, 1936

The remaining years of the twentieth century saw several residents come and go from the house, including Lieutenant-Colonel Douglas 'Duggie' Norman Stewart, who served with the Royal Scots Greys and during the Second World War was awarded a DSO and a Military Cross. On top of his heroic record with the army, he went on take part in the British eventing team at the 1948 and 1952 Olympic Games. In 1952, he was part of the show-jumping team who won Britain's only gold medal of the games. A record also reveals that Colonel Stewart practised his show jumping in the gardens of Holtom House. The house was also home to Mary Grey, who had joined the Women's Voluntary Services in 1938, and, for her services throughout the Second World War and afterwards, was appointed CBE in 1946.

Shakespearean Inspiration

Although obtaining considerable status and wealth, Lopez found himself embroiled in the dangerous power struggles of the Elizabethan court and in 1594 was accused of trying to poison the queen. Accused by Robert Devereux, 2nd Earl of Essex, Lopez was arrested, tortured on the rack and found guilty. He was hanged, drawn and quartered at Tyburn gallows in London on 7 June 1594. However, the drama of Lopez's trial and execution caused such a stir it was believed to be the inspiration for the character of Shylock in Shakespeare's *The Merchant of Venice*.

SHURDINGTON COURT

Shurdington Court, near Cheltenham, was constructed during the late seventeenth century, with the first owner and occupant, Anthony Edwards, moving in during the late 1680s or early 1690s. The Edwards family had been resident in the area of Shurdington from the sixteenth century, becoming a prominent family of yeoman farmers throughout the area. The house passed to William Edwards, the son of Anthony and his wife Mary, who was recorded at the house with his wife Anne by the 1730s. William, who by this time had risen to become a gentleman, and Anne lived at the house throughout the mid 1700s, where they had two daughters, Mary and Anne.

In 1762, Mary Edwards made a very fortunate alliance and married prominent landowner, Robert Lawrence, whose family had owned large portions of surrounding land since the sixteenth century. At the marriage between Robert and Mary Edwards, the house, now known as Shurdington Court, passed into the hands of the Lawrence family. After the marriage,

Name	Relation	Condition	Age	Occupation	Where born
Henry Theyer	Head	Mar	47	Farmer 400 acres employing	Gloucestershire Badgeworth
Elvira D°	Wife	Mar	40	15 men 3 women and 3 boys	D° Huccliceote
Susan D°	Daur		12	Scholar	D° Badgeworth
Mary D°	Daur		11	Scholar	D° D°
Ann D°	Daur		9	Scholar	D° D°
Helen D°	Daur		5	Scholar	D° D°
Edith D°	Daur		3		D° D°
Elizabeth	Daur		1		D° D°
Adelaide Lewis	Governess	Unm	26	Governess	Gloucestershire Cheltenham
Louisa Simpson	Serv	Unm	21	Housemaid Domestic Serv	D° Sandhurst
Helen Dalland	Serv	Unm	15	Nurse maid Domestic	D° Churchdown
Cornelius Green	Serv	Unm	19	Farm Servant Indoor	D° Newent

Census showing the Theyer family, 1871

Mary's father, William Edwards, continued at the house until his death in September 1774, after which time the Lawrences retained ownership but leased it out to tenants.

LASTING MARKS

Having been occupied by several farmers during the late eighteenth and early nineteenth century, land tax records reveal that in 1808 the house became the home of farmer John Theyer. It later passed to Daniel and Elizabeth Theyer, and by the 1850s, it was in the hands of their son, Henry Theyer, and his wife Elvira, along with a growing family. Henry and Elvira continued at the house for many years, and it was during this time that a unique memorial of the Theyer family was etched – still to be discovered on the first-floor windows. These retain scratches made by the Theyer children, including 'Edith' and 'Lilly' [for Elizabeth], as well as the name 'Theyer'. The Theyer family left the house and farm in 1883, at which time it became the home of another farming family, the Sealeys, who continued at the house into the early years of the twentieth century.

THE PALMER FAMILY

During the 1920s several alterations were made to the house, as it changed from a large farmhouse to a gentleman's residence. It was officially named Shurdington Court in 1923, and by 1924 it had been acquired by Frederick and Mabel Palmer. Frederick Palmer was the son of Sir Alfred Molyneux Palmer, 3rd Baronet of Darlington and grandson of Sir Charles Mark Palmer, 1st Baronet, who established Palmer's Shipbuilding & Iron Company at Tyneside in 1852. His grandfather was also MP for Durham and later Jarrow during the late nineteenth and early twentieth centuries, and held several other high-profile positions, including Mayor of Jarrow. However, Frederick did not continue in the footsteps of his father and grandfather, but rather pursued a literary career. He worked as a journalist, poet and playwright, and published under the non-de-plume of 'Stirrup Cup'. However, in 1931, at only 46 years old, Frederick died in a car accident, leaving his 16-year-old son Anthony as heir to the baronetcy, to which he succeeded in 1935 at the death of his grandfather.

In September 1939, Sir Anthony Palmer married Henriette Alice Cadogan, daughter of Commander Francis Charles Cadogan of the Royal Navy.

After the war, war widow Lady Henriette Palmer, and her two children, continued at Shurdington Court with her mother-in-law, Mrs Mabel

Sir Anthony Palmer

Almost immediately after his marriage, Sir Anthony Palmer took an active role at the start of the Second World War, serving with the Royal Artillery; he was in the evacuation of Dunkirk in May 1940, and it is revealed through later records that he, as acting major, went on to serve with the Special Operations Executive (SOE), a special unit created by Winston Churchill to assist resistance forces in occupied territories.

Sir Anthony was deployed to Lebanon and Syria to lead the first mission with the Palmach (the underground army of the Jewish community) against Vichy France forces in Operation Boatswain. However, the operation, whose aim was to destroy oil refineries in Tripoli, was a failure, and Palmer was reported missing in May 1941. Still today there are questions around what happened to Palmer and the twenty-three Palmach commandos, with stories of the boats sinking and some of the men being taken prisoner. After a long wait of over two years, Sir Anthony's family were informed in October 1943 that he had in fact died in May 1941. Major Sir Anthony Palmer is commemorated on the Brookwood Memorial at Brookwood Cemetery in Surrey, and also commemorated on a family gravestone at St Paul's in Shurdington.

Above: Lady Palmer remarries, *The Tatler*, 4 March 1953

Below: Scratching in window by Lilly Theyer,, c. mid nineteenth century

Palmer. However, in 1949 Lady Palmer was appointed lady-in-waiting to the young Princess Elizabeth, future Queen Elizabeth II. Lady Palmer continued serving as lady-in-waiting to Princess Elizabeth during the early 1950s and after she became queen in 1952. In 1953, Lady Palmer remarried, to Alexander Abel-Smith, and the queen and the Duke of Edinburgh attended the wedding at Queen's Chapel at St James's, as did Mrs Palmer of Shurdington Court.

Mrs Mabel Palmer continued at Shurdington Court for many more years, and only sold the house in 1962, when it was described as 'A fine detached double-fronted 17th century stone-built residence …' The house had several owners during the latter years of the twentieth century and was acquired by the current owners in 1993.

Further Reading List

Along with the primary sources described in the Introduction, there are many books that have been useful in my research.

Below is a selected reading list if you wish to explore the history of buildings or your local area.

How to Research the History of Houses

Barratt, N., *Tracing the History of Your House* (The National Archives: Kew, 2006)

Blanchard, G., *Tracing Your House History: A Guide for Family Historians* (Pen & Sword: Barnsley, 2017)

Brooks, P., *How to Research Your House: Every home tells a story* (How To Books Ltd: Oxford, 2007)

Style, C. & Style, O., *House Histories for Beginners* (Phillimore: Andover, 2006)

Thom, S., *Researching London's houses* (Phillimore: London, 2005)

House Stories

Bullman, J., Hegarty, N., and Hill, B., *The Secret History of Our Streets: A Story of London* (BBC Books: London, 2013)

Hutchinson, M., *Number 57: The History of a House* (Headline Book Publishing: London, 2003)

Myerson, J., *Home* (Harper Perennial: London, 2004)

Tindall, G., *The House by the Thames* (Random House: London, 2007)

——, *Three Houses, Many Lives* (Random House: London, 2012)

Architecture

Arnold, D. (ed.), *The Georgian Villa* (Alan Sutton: Stroud, 1996)

——, *The Georgian Country House* (Alan Sutton: Stroud, 1998)

Aslet, C., *The English House: The Story of a Nation at Home* (Bloomsbury: London, 2008)

Ayres, J., *Building the Georgian City* (Yale University Press: New Haven and London, 1998)

Binney, M., *Town Houses* (Mitchell Beazley: London, 1998)

Brunskill, R.W., *Illustrated Handbook of Vernacular Architecture* (Faber: London, 2000)

Bryson, B., *At Home: A Short History of Private Life* (Doubleday: London, 2010)

Cave, L.F., *The Smaller English House: Its History and Development* (Robert Hale: London, 1985)

Colvin, H., *A Biographical Dictionary of British Architects, 1600–1840* (Yale University Press: New Haven, 2007)

Cruickshank, D. & Wyld, P., *Georgian Town Houses and Their Details* (Butterworth Architecture: Oxford, 1990)

Cunnington, P., *How Old is Your House?* (Marston House: Yeovil, 2002)

Flander, J., *The Victorian House* (Harper Perennial: London, 2004)

Gomme, A. & Maquire, A., *Design and Plan in the Country House: From Castle Donjons to Palladian Boxes* (Yale University Press: New Haven and London, 2008)

Gray, E., *The British House: A Concise Architectural History* (Barrie & Jenkins: London, 1994)

Highmore, B., *The Great Indoors: At Home in the Modern British House* (Profile Books: London, 2014)

Hole, C., *English Home Life 1500–1800* (B.T. Batsford: London, 1947)

Laws, A., *Understanding Small Period Houses* (Crowood: Ramsbury, 2003)

Lawrence, R.R., *The Book of the Edwardian and Interwar House* (Aurum Press: London, 2009)

Lewis, P., *Everyman's Castle* (Francis Lincoln: London, 2014)

Muthesius, S., *The English Terraced House* (Yale University Press: New Haven and London, 1982)

Pevsner, N. et al., *The Buildings of England* (Penguin and Yale University Press: London, 1951)

Quiney, A., *House and Home: A History of the Small English House* (BBC: London, 1986)

Upton, C., *Living Back-to-Back* (Phillimore: Chichester, 2005)

Wood, M., *The English Medieval House* (Studio Editions: London, 1994)

Woodward, C., *A Guide to the Architecture of London* (Weidenfeld & Nicolson: London, 1992)

Worsley, L., *If Walls Could Talk: An Intimate History of the Home* (Faber and Faber: London, 2011)

England's Living History series, including *The Edwardian House Explained* and *Georgian & Regency Houses Explained*, both by Trevor Yorke (Countryside Books: Newbury)

Further Sources

The Survey of London (published for a selection of boroughs from 1894)

Victoria County Histories (published for counties across the country from 1899)

Listed Building descriptions for listed buildings – Historic England

County and Local Borough Conservation area audits

Oxford Dictionary of National Biography (Oxford University Press: Oxford, 2004)

Burke's Peerage and Gentry (Published since 1826)

Who's Who (published since 1849)

LONDON

Barker, F. & Jackson, P., *London: 2000 years of a city and its people* (Macmillan: London, 1974)

Bebbington, G., *Street Names of London* (B.T. Batsford Ltd: London, 1988)

Cameron, D.K., *London's Pleasure: From Restoration to Regency* (The History Press: Stroud, 2001)

Cruickshank, D. & Burton, N., *Life in the Georgian City* (Penguin: London, 1990)

Inwood, S., *City of Cities: The Birth of Modern London* (Macmillan: London, 2005)

London County Council, *LCC List of the Streets and Places within the Administrative County of London* (London County Council: London, 1929 and 1955)

Lysons, D., *The Environs of London, being an Historical Account of the Towns, Villages and Hamlets within twelve miles of that Capital* (London, 1792)

Olson, D.J., *The Growth of Victorian London* (Holmes & Meier: London, 1976)

Porter, R., *London: A Social History* (Penguin: London, 2000)

Richardson, A.E. & Gill, C.L., *London Houses from 1660 to 1820* (Charles Scribners & Sons: London, 1911)

Rosen, B. & Zuckerman, W., *The Mews of London* (Magnolia: London, 1982)

Stamp, G. & Amery, C., *Victorian Buildings of London: 1837–1887* (Architectural Press: London, 1980)

Summerson, J., *Georgian London* (Yale University Press: New Haven and London, 2003)

Thorold, P., *The London Rich* (Penguin: London, 2000)

Walford, E. & Thornbury, W., *Old and New London* (Cassell & Company Ltd: London, 1881)

Weightman, G. & Humphries, S., *The Making of Modern London* (Ebury Press: London, 2007)

Weinreb, B. & Hibbert, C., *The London Encyclopaedia* (Macmillan: London, 2010)

White, J., *London in the Nineteenth Century* (Random House: London, 2007)

Bankside & Spitalfields

Bennett, J.G., *E1: A Journey through Whitechapel and Spitalfields* (Five Leaves Publications: London, 2009)

Besant, W., *South London* (Chatto and Windus: London, 1901)

Constable, J., *Secret Bankside: Walks in the Outlaw Borough* (Oberon Books: London, 2007)

Cox, M., *Life and Death in Spitalfields 1700–1850* (Council for British Archaeology: London, 1996)

Girouard, M., Cruickshank, D. et al., *The Saving of Spitalfields* (The Spitalfields Historical Buildings Trust: London, 1989)

Golden, G., *Old Bankside* (Williams and Norgate Ltd: London, 1951)

Reilly, L. & Marshall, G., *The Story of Bankside* (London Borough of Southwark: London, 2001)

Tames, R., *Southwark Past* (Historical Publications: London, 2001)

Barnes, Putney & Battersea

Brown, M., *Barnes and Mortlake Past with East Sheen* (Historical Publications: London, 1997)

Gerhold, D. (ed.), *Putney and Roehampton Past* (Historical Publications: London, 2000)

Hammond, E., *Bygone Putney* (Surrey Comet: Kingston-on-Thames, 1898)

Loobey, P., *Battersea Past* (Historical Publications: London, 2002)

MacRobert, S., *A Brief History of Putney & Roehampton* (Putney History Society: Putney, 2009)

Mitton, G.E. & Geike, J.C., *Hammersmith, Fulham and Putney*, ed. W. Besant (London, 1903)

Renier, H., *Lambeth Past: Kennington, Vauxhall, Waterloo* (Historical Publications: London, 2006)

Stevens, J.W., *The History of the Shaftesbury Park Estate* (Dissertation, no date)

Unwin, T.F., *Wimbledon, Putney and Barnes: A Handy Guide to Rambles in the District* (T. Fisher Unwin: London, 1883)

Woods, M., *Proof of Evidence* (English Heritage: London, 1992)

Camden

Camden History Society, *Streets of Camden Town* (Camden History Society: London, 2003)

Hart, V., Knight, R. & Marshall, L., *Camden Town 1791–1991* (London Borough of Camden: London, 1991)

Richardson, J., *Camden Town and Primrose Hill Past* (Historical Publications: London, 1991)

——, *The Camden Town Book* (Historical Publications: London, 2007)

Whitehead, J., *The growth of Camden Town: AD 1800–2000* (self-published: London, 2000)

Chelsea & Kensington

Borer, M.C., *Two Villages: The Story of Chelsea and Kensington* (W.H. Allen: London, 1973)

Denny, B., *Chelsea Past* (Historical Publications: London, 1996)

Denny, B. & Starren, C., *Kensington Past* (Historical Publications: London, 1998)

Edmonds, R., *Chelsea: From Five Fields to the Worlds End* (Phene Press: London, 1956)

Evans, G., *Kensington* (Hamish Hamilton: London, 1975)

Garceau, E., (translated from French by Chappell, V.A.) *The Little Doustes: A biography of Louise and Jeanne Douste* (Frederick Muller: London, 1935)

Gaunt, W., *Kensington & Chelsea* (B.T. Batsford: London, 1975)

Holme, T., *Chelsea* (Hamish Hamilton: London, 1972)

Richardson, J., *The Chelsea Book: Past and Present* (Historical Publications: London, 2003)

Tames, R., *Earl's Court and Brompton Past* (Historical Publications: London, 1998)

Walker, A. & Jackson, P., *Kensington & Chelsea* (John Murray Publishers: London, 1987)

Chiswick

Arthure, H., *Life and Work in Old Chiswick* (Old Chiswick Protection Society: London, 1998)

Clegg, G., *Chiswick Past* (Historical Publications: London, 1995)

——, *The Chiswick Book: Past and Present* (Historical Publications: London, 2004)

Draper, W., *Chiswick* (Ann Bingley: London, 1973)

Phillimore, W.P.W. & Whitear, W.H., *Chiswick* (Phillimore & Co.: London, 1897)

Fulham

Croker, T.C., *A Walk from London to Fulham* (William Tegg: London, 1860)

Denny, B., *Fulham Past* (Historical Publications: London, 1997)

——, *Hammersmith and Shepherd's Bush Past* (Historical Publications: London, 1995)

Feret, C.J., *Fulham Old and New being an exhaustive history of the ancient Parish of Fulham* (Leadenhall Press Ltd: London, 1900)

Hasker, L., *The Place which is called Fulanham* (Fulham & Hammersmith Historical Society: London, 1981)

Whitting, P.D. (ed.), *A History of Fulham* (Fulham History Society: London, 1970)

Hampstead & Highgate

Barratt, T.J., *The Annals of Hampstead Volumes I–III* (Lionel Leventhal Ltd and The Camden History Society: London, 1972)

Bohm, D. & Norrie, I., *Hampstead: London Hill Town* (High Hill Press: London, 1981)

Camden History Society, *Streets of Highgate* (Camden History Society: London, 2007)

Farmer, A., *Hampstead Heath* (Historical Publications: London, 1984)

Ikin, C.W., *Hampstead Garden Suburb Dreams and Realities* (The New Hampstead Garden Suburb Trust: London, 1990)

Miller, M., *Hampstead Garden Suburb Arts and Crafts Utopia* (Phillimore: London, 2006)

Norrie, M. & Norrie, I. (eds), *The Book of Hampstead* (High Hill Books: London, 1968)

Richardson, J., *Hampstead One Thousand AD 986–1986* (Historical Publications with London Borough of Camden: New Barnet, 1985)

Richardson, J., *Highgate Past* (Historical Publications: London, 2004)

Service, A., *Victorian and Edwardian Hampstead* (Phillimore: London, 1989)

Thompson, F.M.L., *Hampstead: Building a Borough 1650–1964* (Routledge: London, 1974)

Wade, C., *Hampstead Past* (Historical Publications: London, 1989)

——, *The Streets of Hampstead* (Camden History Society: London, 2000)

——, *The Streets of West Hampstead* (Camden History Society: London, 1992)

Hyde Park & Marylebone

Brandon, D. & Brook, A., *Marylebone & Tyburn Past* (Historical Publications: London, 2007)

Chancellor, E.B., *Wanderings in Marylebone* (Dulau: London, 1926)

Clinch, G., *Marylebone and St Pancras: Their History, Celebrities, Buildings and Institutions* (Truslove & Shirley: London, 1890)

Mackenzie, G., *Marylebone: Great City North of Oxford Street* (Macmillan: London, 1972)

Whitehead, J., *The Growth of St Marylebone and Paddington* (Jack Whitehead: London, 2001)

Wittich, J. & Dowsing, J., *Guide to Bayswater* (Sunrise Press: London, 1989)

Islington & Covent Garden

Cosh, M., *A History of Islington* (Historical Publications: London, 2005)

Lewis, S., *The History and Topography of the Parish of St Mary, Islington in the County of Middlesex* (John Nichols: London, 1811)

Nelson, J., *The History, Topography, and Antiquities of Islington* (Philip Wilson Publishers: London, 1980)

Richardson, J., *Islington Past* (Historical Publications: London, 2000)

——, *Covent Garden Past* (Historical Publications: London, 1995)

Tames, R. & Tames, S., *Covent Garden and Soho: The illustrated A–Z historical guide* (Historical Publications: London, 2009)

Willats, E.A., *Islington – Streets with a Story* (Islington Local History Education Trust: London, 1988)

Zwart, P., *Islington: A History and Guide* (Sidgwick & Jackson Ltd: London, 1973)

Knightsbridge, Belgravia & Mayfair

Borer, M.C., *Mayfair: The Years of Grandeur* (W.H. Allen: London, 1975)

Chancellor, E.B., *Knightsbridge and Belgravia: Their History, Topography and Famous Inhabitants* (Sir Isaac Pitman & Sons: London, 1909)

Clinch, G., *Mayfair and Belgravia: being an historical account of the parish of St. George, Hanover square* (Truslove & Shirley: London, 1892)

Colby, R., *Mayfair: A Town within London* (Country Life: London, 1966)

Dowsing, J., *Belgravia: A Guide to History and Landmarks* (Sunrise Press: London, 2000)

Johnson, B.H., *Berkeley Square to Bond Street: The Early History of the Neighbourhood* (John Murray: London, 1952)

Kennedy, C., *Mayfair: A Social History* (Hutchinson: London, 1986)

Little Venice & Paddington

Ashford, E.B., *St John's Wood: The Harrow School and Eyre Estates* (St Marylebone Society: London, 1965)

Tames, R., *St John's Wood and Maida Vale Past* (Historical Publications: London, 1998)

Margetson, S., *St John's Wood: An Abode of Love and the Arts* (St John's Wood Society: London, 1988)

O'Sullivan, K., *Dial 'M' for Maida Vale* (Historical Publications: London, 2000)

Westminster & Pimlico

Baker, E.C., *Preece and Those Who Followed: Consulting Engineers in the Twentieth Century* (Reprographic Centre Ltd: London, 1980)

Dowsing, J., *Guide to Pimlico* (Sunrise Press: London, 2001)

Mee, A., (revised and rewritten by Saunders, A., 1975) *London: The City and Westminster* (Hodder and Stoughton: London, 1975)

Tames, R., *The Westminster & Pimlico Book* (Phillimore: Andover, 2005)

Watson, I., *Westminster and Pimlico Past* (Historical Publications: London, 2002)

Woolwich & Blackheath

Rhind, N., *Blackheath Village and Environs 1790–1990: Volume 1* (Bookshops Blackheath Ltd: London, 1976)

Burford, B. & Watson, J., *Aspects of the Arsenal: The Royal Arsenal, Woolwich* (Greenwich Borough Museum: London, 1997)

THE SOUTH WEST
Devon & Dorset
McDonald, K., *The Story of Thurlestone, Bantham and West Buckland* (Neil Girling: Plymouth, 1993)

——, *More than Just a Cottage: A Village in the South Hams* (Ashgrove Press: Kent, 1981)

Lysons, D. & Lysons, S., *Magna Britannia: Volume 6* (T. Cadell & W. Davies: London, 1822)

Fox, C., *Exhibition of Village History: Bantham 2000 BC – 1953 AD* (Kingsbridge, 1953)

Beacham, P. et al., *Devon's Heritage: Building and Landscape* (Devon County Council Planning Department: Exeter, 1982)

Giraud, M. (ed.), *House for Mr Curry* (Dartington Hall Trust: High Cross House, 2000)

Gray, J. (ed.), *Dorset Constabulary 1856–1956* (Dorchester, 1956)

Hann, M., *Bobbies on the Beat: 150 Years of the Dorset Police* (The Dovecote Press: Wimborne Minster, 2006)

Milne, O.P., 'The New Rural England: The Buildings of Dartington Hall Ltd, Totnes, South Devon', *The Architect and Building News*, Parts I–IV, Volume 135 (1933)

Hall, M., 'High Cross House, Devon' in *Country Life*, Volume 189, No 31, 3 August 1995

Hussey, C., 'High Cross Hill, Dartington, Devon: The Residence of Mr W.B. Curry' in *Country Life*, Volume 73, No 1882, 11 February 1933

Yorke, F.R.S., *The Modern House* (Architectural Press: London, 1934)

Wodehouse, L., 'William Lescaze and Dartington Hall' in *Architectural Association Quarterly*, Volume 8, No 2 (1976)

Pearson, E.H., *Do Not Lie! The Notleys of Somerset and Dorset* (E.H. Pearson: Cardiff, 1991)

Polwhele, R., *The History of Devonshire: Volume II* (Cadell Johnson Dilley: London, 1793)

Gloucestershire & Worcestershire
Aslet, C., *The Last Country Houses* (Yale University Press: New Haven and London, 1982)

Beckwith, E.G.C., *Blockley and Northwick Gloucestershire and What to See in Historical Blockley* (Blockley Antiquarian Society, Blockley: 1985)

Bigland, R. [Frith, B. (ed.)], *Historical, Monumental and Genealogical Collections Relative to the County of Gloucester* (The Bristol and Gloucestershire Archaeological Society: Gloucester, 1995)

Blockley Antiquarian Society, *Walks Around Blockley* (Blockley Antiquarian Society: Blockley, 2000)

Blockley Historical Society, *Walks in Blockley Village: Buildings of Historical and Archaeological Interest* (Blockley Historical Society: Blockley, 2011)

Bourne, J. (ed.), *Blockley Yesterday: A Third Miscellany* (Blockley Antiquarian Society: Blockley, 2000)

Hussey, C., 'Hilles, Stroud, Gloucestershire: The Home of Detmar Blow' in *Country Life*, Volume 88 (7 and 14 September 1940)

Lee-Milne, J., *Some Cotswold Country Houses* (The Dovecote Press: Stanbridge, 1987)

Nash, T.R., *The History and Antiquities of Worcestershire* (T. Payne: London, 1781–99)

Rudder, S., *A New History of Gloucestershire* (Nonsuch Publishing Ltd: Stroud, 2006; first published 1779)

Rudge, T., *The History of the County of Gloucester, Volume II* (G.F. Harris: Gloucester, 1803)

Williams, A., *Lechlade: Being the History of the Town, Manor & Estates, the Priory and the Church* (E.W. Savory: Cirencester, 1888)

Oxford & Didcot
Gardiner, J., *Brunel's Didcot: Great Western Railway to Great Western Society* (Runpast Publishing: Cheltenham, 1996)

Hibbert, C. (ed.), *The Encyclopaedia of Oxford* (Macmillan: London, 1998)

Hinchcliffe, T., *North Oxford* (Yale University Press: New Haven and London, 1992)

Lingham, B., *The Railway Comes to Didcot: A History of the Town 1839–1918* (Alan Sutton: Stroud, 1992)

——, *A Poor Struggling Little Town: A History of Didcot 1918 to 1945* (Didcot Town Council: Didcot, 2000)

Lingham, B. & Hall, M.J., *Changing Face of Didcot: A Photographic Record Covering the Past One Hundred Years* (Didcot Archaeological & Historical Society: Didcot, 1977)

Bristol & Bath
Gomme, A., Jenner, M. et al., *Bristol: An Architectural History* (Lund Humphries: London, 1979)

Haddon, J., *Portrait of Bath* (Robert Hale: London, 1982)

Ison, W., *The Georgian Buildings of Bath* (Spire Books Ltd and The Bath Preservation Trust: Reading, 2004)

——, *The Georgian Buildings of Bristol* (Kingsmead Press: Bath, 1978)

Jones, D., *A History of Clifton* (Phillimore: Chichester, 1992)

Manco, J., *The Hub of the Circus* (Bath & North East Somerset Council: Bath, 2004)

Mowl, J. & Earnshaw, B., *John Wood: Architect of Obsession* (Millstream Books: London, 1988)

Thomson, F.G. for the Ninety-Third Annual Meeting of the BMA, *The Book of Bath* (British Medical Association: Bath, 1925)

Walcot & Larkhill Townswomen's Guild, *A History of the Parish and Manor of Walcot* (Walcot & Larkhill Townswomen's Guild: Bath, 1987)

Somerset & Wiltshire
Levinge, E.M. & Radway, R.S., *About Blunsdon: A North Wiltshire Village* (The Authors: Blunsdon, 1976)

Green, E., *Downton and the First World War* (Meerstone: Downton, 2002)

Wales (Bute Town)
Hilling, J.B., *Cardiff and the Valleys* (Lund Humphries: London, 1973)

——, *The Historic Architecture of Wales: An Introduction* (University of Wales Press: Cardiff, 1975)

Harwood, E.M., 'Bute Town: The Recovery of a Village' in *Journal of the Faculty of Architects and Surveyors*, Volume 83, No 4, pp. 14–17 (1979)

Rees, D.M., *The Industrial Archaeology of Wales* (David & Charles: Newton Abbot, 1975)

——, *Mines, Mills and Furnaces* (HMSO: London, 1969)

SOUTH EAST & EAST ANGLIA

Huntingdonshire

Carter, M., *Hemingford Grey is Famous for its Enormous Gooseberries: History through Road Names* (Westmeare Publications: St Ives, 1998)

Dady, J., *Beyond Yesterday: A History of Fenstanton* (Fenstanton, 2002)

Dickenson, G.M., *Historic Hemingford Grey: An Account of a Huntingdonshire Village* (W.H. Smith & Sons: Huntingdon, 1946)

Kent

Brown, J.C., *History of Brasted* (J.H. Jewell: Westerham, 1874)

Cox, J.C., *Rambles in Kent* (Methuen & Co.: London, 1913)

Downes, D., *Ash: An East Kent Village* (The History Press: Stroud, 2000)

Dunlop, J., *The Pleasant Town of Sevenoaks: A History* (The Author: Sevenoaks, 1965)

Gardiner, D., *Companion into Kent* (Spurbooks: Bourne End, 1973)

Hasted, E., *The History and Topographical Survey of the County of Kent*, 1797 (reprinted by P.M.E. Erwood: Sidcup, 1981)

Ireland, W.H., *A New and Complete History of the County of Kent* (G. Virtue: London, 1830)

Jewell, J., *St Margaret's Bay: The Piccadilly of the Sea* (St Margaret's Local History Society: Kent, 1980)

Kent Archaeological Society, *Archaeologia Cantiana* (Kent Archaeological Society: Kent, 1858)

Macfie, A.L. (ed.), *Historical Sketches of St Margaret's at Cliffe 1086–1911* (A.L. Macfie, 1977)

Plancé, J.R., *A Corner of Kent* (London, 1864)

Rayner, C., *Sevenoaks Past* (Phillimore: London, 1997)

Terry, R., *Old Corners of Sevenoaks* (Caxton & Holmesdale Press: Sevenoaks, 2000)

Watson, I., *The History of the Parish of Chevening* (Chevening Parish History Group: Sevenoaks, 1999)

Norfolk & Suffolk

Becker, M.J. (ed.), *Story of Southwold* (F. Jenkins: Southwold, 1948)

Blomefield, F., *An Essay towards a Topographical History of the County of Norfolk: Volume II* (William Miller: London, 1805)

Bottomley, A.F. (ed.), *The Southwold Diary of James Maggs 1818–1876* (Boydell Press, Suffolk Records Society: Woodbridge, 2007)

Bottomley, A.F., *A Short History of the Borough of Southwold* (Southwold Corporation: Southwold, 1974)

Carter, J.I. & Bacon, S.K., *Southwold, Suffolk: The Fortified Anchorage of Sole Bay* (Segment Publications: Suffolk, 1976)

Clegg, R. & S., *Southwold: Portraits of an English Seaside Town* (Phillimore: Chichester, 1999)

Lyng History Group, *Lyng: A Village in the Wensum Valley. A Miscellany* (Lyng History Group: Lyng, 1993)

Sayer, M.J., *Lyng* (F.C. Barnwell: Aylsham, 1983)

Tennyson, A., *The Charge of the Light Brigade* (1854)

Wake, R., *Southwold and its Vicinity, Ancient and Modern* (W.H. Dalton: London, 1842)

Surrey & Sussex

Cunningham, M., *The Story of Little Woodcote and Woodcote Hall* (Heritage in Sutton Leisure: Surrey, 1989)

Beresford, M.W., *The Lost Villages of England* (Sutton Publishing: Stroud, 1998)

Bingham, N., *C.A. Busby: The Regency Architect of Brighton and Hove* (RIBA Heinz Gallery Exhibition: Bath, 1991)

Creese, M., *The Regency Town House: An Illustrated Guide and History to 13 Brunswick Square, Hove* (The Brunswick Town Charitable Trust: Brighton, 2000)

Dale, A., *Fashionable Brighton 1820–1860* (Oriel: London, 1987)

——, *Brighton Town and Brighton People* (Phillimore: Chichester, 1976)

Fines, K., *A History of Brighton and Hove: Stone Age Whitehawk to Millennium City* (Phillimore: Chichester, 2002)

Farrart, S., *Georgian Brighton 1740–1820* (University of Sussex Centre for Continuing Education: Brighton, 1980)

Middleton, J., *Encyclopaedia of Hove and Portslade: Volume I* (Judy Middleton, 2001)

——, *A History of Hove* (Phillimore: London, 1979)

Reger, J., *Chichester Harbour: A History* (Phillimore: London, 1996)

Smith, K. & Smith, J., *Birdham and Itchenor: Then and Now* (Mill Press, 1987)

MIDLANDS & NORTH EAST

Lincolnshire

Allen, T., *The History of Lincoln: From the Earliest Period to the Present Time, Volume II* (John Saunders, Junior: London and Lincoln, 1834)

Deepings Heritage, *A Glimpse of the Past* (Deepings Heritage: Lincolnshire, 1998)

Taylor, G., 'Long Sutton: Seagate Hall' in *Lincolnshire History and Archaeology*, Volume 36, p. 59 (Society for Lincolnshire History and Archaeology: Lincoln, 2001)

Marrat, W., *The History of Lincolnshire, Topographical, Historical and Descriptive*, Volumes I–IV (Marat, W.: Boston, 1816)

Turnor, E., *Collections for the History of the Town and Soke of Grantham* (W. Bulmer, 1806)

Manchester (Hulme)

Stewart, C., *The Stones of Manchester* (Edward Arnold: London, 1956)

Parkinson-Bailey, J.J., *Manchester: An Architectural History* (Manchester University Press: Manchester, 2000)

Hartwell, C., *Manchester: Pevsner Architectural Guides* (Penguin: London, 2001)

Nottinghamshire

Arundal, B.M., *Southwell: A History Walk* (The Southwell Civic Society: Southwell, 2001)

Chapman, S. & Walker, D. (eds), *Southwell: The Town and its People, Volume II* (Southwell & District Local History Society: Southwell, 2006)

Payne, M., *Victorian Nottingham* (Nonsuch Publishing: Stroud, 2007)

Kaye, D., *A History of Nottinghamshire* (Phillimore: Chichester, 1987)

Kirkland, R., *Memories of a Villager: Syerston Village* (1960)

Pratt, W. W., *Byron at Southwell: Making of a Poet with New Poems & Letters from the Rare Books Collection of the University of Texas* (Texas University Press: Austin, 1948)

Russenberger, L., *The Villa Estate in Nineteenth Century England* (Dissertation – University of Chicago, 1988)

Schoenfield, M., 'Private Souvenirs: Exchanges among Byron's Southwell Set' in *Wordsworth Circle*, Volume 39 (2008)

Shilton, R.P., *The History of Southwell in the County of Nottingham* (Newark, 1818)

Summers, N., *A Prospect of Southwell: An Architectural History of the Church and Domestic Buildings of the Collegiate Foundation* (Phillimore: Chichester, 1974)

Transactions of the Thoroton Society of Nottinghamshire (Nottingham, 1897)

Warwickshire

Alcock, N. W., *People at Home: Living in a Warwickshire Village 1500–1800* (Phillimore: Chichester, 1993)

Alcock, N. W. et al., 'Timber-Framed Building in Warwickshire: Stoneleigh Village' in *Birmingham and Warwickshire Archaeological Society: Transactions for 1971–73*, Volume 85

York (Micklegate)

Nuttgens, P., *York: The Continuing City* (Faber: London, 1976)

Gee, E.A., *The Architecture of York* (Cerialis Press: York, 1979)

Royal Commission on Historical Monuments, *City of York, Volume III, South-West of the Ouse* (HMSO: 1972)

List of Illustrations